WHAT'S THE BEST TRIVIA BOOK?

Fun Trivia Games with 4,000
Questions and Answers

Louis Richards

MONKEY
PUBLISHING

OUR HAND-PICKED
BOOK SELECTION FOR YOU.

LEARN
SOMETHING NEW
EVERYDAY.

Content

Animals

TRIVIA

DID YOU KNOW?

HORSES SLEEP ONLY 2 HOURS A DAY ON AVERAGE.

Quiz 1

1. What famous bear did Michael Bond create?
2. What color are the spots on a common lady bug? Black
3. What mammals use echolocation to fly?
4. What is the food source for a carpophagus animal?
5. What was the name of the first dog in outer space?

Quiz 2

6. What sea creature is more abundant than any other?
7. What is the name for the offspring of a female horse and a male donkey?
8. What animal is used in the symbol for modern medicine?
9. Who rode the famous horse Black Bess?
10. What kind of animal is a mandrill?

Quiz 3

11. What is the name for a group of frogs?
12. Animals of the Vespertilio genus are more commonly known as _____.
13. What color are the spots on a plaice?
14. The star-nosed mole is extremely sensitive to touch and smell, which is due to the 22 _____ on its snout.
15. In the movie Free Willy, what kind of mammal was Willy? whale

Quiz 4

16. What animal will always give birth to same-sex twins?
17. What insect is known for eating its mate after reproduction?
18. Yes or No: Mosquitoes have teeth.
19. There is only one kind of venomous snake in Britain; what kind is it?
20. What is the common name of the wild pig of Central & South America? Boar

Quiz 5

21. What land animal is the second heaviest?
22. What ape species is the largest?
23. What is the name of Dorothy's dog in the movie The Wizard of Oz?   Toto
24. What is the common name for the Syncerus caffer?
25. What percentage of all mammal species are bats?

Quiz 6

26. Which is faster; a hare, a horse, or a greyhound?
27. What animal (besides humans) is the only animal that can catch leprosy?
28. What animal lives in a formicary enclosure?
29. What is the name of an animal that can live on land or in the water?
30. What kind of animal was a Tarka?

Quiz 7

31. What is the name for a female donkey?
32. What animal symbolizes a long life in Korea?
33. What animal can sleep for 3 years and only mates once in its life?
34. What animal symbolized the Egyptian god Sobek?
35. What reptile is known for changing its color?

Quiz 8

36. What is the name for the field of science that studies animals in their natural environment?
37. What kind of animal produces the substance gossamer?
38. What is the name for plants and animals on the lake bottom?
39. What is the largest deer species?
40. What animal is used in the Toys-R-Us logo?

Quiz 9

41. The Macaw is a species of _____, and is the largest and most colorful of its kind.
42. What intestinal parasite affects both man and animals?
43. What two famous bears lived at Jellystone Park?
44. What animal comes last, alphabetically, in Chinese horoscopes?
45. What animal's shell is a popular material for jewelry?

Quiz 10

46. What animal symbolizes the World Wide Fund for Nature?
47. Chi Chi and An An were what kind of animals?
48. What is a mole's main food source?
49. Myxomatosis is a disease commonly associated with what animal?
50. What is the common name for the Pulex irritans?

Quiz 11

51. How many different kinds of panda are there?
52. What was the name for Tarzan's chimpanzee friend?
53. An ocelot is what color?
54. How long is the longest beetle in the world?
55. What animal produces young that are named elver?

Quiz 12

56. What is the sacred animal of Thailand?
57. What kind of animal only eats plants?
58. A marmoset is what kind of animal?
59. Hannibal brought large animals with him across the Alps; what were they?
60. How many hearts does an earthworm have?

4

Quiz 13

61.   What is the common name for a Lupus?
62.   What is the formal name for the study of animals?
63.   What kind of animal is an abalone?
64.   Asiatic _____ have the largest ears of all bear species.
65.   A cat uses its whiskers like an insect uses its _____, which help it to navigate tight spaces.

Quiz 14

66.   What bird takes over the nests of other species?
67.   What animals are in the Suidae family?
68.   A rodent wears down its teeth by chewing on bark, leaves and other _____.
69.   What is the name for a queen bee's closest servants?
70.   What animal provides 50% of the protein for the inhabitants of Peru?

Quiz 15

71.   Javelinas snort, squeal, and click their teeth in an effort to _____.
72.   What sea creature has the largest eyes?
73.   What animal is first in the Chinese horoscopes, alphabetically?
74.   What animals live in an apiary enclosure?
75.   What is the name for a fox's home?

Quiz 16

76.   Reptiles are in the class Reptila, and birds are in the class _____.
77.   What animal (besides humans) is the only animal to have unique prints?
78.   Man of the Forest is the name for what animal?
79.   What reptile cannot stick out its tongue?
80.   Where is the largest natural population of Asian elephants?

Quiz 17

81. What do Tasmanian Devils, Koalas, and Possums have in common?
82. What is the only animal where both males and females are born with horns?
83. What three animal species have stereoscopic vision?
84. As an Ozark blind salamander matures, its eyes and gills _____.
85. What was Tonto's horse's name in the Western series Lone Ranger?

Quiz 18

86. What is the formal name for the study of bird eggs?
87. What species of penguin is the largest?
88. What is the name for animals that do not eat meat?
89. What is the name for the relationship between coral and algae?
90. What animal is groomed with a curry comb?

Quiz 19

91. What is the name for a fruit-eating animal?
92. What fictional animal had a wife named Celeste?
93. What is the name for the fur produced by a stoat?
94. What is the name of Walt Disney's famous animated deer?
95. What kind of animal is a skua?

Quiz 20

96. Where is the scut on a rabbit?
97. Rain forest birds migrate from South America to Canada to _____ each summer.
98. Nuzzing is a sound made by what animal?
99. Only 18 of the 250+ known species of shark are _____.
100. What is the name for animals without backbones?

Quiz 21

101.   What is the name for the semi-aquatic animal lutra-lutra?
102.   What is it called when a caterpillar turns into a butterfly?
103.   Mohair is a fiber sourced from what animal?
104.   What is a borzoi?
105.   What animal can survive the longest in captivity?

Quiz 22

106.   What kind of animal is a fennec?
107.   Rectangular pupils are a unique feature of a _____.
108.   What insect is known for having the best eyesight?
109.   A fluke is what type of animal?
110.   Lincoln Park Zoo bought its first animal in 1874 for $10; what was it?

Quiz 23

111.   A Guinea pig has another common name, what is it?
112.   Sika, roe, and fallow are common names for what?
113.   What is the most intelligent non-human primate?
114.   On average, 30% - 60% of animals brought into shelters are
        _____.
115.   In the ocean, there are 2,000 known species of _____.

Quiz 24

116.   What species of beetle is the largest?
117.   How many chambers are in a cow's stomach?
118.   Who hosted the show Animal Magic?
119.   How long is the largest seahorse species?
120.   Bees communicate through _____.

121.   What leaves do koala bears eat?
122.   What reptile has the longest lifespan?
123.   According to Inuit people, what is a Nanook?
124.   What does arboreal mean in reference to an animal's habitat?
125.   What is the best known animal that is in the same family as a llama?
126.   What cartoon family had a pet named Dino?

Animals TRIVIA Answers

Answers – Quiz 1

1. Paddington Bear
2. Black
3. Bats
4. Fruit
5. Laika

Answers – Quiz 2

6. Sea worm
7. A mule
8. Snake
9. Dick Turpin
10. Monkey

Answers – Quiz 3

11. Army
12. Bats
13. Orange
14. Tentacles
15. A killer whale

Answers – Quiz 4

16. Armadillo
17. Praying mantis
18. Yes
19. Adder
20. Peccary

Answers – Quiz 5

21. The hippopotamus
22. Gorilla
23. Toto
24. Cape buffalo
25. 25%

Answers – Quiz 6

26. Hare
27. The armadillo
28. Ant
29. Amphibians
30. An otter

Answers – Quiz 7

31. Jenny
32. The deer
33. Snail
34. Crocodile
35. A chameleon

Answers – Quiz 8

36. Ethology
37. Spider
38. Benthos
39. The moose
40. Giraffe

Answers – Quiz 9

41. Parrot family
42. Tapeworm
43. Yogi and Boo Boo
44. Tiger
45. Abalone

Answers – Quiz 10

46. Giant panda
47. Panda bears
48. Earthworms
49. Rabbits
50. Flea

Answers – Quiz 11

51. Two, the giant and the lesser
52. Cheta
53. The ocelot is white, black, and tawny
54. Six inches
55. The eel

Answers – Quiz 12

56. The white elephant
57. Herbivore
58. A monkey
59. Elephants
60. 5

Answers – Quiz 13

61.   Wolf
62.   Zoology
63.   Marine snail
64.   Black bears
65.   Antennae

Answers – Quiz 14

66.   Cuckoo
67.   Pigs
68.   Vegetable matter
69.   Drones
70.   The guinea pig

Answers – Quiz 15

71.   Communicate
72.   The giant squid
73.   Boar
74.   Bees
75.   A den

Answers – Quiz 16

76.   Aves
77.   Koala bears
78.   Orang-utan
79.   Crocodile
80.   India

Answers – Quiz 17

81. They're all marsupials
82. Giraffes
83. Monkeys, apes And humans
84. Disappear
85. Scout

Answers – Quiz 18

86. Oology
87. Emperor
88. Herbivore
89. Symbiotic
90. Horse

Answers – Quiz 19

91. Frugivore
92. Babar the Elephant
93. Ermine
94. Bambi
95. A bird

Answers – Quiz 20

96. The tail
97. Breed
98. Camels
99. Dangerous to humans
100. Invertebrates

Answers – Quiz 21

101.	Otter
102.	Metamorphous
103.	Angora goat
104.	A dog, also known as the Russian wolfhound
105.	Giant tortoise

Answers – Quiz 22

106.	A desert fox
107.	Goat
108.	Dragonfly
109.	Worm
110.	Bear cub

Answers – Quiz 23

111.	Cavy
112.	Deer
113.	Chimpanzee
114.	Euthanized
115.	Starfishes

Answers – Quiz 24

116.	The Goliath Beetle
117.	4
118.	Johnny Morris
119.	8 inches
120.	Dancing

121.   Eucalyptus
122.   The giant tortoise
123.   Polar Bear
124.   In or amongst trees
125.   Camel
126.   The Flintstones

Nature & Science
TRIVIA

DID YOU KNOW?

HUMAN DNA AND BANANA DNA ARE 50% THE SAME.

Quiz 1

1. What does the constellation name Corona Borealis mean?
2. The average human being has 206 _____.
3. What Russian physiologist studied the reflexive behavior of dogs?
4. The interrupter gear enabled machine guns to shoot through a plane's propeller; which German company produced it?
5. What is the formal name for the study of air movement and objects moving through the air?

Quiz 2

6. A _____ bear's mark is distinct due to its 5 claw marks.
7. What bird species was the first to be domesticated?
8. What bird is the only one that can fly backward?
9. What temperature is considered to be absolute zero?
10. What male fish can give birth?

Quiz 3

11. The chemical symbol for lead is _____.
12. What field would you work in if you studied histology?
13. What are the ingredients of gunpowder, besides potassium nitrate?
14. Who was the inventor of the British jet engine?
15. The initials IATA stand for _____.

Quiz 4

16. Ants, bees, and wasps are in the order _____.
17. What is something that babies can do, but adults can't?
18. Cocci, spirilla, and streptococci are examples of _____.
19. The spitfire was produced by what aircraft manufacturer?
20. What is the European common name for the caribou?

Quiz 5

21. In 1948, what hook-and-eye fastener was invented by Georges De Mestral?
22. What trunkless plant is the largest?
23. What animal (besides humans) has sex for reasons of pleasure, not only reproduction?
24. In the U.K., how many lines are on the television?
25. What is the name for repetitive spasms in the diaphragm?

Quiz 6

26. What is the name for a growing method that does not use soil?
27. If a female honeybee receives royal jelly as a larva, what will it become?
28. What primate native to Madagascar meows like a cat?
29. What is A+Cos (Sin) equal to?
30. Which nation is responsible for inventing the wheelbarrow?

Quiz 7

31. What kind of glass gets darker when it is exposed to light?
32. How long can a flamingo live?
33. What is the name for an artificial ant's habitat?
34. Who first used gloves during surgery?
35. Is earth's gravity pull stronger at the poles or the equator?

Quiz 8

36. What is the sun made of?
37. What is another name for German measles?
38. What is the name scientists use for how the universe will collapse?
39. The Himalayan yeti is also known as what?
40. What do the letters URL stand for in relation to computers?

Quiz 9

41. Aberdeen Angus is what kind of mammal?
42. What are the 2 components of complex numbers?
43. How do white blood cells function?
44. How many legs are in each segment of a millipede?
45. What can invertebrates live without?

Quiz 10

46. Who is the father of the child who flew too close to the sun with feathers held together by wax?
47. What species of pig weighs an average of 2 pounds as an adult?
48. What do chiropodists treat?
49. How long has the earth been around?
50. What system is measured in farads?

Quiz 11

51. Where is the carotid artery located?
52. What type of animal are frogs?
53. Who discovered Penicillin?
54. Nyctophobia is the fear of what?
55. Who was the inventor of the Centigrade scale?

Quiz 12

56. What is the only undomesticated monkey in Europe?
57. ATP stands for what?
58. The word "puppy" comes from which French word?
59. What physical print on the human body is singular?
60. A woman's ceasing of menstruation is known as what?

Quiz 13

61.   What is Polyvinyl Chloride better known as?
62.   Which part of the brain does a lobotomy effect?
63.   What is another common name for the crane fly?
64.   What were pterosaurs?
65.   Which female pilot flew solo across the Atlantic Ocean?

Quiz 14

66.   What is the smallest living mammal in Europe?
67.   What are fly larvae called?
68.   What does ROM stand for in computer technology?
69.   In computing terminology, what does BASIC stand for?
70.   Which planet spins quicker than the rest?

Quiz 15

71.   What are the 3 parts of an insect's body?
72.   What star is closest to the earth (besides the sun)?
73.   The oyster is _____, which means it will change from male to
       female many times throughout its life.
74.   What mammal has the longest life span?
75.   What does the acronym LPG stand for?

Quiz 16

76.   What two-dimensional shape has four equal sides but no right
       angles?
77.   Which country produced the first alarm clock?
78.   Why was the seismosaurus given its name?
79.   What kind of creature is kept by an apiarist?
80.   Including pincers, how many legs does a crab have?

Quiz 17

81. The largest jellyfish in the world has tentacles that are longer than half of a _____.
82. Hyraxes, a small mammal known as conies in the Bible, share their ancestry with which large animal?
83. What is a winkle?
84. Trepanning is used for _____.
85. The road from Alaska to Chile is called _____.

Quiz 18

86. Does a person generally become farsighted or nearsighted as they get older?
87. Common, white-winged, and hairy-legged, are all types of which kind of bat?
88. What pressure and temperature conditions are necessary to transform graphite into a diamond?
89. A dromedary has _____ humps.
90. What does MG stand for in the automotive world?

Quiz 19

91. During hibernation, a bear will lose up to 25% of its _____.
92. What are the most common colors people will confuse when they are color blind?
93. What country has the longest coastline?
94. The second most common element on planet earth is _____.
95. What substance uses the Greek words meaning non-flammable?

Quiz 20

96. What is the fastest flying bird in the world?
97. What language does the term eureka come from?
98. What is the average life expectancy of a leopard in captivity?
99. What is the oldest organism still alive on planet earth?
100. The cheese plant is native to what region?

101.   What city is home to the first heart transplant?
102.   What is the main food source of the pangolin?
103.   What is the name of the instrument that measures atmospheric pressure?
104.   Who is credited with the original concept of the computer?
105.   What important scientific first creation was completed in 1996 at the Roslin Institute?

Quiz 22

106.   Who is the inventor of the telephone?
107.   What was later invented in the same lab using the prize money from the telephone invention?
108.   Who invented geodesic dome construction?
109.   How big is the Milky Way galaxy?
110.   A baby hare is called _____.

Quiz 23

111.   The Jay belongs in what family?
112.   Who designed the Wellington bomber of WWII?
113.   A lady slipper is what kind of plant?
114.   What word describes both a part of your hand and a part of a tree?
115.   What scientist proposed the theory of relativity?

Quiz 24

116.   Henry Ford is known for saying, "You can have any color you want, as long as it's black." Why?
117.   What is a mass of food moving from your mouth to your stomach called?
118.   What do you call an emasculated male pig?
119.   What chemical compound is responsible for pain after exercise?
120.   Where did the term nylon originate?

Quiz 25

121.   What does the number 40 reference in the GT40?
122.   Who is responsible for the uncertainty principle?
123.   What are the ulna, radius, and clavicle?
124.   A mother cat's purring acts as a _____, signaling kittens to nurse before their eyes have opened.
125.   The Milky Way is an example of what?

Quiz 26

126.   The tsetse fly carries what disease?
127.   Brontosaurus had a hit with what British pop group?
128.   The shortest wavelength in radiation is _____.
129.   What is the smallest bird?
130.   A mean-spirited woman gets her nickname from what rodent?

Quiz 27

131.   What animal is male when it is first born, and then slowly evolves into a female?
132.   Which cell is the largest?
133.   The activity of a radioactive source is measured with what?
134.   What was first performed by Dr. Richard Lower in 1665?
135.   During a _____, a camel can shut its nostrils.

Quiz 28

136.   Earth is the _____ planet from the sun.
137.   How long can the lungfish survive out of water?
138.   pH is a measure of what?
139.   Which flying insect is responsible for the spread of malaria?
140.   A cross between a _____ and a male donkey is a mule.

Quiz 29

141. What are the first 6 values of PI?
142. What is the cause of an aurora?
143. How do vets determine a horse's age?
144. What modern scientist suffered from motor neurone disease?
145. What is the common name for the patella bone?

Quiz 30

146. Toxicology is the study of _____.
147. What is the Ishashara test used to determine?
148. Instead of drinking water, frogs absorb water by _____.
149. Do humans have the same number of vertebrae as a giraffe?
150. What percentage of people are left-handed?

Quiz 31

151. What is the largest rodent alive today?
152. The hardest bone in the human body is the _____.
153. What did the lion need in the Wizard of Oz?
154. The ancient Greeks proposed 4 elements; what were they?
155. What is the name of the system blind people use to read?

Quiz 32

156. What small organ is attached to the large intestine?
157. If you break the sound barrier, what happens?
158. The color of the redstart's eggs are _____.
159. What creature had a short nose horn and two larger brow horns?
160. What compound is responsible for the green color of plants?

Quiz 33

161.   Who were the inventors of the aqua lung?
162.   What type of pine tree was alive during the time of Christ and is still alive today?
163.   The three smallest bones in the human body are located where?
164.   What planet in our solar system is the hottest?
165.   Who is famous for running through the streets shouting,"Eureka!?"

Quiz 34

166.   What organ are deer missing?
167.   How long is the gestation period of an Asiatic elephant?
168.   What's an usual characteristic of sleeping goats?
169.   How long is a stag beetle in the larva stage?
170.   What is the technical term for the period after childbirth?

Quiz 35

171.   Stewart Springer, the scientist, was bitten by a tiger shark while examining its _____.
172.   What spikey African succulent is an ingredient in lotions and creams?
173.   It takes 69,000 venom extractions from a coral snake to fill a _____.
174.   A healthy human adult has _____ teeth.
175.   What type of particle is emitted by cathode ray tubes?

Quiz 36

176.   What planet in our solar system is the coldest?
177.   What is the name of the comet that appears once every 76 years?
178.   Who patented the Magic & Infallible burglar-proof lock?
179.   Why do woodpeckers peck on wood?
180.   Where is earth's largest meteor crater?

Quiz 37

181. Can a human lick their elbow?
182. What meteor shower occurs around the 4th of November?
183. Herpes Zoster is more commonly known as _____.
184. In the late 1800s, who discovered x-rays?
185. What is the distance between the moon and the earth?

Quiz 38

186. Where does a car mix fuel with air?
187. At least 100 whales are killed each day by _____.
188. Who won the Nobel Peace Prize in 1944 for discovering nuclear fission?
189. The mating dance of the wandering _____ includes spreading wings, clacking bills, and shaking heads.
190. Brass is made of what two metals?

Quiz 39

191. What is the smallest mammal in North America?
192. A leech can eat up to _____ its body weight in one feeding.
193. A woman's first menstrual cycle is known as _____.
194. What creature was named by scientists who thought it ate eggs?
195. Who was the designer of the VW Beetle?

Quiz 40

196. What is the definition of hypoglycemia?
197. What do you call planets outside our solar system?
198. Porpoises differ from dolphins by being more _____.
199. Loss of appetite and excessive weight loss are characterized by _____.
200. The owl parrot builds its nest under tree _____ because it can't fly.

Quiz 41

201.   What vegetables are in the allium family?
202.   The _____'s armor is not as tough as it appears, and is only as rigid as a human fingernail.
203.   What is the name for a triangle with two equal sides?
204.   Where in the world were the first windmills?
205.   What bird has a distinct green crest and is sometimes called the peewit?

Quiz 42

206.   What is the name of a female's two sex hormones?
207.   What unit of measurement is used for supersonic speed?
208.   What African eagle hunts over a 250-mile area each day?
209.   Racehorses can wear out a pair of _____ in each race.
210.   What is the name for the liquid in blood?

Quiz 43

211.   Do you use more muscles to smile or to frown?
212.   What is the name for the study of low temperatures?
213.   The King crab walks in what way?
214.   What is the name scientists use for the skull?
215.   What is the common name for the scapula?

Quiz 44

216.   What is the smallest breed of hunting dog?
217.   What did the Caroline Institute of Stockholm win the Nobel Peace Prize for?
218.   What is the name for the lowest theoretical temperature?
219.   What do the initials A.M. stand for on a radio?
220.   The elements cerium, praseodymium, and promethium belong to what group?

Quiz 45

221. What is the name of the largest gold nugget ever discovered?
222. A monotreme is what?
223. What hormone does the adrenal gland produce?
224. What disease is the BCG vaccine used for?
225. What hormone is responsible for controlling the sugar supply between blood and muscles?

Quiz 46

226. Why did the Psittocosaurus get its name?
227. What did ancient Egyptians believe about cats?
228. How high can a bison jump?
229. How long does a human red blood cell live?
230. A cat can't move its _____ sideways.

Quiz 47

231. What is the short, dog-like extinct ancestor of the horse?
232. Due to an ability to purify water, mussels can survive in

      _____.
233. What is a group of rhinoceros called?
234. What does a blue moon refer to?
235. If a drug reduces edema swelling, what is it called?

Quiz 48

236. What flower grows on the flat of India?
237. What detective tried to discover who framed Roger Rabbit?
238. What whale is also known as the sea canary?
239. What protein gives blood its red color?
240. What term is used to describe 3D simulated environments?

Quiz 49

241.   What Latin word is responsible for iron's chemical symbol, Fe?
242.   A snail mates only once in its life, but the process can last up to _____ hours.
243.   GTA refers to what video game series?
244.   What percentage of the population has a 100 IQ or better?
245.   What creature is also known as a fluke?

Quiz 50

246.   What does prosthetic refer to?
247.   Water beds are said to help cattle by helping to relieve _____.
248.   The average human has _____ vertebrae.
249.   The oldest known fossil contains what organism?
250.   A buret is a what?

Quiz 51

251.   What reptile had two plates running down its back to its tail?
252.   What is the name of the rear part of a horse's head?
253.   What insect has large pincers at the base of its abdomen?
254.   How did the mole cricket get its name?
255.   The woolly _____ has been extinct since the Ice Age.

Quiz 52

256.   What is another name for the bishop's stone?
257.   A manometer measures _____.
258.   If quinine is added to water, what does it make?
259.   What beneficial insect is loved by gardeners because it eats aphids?
260.   Plumbism is what kind of poisoning?

Quiz 53

261. What does a conchologist study?
262. What does A.I.D.S. stand for?
263. Where does Fahrenheit and Celsius coincide on their respective scales?
264. What type of plant is an Allium cepa?
265. Who discovered electricity?

Quiz 54

266. Saliva production increases by _____ when cows bend down to graze.
267. Who designed the first vehicle with a combustion engine?
268. What makes up a shark's skeleton?
269. The chemical symbol for radon is _____.
270. What is the common name for Acetylsalicylic acid?

Quiz 55

271. What is the common name for sound navigation ranging?
272. The sun is _____ times bigger than the earth.
273. What does the comet's name Coma Berenices mean?
274. What metal is the only metal that is liquid at room temperature?
275. What is the name for the device inside a microwave?

Quiz 56

276. Which of the five senses is the most sensitive?
277. E.J. Claghorn patented what vehicular safety device?
278. A butterfly uses what part of its body to taste?
279. What metal is the most common metal on earth?
280. The kinkajou uses its long tail for an _____.

Quiz 57

281.   The largest insect on earth is a _____.
282.   Stephen Hawking studied what field of science?
283.   Is a tomato a fruit or a vegetable?
284.   V + IR is also known as _____.
285.   E.C.T. stands for _____.

Quiz 58

286.   What does the blue and white circle stand for in the BMW logo?
287.   Ursa Major stands for what in English?
288.   The scientific study of birds is called _____.
289.   The Nile crocodile can live 80 years in _____.
290.   What is the scientific name of the Sydney blue gum?

Quiz 59

291.   What is the common name for sodium hydroxide?
292.   Richard Drew invented Scotch tape when he worked for what company?
293.   What video game character made its debut on May 10th, 1980?
294.   What carnivorous plant lives on a small portion of the coastline of the Carolinas?
295.   What instrument is used for measuring humidity?

Quiz 60

296.   A group of bees can be called a hive, swarm, or _____.
297.   What was the original name of the tomato?
298.   The archaeopteryx bore the physical features of what modern-day creature?
299.   Cows produce more milk when they _____.
300.   The USPS introduces the Telex service in what decade

Quiz 61

301.   What substance in the human body is the hardest?
302.   What is the life span of a Mayfly?
303.   Why does a jumping bean jump?
304.   What animal pretends to be dead when captured, but hops away if let go?
305.   What fruit/vegetable is the least nutritious?

Quiz 62

306.   What compound is made from thiamine, niacin, and riboflavin?
307.   The anaconda gives live birth as opposed to _____.
308.   The largest egg ever laid came from the Madagascar _____ and was almost 10" long.
309.   An entire litter of baby opossums can fit into a _____.
310.   What shape is characterized by a constant distance between two points?

Quiz 63

311.   Are tidal waves and tsunamis the same thing?
312.   Negative 40 Fahrenheit is the same as what?
313.   Renal refers to what major organ?
314.   What is the fear of reptiles called?
315.   What is the largest carnivore on land?

Quiz 64

316.   One gram of gold can be drawn out how far?
317.   What is the purpose of ethylene glycol in vehicles?
318.   Pig is to _____ as horse is to equine.
319.   True or False: pure silver and sterling silver are the same.
320.   What country houses the world's largest blast furnace?

Quiz 65

321.   A Geiger counter measures what?
322.   A cod will deposit between 4 and 6 million eggs during _____.
323.   What phenomenon can be sheet, ball or forked?
324.   What does MRM stand for in the food industry?
325.   A condenser is also known as a _____.

Quiz 66

326.   In 1868, what appeared on the roads outside the houses of parliament?
327.   Struthious refers to something that resembles or is related to _____.
328.   When a seabird swallows a fish that is too large to swallow, the tail will stick out of its _____.
329.   Walk, trot, and gallop are the three gaits of a _____, a type of equid.
330.   Duncan and Alonso _____ were the inventors of the lightweight portable drill.

Quiz 67

331.   FTL stands for _____ in the field of space study.
332.   What field studies the movement of projectiles?
333.   Light-colored horses, pigs, and walruses can be _____.
334.   The smallest irreducible constituent of a chemical compound is known as _____.
335.   The 21st of October is the date of what meteor shower?

336. In 1939, what country began to produce polythene plastic commercially?
337. Bald eagles get their name because the white feathers on their head make them appear _____.
338. Which American car was patented in 1909?
339. What person is known as the father of medicine?
340. Ferdinand De Lesseps helped open what canal in 1869?

Quiz 69

341. In proportion to its body, what creature has the largest brain?
342. Artificial dialysis replaces the function of what organ?
343. What is the title of the famous cosmology book written by Stephen Hawking in 1998?
344. How long does it take an elephant to consume 60 gallons of water?
345. What do Flamsteed Halley, Bliss, and Bradley have in common?

Quiz 70

346. Small packets of energy called _____ make up light rays.
347. What port has the most trade traffic in the world?
348. What is the name for the middle of a black hole?
349. What newspaper had its own private office on the second floor of the Eiffel Tower?
350. 12 hours of a panda's day is spent eating _____.

Quiz 71

351. What does EEG stand for in medicine?
352. What company released the first instamatic camera in the early 60s?
353. Which star is the brightest visible star from earth?
354. How did the Edmontosaurus get its name?
355. Name the four types of adult teeth.

Quiz 72

356.   What is the most widespread disease?
357.   What do you call a group of geese?
358.   How many ribs does a human being have?
359.   Percy Shaw is credited with inventing what road safety device?
360.   What standard vehicle fittings were first released in 1916?

Quiz 73

361.   What does the name of the constellation Leo Minor mean?
362.   What famous dam uses the Colorado River?
363.   Ceres, Juno, Iris, and Florida are examples of what?
364.   An ammeter is a tool to measure _____.
365.   What is the name for the soft spot on a baby's head?

Quiz 74

366.   What is the name for the curved line between two points on a circle?
367.   What eye condition makes the lens of the eye turn opaque?
368.   If you were to mix all the colors of light, what color would it make?
369.   Thiamine is the name of what vitamin?
370.   What is Charles E. Yeager known for?

Quiz 75

371.   What is the common name for the Clorophytum?
372.   What planet in our solar system is closest to the sun?
373.   What technological innovation celebrated 25 years in 2007?
374.   The flying squirrel does not fly, but rather _____.
375.   The opposite of matter is _____.

Quiz 76

376. Edward Jenner helped develop what vaccine?
377. Who is the inventor of dynamite?
378. What are baby rattlesnakes lacking at birth?
379. Name the two kinds of corpuscles in invertebrates.
380. What is the name for the colored part of the eye?

Quiz 77

381. What kind of mathematician deals with the sides and angles of triangles?
382. What are the two initials that represent Chronic Fatigue Syndrome?
383. What gland produces tears?
384. What is the largest European curved-billed bird?
385. What is the main food source of silk worms?

Quiz 78

386. What is the term that denotes a bell-shaped flower?
387. What is the average weight of a human liver?
388. Paleontology is the study of _____.
389. Utah _____ exchange kisses as a way to recognize members of their group.
390. What was the focus of the research in the Manhattan Project?

Quiz 79

391. What do amps measure?
392. What is 1,000,000 in binary code?
393. Where does the world's most rare plant live?
394. The whistling swan has how many feathers?
395. Some octopi will eat their own tentacles under stress, but they will eventually _____.

396.   Who invented the self-lit match?

397.   What is the instrument used to measure angles in geometry?

398.   What blood group is the most common?

399.   The pronghorn _____ can reach speeds of up to 61 MPH.

400.   What Australian mammal can only be found in alpine environments?

Quiz 81

401.   What was the name of the first director at the Los Alamos Atomic Lab?

402.   What theory of creation is the most widely accepted?

403.   What is the name for sugar that is found in fruit?

404.   Which 3 colors make up the images on a screen?

405.   What is the common name of calcium carbonate?

Quiz 82

406.   What famous person developed the automatic telephone exchange?

407.   The value of Sine 30° is _____.

408.   What is another name for hemophilia?

409.   These three types of plague are the result of the route of infection: bubonic plague, septicemic plague, and _____.

410.   Who discovered canals on Mars?

Quiz 83

411.   What is the name of the green compound found only in plants?

412.   What birds saved Rome from attack by the Gauls because they were kept at the capitol?

413.   What comes between x-rays and visible light on the electromagnetic spectrum?

414.   As you age, why does your eyesight deteriorate?

415.   What was the first book produced by the first printing press?

Quiz 84

416.   Diazepam is more commonly known as what?
417.   What family of plants is the most common plant on earth?
418.   What kind of eagles hunt in a 100 mile span to feed their young?
419.   Do you get taller in outer space?
420.   Researchers believe Orca whales rub their bellies on the bottom of shallow beaches as a form of _____.

Quiz 85

421.   What American aircraft designer was born in Russia and created the helicopter?
422.   The small red deer is the only deer found in _____.
423.   The chemical symbol for gold is _____.
424.   What does the name of the constellation Ophiucus mean?
425.   The axilla is what part of the human body?

Quiz 86

426.   A moose may also be known as what?
427.   Which will survive an impact with earth: a meteor, a meteorite, or an asteroid?
428.   Rhinitis affects what part of the human body?
429.   Who is known for taking the first real photograph?
430.   What is the name for a particle of light?

Quiz 87

431.   Birds eat at least half of their own weight in food in what time period?
432.   The _____ mode is also known as the standard major scale.
433.   How do butterflies usually rest; with their wings open or shut?
434.   What are Chang and Eng Bunker known for?
435.   What is the purpose of bile in the human body?

Quiz 88

436.   What is the name of the clear liquid in a nuclear protoplasm?
437.   Ducks will only lay eggs in the _____.
438.   The human body's largest artery is the _____.
439.   The ocean sunfish can lay up to _____ eggs at one time.
440.   What do the letters BCG stand for?

Quiz 89

441.   What makes up the horn of a rhino?
442.   Hydrophytic plants grow in what conditions?
443.   Whose flight did Rimsky Korsakov compose a musical piece about?
444.   What kind of tree drops its leaves in the fall?
445.   What carnivore is the largest UK native?

Quiz 90

446.   What is a micron?
447.   What is the name for a hare's home?
448.   Is obsidian igneous, sedimentary, or metamorphic?
449.   Cave ceilings have which type of crystal formation; stalactites or stalagmites?
450.   If you wanted to walk in a straight line, would you eventually walk in a circle?

Quiz 91

451.   A chuckwalla is a _____.
452.   What is the unusual feature of a wombat's pouch?
453.   The adult human brain weighs approximately how much?
454.   The _____ can have an incredibly long lifespan for a mammal of nearly 200 years.
455.   The shoebill _____, a native African bird, will stand as still as a statue while hunting.

Quiz 92

456. Where do gophers live?
457. Why are the fossils of long-necked dinosaurs found with the head bent back over their bodies?
458. What is the name of the largest webbed-footed bird?
459. What is the name for the rate of increase in velocity?
460. What would you call 1 followed by 100 noughts?

Quiz 93

461. What is the name for inserting a shoot or twig of one species plant into another?
462. What do you call a rabbit's short tail?
463. Where on the human body is the trapezius?
464. A cow won't _____ until after she's calved.
465. What is the Russian's equivalent of Sky Lab?

Quiz 94

466. Who was the inventor of the first battery?
467. In Britain, does the water drain clockwise or counterclockwise?
468. What was the cause of Cleopatra's death?
469. What part of a camel may slump over if it is starving?
470. What does E.C.G. stand for in medicine?

Quiz 95

471. What is the rarest human blood type?
472. Most birds only sing when sitting off the _____.
473. How would you convert a measurement in Centigrade into Fahrenheit?
474. Who was the first person to use electric ignition with a battery and coil in an automobile in the late 1800s?
475. What British car won the 1964 Monte Carlo Rally?

476. What is the volume of an average human's gastric juices in pints?
477. Where are a grasshopper's ears located?
478. Xylem is _____.
479. Whales and dolphins likely had ancestors that lived on land, although we don't know how they _____.
480. What is considered a normal temperature for the human body?

Quiz 97

481. Who is the inventor of the ball point pen?
482. Which horsefly feeds on blood; the male or the female?
483. The sea wasp and cubozoa are examples of what type of fish?
484. The ancient nautilus is said to be as intelligent as a _____.
485. What toadstool is the most poisonous?

Quiz 98

486. Once a month, goats need their _____ trimmed.
487. What substance coming from a whale is used to make perfume (or used to be)?
488. Where is the stratosphere in relation to the troposphere?
489. What substance makes up hair and fingernails?
490. What port in Spain is the largest?

Quiz 99

491. What part of the human body can receive oxygen without any blood supply?
492. Who is the inventor of the elevator?
493. Where did the Chihuahua get its name?
494. Where was the first full scale public performance of a Wright brothers airplane?
495. A single king cobra has enough venom in a single bite to kill _____ men?

Quiz 100

496. In relation to Aston Martin, what does DB stand for?
497. What will other types of milk do that camel's milk won't?".
498. Where is your uvula?
499. Procumbent plants grow how?
500. On average, how many pounds of salt are in a gallon of ocean water?

Quiz 101

501. What type of tree produces hardwood?
502. How much salt is in the average human body?
503. What is the term for electronic systems used for aviation?
504. How long do baby mink remain blind?
505. The hummingbird is known for being the only bird that can _____.

Quiz 102

506. Psalm 23 reads, "He leadeth me beside _____" because sheep cannot drink from running water.
507. What kind of bird will gorge itself until it is unable to fly, and then vomit to make itself light enough to avoid attack?
508. Approximately how old is the universe?
509. Arctic terns migrate over 18,000 miles each year, making their _____ the longest.
510. The world's first commercial jet liner was produced by what company?

Quiz 103

511. Hawkers, clubtails, and biddies are examples of what type of insect?
512. What name is given to the theory that the earth originated from an explosion millions of years ago?
513. Is your stomach above or below your large intestine?
514. Alphabetically, which noble gas comes first?
515. What large Asian cat is also known as an ounce?

Quiz 104

516.   What disease is the most infectious?

517.   What is a carcinogen?

518.   Was the T-rex or iguanodon more aggressive during their fights?

519.   Cytology is the study of what?

520.   What breed of dog is generally considered to be the most intelligent?

Quiz 105

521.   Who is the inventor of the hovercraft?

522.   What portion of the earth's atmosphere is home to clouds?

523.   The group of 8 industrialized nations are known by what abbreviation?

524.   What substance makes up a pencil's lead?

525.   What is another name for the Black Death?

Quiz 106

526.   The Rowan tree is also known as the what?

527.   True or False: There are 94 more bones in an infant's body than an adult's.

528.   What common chewable item is flavored by mentha piparita or mentha viridis?

529.   What is the most common term for a baby kangaroo?

530.   What does S.A.D. stand for in medicine?

Quiz 107

531.   What cell is the smallest?

532.   The luminous intensity of light is measured in what?

533.   What does tinnitus cause?

534.   African sleeping sickness is transmitted by what insect?

535.   What surface wind speed is the highest to ever be recorded on Earth?

536.   What does the name of the constellation Cepheus mean?
537.   What is the common name of sodium carbonate?
538.   What part of a Cat's Eye is responsible for the reflection at night?
539.   What part of the body does gingivitis affect?
540.   A pyrogen is _____.

Quiz 109

541.   What pistol was patented in 1835 and was named after the person who patented it?
542.   Blue eyes are the characteristic of what breed of cat?
543.   Who is the only person to win two Nobel Peace Prizes?
544.   What is the world's most dangerous jellyfish?
545.   What is the name for the pivot point of a level?

Quiz 110

546.   What is the world's largest plant?
547.   What is the name for a breeding spot for seals?
548.   When and where did people first start using spectacles?
549.   Which British car company released the 2-seater Oxford in 1913?
550.   What kind of animal is a salamander?

Quiz 111

551.   What kind of animal is a glow worm?
552.   How often are twins born in the United Kingdom?
553.   What number relates the diameter of a circle to its circumference?
554.   Male _____ may go more than 3 months without eating, and can have over 100 mates in their lifetime.
555.   How often does a bamboo plant flower?

Quiz 112

556.   What dinosaur's fossils were originally confused with the Apatosaurus?

557.   While its mouth is only an inch wide, an _____ may be up to 6 feet in length.

558.   What muscle is the only one that is not attached on both ends?

559.   What part of a computer carries out instructions?

560.   How much does a mountain lion weigh on average?

Quiz 113

561.   What solid element is the lightest?

562.   What layer of air is closest to humans in the atmosphere?

563.   Who is known for first using antiseptics in surgery?

564.   What is the chemical symbol for silver?

565.   The British civil Engineer Brunel's first names were

        _____.

Quiz 114

566.   What is the definition of the Law of Conservation of Energy?

567.   What is the name of the process by which a plant converts sunlight into glucose?

568.   What purpose does the labyrinth in your ear serve?

569.   When submerged in _____, dead sponges can resist decay for nearly 5 years.

570.   Nauru is an island known for their export of bird droppings, and they are an island located in which ocean?

Quiz 115

571.   The Scoville heat unit scale measure what?

572.   What tiny organisms are found floating near the water's surface of lakes and oceans?

573.   Who founded the periodic table?

574.   How many degrees can the great horned owl rotate its head?

575.   Who is the author of A Brief History of Time?

Quiz 116

576. The first transcontinental railroad was completed in the US in _____.

577. Elephants have large ears to help with _____.
578. What field of science studies sound?
579. What is the scientific name for a 3-legged frog?
580. What time period came after the Triassic?

Quiz 117

581. How old is the sun in our solar system?
582. What does the 220 reference in the JaguarXj220?
583. The chemical symbol for einsteinium is _____.
584. Who was the inventor of the Spinning Jenny?
585. Which part of rhubarb is poisonous if eaten?

Quiz 118

586. What fish has green bones?
587. What Italian company has an angry bull as their logo?
588. In E- Numbers, what does the E stand for?
589. The Arctic tern migrates to where?
590. What is the largest bird still alive today?

Quiz 119

591. Crabs can evade danger by dropping a _____.
592. True or False: nitroglycerin is a heart attack treatment.
593. What is the largest cat in the Americas?
594. The potter's wheel was first used in what region?
595. If you stood on the equator, what would be the brightest star?

596.   In 1512, what astronomer discovered that the sun was the center of the solar system?

597.   What pharmaceutical company originally sold the morphine brand Heroin?

598.   What Australian-sourced wood was used to construct the London docks?

599.   What purpose does the thyroid serve?

600.   What is the cause of swelling after touching a stinging nettle?

Quiz 121

601.   What is the common name of sodium bicarbonate?

602.   What camera did Edwin Land create?

603.   What is another name for the freshwater lobster?

604.   Thoracic medicine specializes in what part of the body?

605.   Pigeons and hummingbirds have tiny magnetic particles in their heads that they use for _____.

Quiz 122

606.   The longest side of a right-angled triangle is called _____.

607.   The term "Ass" can refer to several hoofed animals in the Equus family, including the donkey and the _____.

608.   What is the name of space without matter?

609.   What solid has the largest volume per surface area?

610.   What does a low wing bearing mean?

Quiz 123

611.   _____ can tolerate freezing temperatures, and will thaw out in the spring in time for reproduction in vernal ponds.

612.   How many millimeters is one inch?

613.   What is the more common name for frozen carbon dioxide?

614.   What radioactive element is the most abundant?

615.   What is a cow's gestation period?

Quiz 124

616. Hypotension is the medical term for _____.
617. How many pints of blood does an average man have?
618. When was the seismograph first invented?
619. Bracket fungus grows where?
620. How many patents did inventor Thomas Edison file?

Quiz 125

621. If a number is equal to the sum of the numbers it is divisible by, what is the name of the number?
622. What is the name for a clot or blockage in a blood vessel?
623. What common kitchen item was released by GE in 1909?
624. A reduced British national rail system was due to a report written by whom?
625. Where is Edelweiss grown?

Quiz 126

626. How fast is Mach II?
627. Who is the inventor of Nylon?
628. What large rodent has fur?
629. Why does a duck's quack not echo?
630. What is something snails, oysters, and squid have in common?

Quiz 127

631. What is the dinosaurs' smallest living relative?
632. What instrument is used by doctors to listen to the heart and lungs?
633. What railway line is the longest in the world?
634. Dipsomania is another name for what?
635. Maasai tribesmen in Africa use the nests of the penculine _____ as purses.

Quiz 128

636.   What is the name of a badger's habitat?
637.   What company started producing the Jeep in 1943?
638.   A tiger's vision is six times better than a _____.
639.   What is the chemical symbol of iron?
640.   It can take up to ____ days for a cow's food to become milk.

Quiz 129

641.   What is a characteristic of the pitcher plant?
642.   What vitamin deficiency causes scurvy?
643.   What kitchen item did Percy Spencer patent in 1945?
644.   Who is the first man to visit space twice?
645.   A hibernating woodchuck breathes only 10 times per hour, as opposed to an _____ woodchuck, which breathes nearly 2,100 times per hour.

Quiz 130

646.   What mammal is the largest?
647.   The toy _____ is one breed of dog that does not tolerate children.
648.   What writes once but reads many times in the computer world?
649.   The first successful steam engine was installed where?
650.   What venomous snake is known as the gentlemen among all snakes?

Quiz 131

651.   What novel item was built in the USSR at the Obrusk?
652.   A cumulus or cirrus are examples of _____.
653.   The first gas lamps lit up what British street?
654.   What term is used to denote the disintegration of a nuclear reactor?
655.   Are worker ants female or male?

Quiz 132

656. American undertaker Almon Strowger invented what communication aid in the early 1900s?
657. Larry Paige and Sergei Brin formed what company in the late 1900s?
658. What was the name of Marie Antoinette's spaniel?
659. Decibels is the measure of what?
660. Louise Brown is famous because why?

Quiz 133

661. What is dust?
662. What reptile can go through 3,000 teeth in one lifetime?
663. Dachshunds were bred to hunt what animal?
664. What term is used for the annual tradition of marking of swans on the Thames?
665. Birds sing because it is a _____.

Quiz 134

666. What metal alloy is 9 parts tin and 1 part lead?
667. The world's largest atomic establishment is located where?
668. What is the name of the process in which a snake sheds its skin?
669. What creature is always late in Alice in Wonderland?
670. What is the scientific name for the Adam's apple?

Quiz 135

671. The world's longest manmade waterway is the _____.
672. The Great Dane is most generally what color?
673. Who first demonstrated TV?
674. African, chinstrap, and emperor are all types of what?
675. Who is credited with discovering Uranus?

Quiz 136

676. Most _____ cannot penetrate the skin of a hippo.
677. What is the common name of the flower Bellis perennis?
678. What is dry ice made of?
679. What is the common name of trinitoluene?
680. What TV astronomer was the most 'durable'?

Quiz 137

681. Yes or No: The sun rotates.
682. The world's first commercial railway connected what two towns?
683. What human cell is the longest?
684. May 4th is the date of what meteor shower?
685. What is the name of the largest aviation company in the world, who was started as the Pacific Aero Products Company in 1916?

Quiz 138

686. What is the more common name for acute nasopharyngitis?
687. What animals mate in February?
688. What is the chemical symbol of helium?
689. A one-humped camel is a dromedary, while a two-humped camel is a _____.
690. Mercury has a chemical symbol of _____.

Quiz 139

691. Pineapple is technically what kind of fruit?
692. Bubbles pop because _____.
693. Alopecia is more commonly known as what?
694. The Wilson's Storm Petrel is the smallest bird that breeds on the _____.
695. What do the initials BBIAM stand for in an internet chat?

Quiz 140

696. Ostriches can reproduce for _____ years.
697. In our solar system, which planet comes between Mars and Saturn?
698. What crop is the main crop of the UAE?
699. Does a crow or a rook have a black bill?
700. What magnet is the strongest?

Quiz 141

701. Acetaminophen is more commonly known as what?
702. Define rubella.
703. What is the process of water changing to vapor?
704. What grass is the world's tallest?
705. Bird of paradise are native to what country?

Quiz 142

706. What vitamin deficiency causes rickets?
707. A wood louse has how many legs?
708. What kind of dog can't bark?
709. What is the second part of a scientific name?
710. What bird uses a stone to break down its prey?

Quiz 143

711. What natural formation can be termed blocky, pinnacle, dry dock, or growler?
712. In the Windows XP operating system, what does XP stand for?
713. Besides the sun, what star is closest to earth?
714. What does a Bessemer converter produce?
715. If a cell converts glucose to energy, what process is it?

Quiz 144

716.   Ostriches are so fast they can outrun a horse, and male ostriches can _____.
717.   What is another word for a cancerous tumor?
718.   What did Douglas Englebart invent?
719.   Where is your pinna?
720.   Blinky, Pinky, Inky, and Clyde are characters in what video game?

Quiz 145

721.   What is the term for growing dwarf trees?
722.   Sloths spend up to 80% of their lives sleeping or _____.
723.   Manatees live a maximum of 60 _____.
724.   What was the nickname of the Mitsubishi A6M fighter aircraft?
725.   If a male lion and a female tiger have offspring, what are they called?

Quiz 146

726.   In the classic nursery rhyme, what frightens Miss Muffet?
727.   Who was the author of Sexual Behavior in The Human Male?
728.   What do you call .1 Newton?
729.   The mudskipper is a fish with the unique ability to _____.
730.   What is between Jupiter and Mars?

Quiz 147

731.   SI is what kind of unit of energy?
732.   Where do thermophilous plants survive?
733.   What kind of acid is in a human stomach?
734.   Are males or females more likely to commit suicide?
735.   The African tailorbird sews leaves together by using its bill as a _____.

Quiz 148

736.   Hyena clans are dominated by the _____.
737.   Who founded the modern periodic table?
738.   Which British sports car company was founded by Jem March & Frank Costin?
739.   If a shrew is deprived of food for even a day, it may _____.
740.   What chemical is responsible for the burning sensation when something is spicy?

Quiz 149

741.   What will PC World no longer be selling due to a lack of demand?
742.   What does the name of the constellation Auriga mean?
743.   What is the average temperature of a Clydesdale horse?
744.   Is white gold the same as pure gold?
745.   There are 32 muscles in a cat's _____.

Quiz 150

746.   A group of whales is called a _____.
747.   The largest living structure, _____, is found in Australia.
748.   What bird has to juggle its food before swallowing?
749.   What bird was the symbol of Prussia?
750.   On average, an elephant produces 50 pounds of_____ on a daily basis.

Quiz 151

751.   Who is credited with discovering vitamin C?
752.   What nationality was the man who built the first pedal-propelled bicycle?
753.   Female turkeys make a clicking noise, while male turkeys _____.
754.   What does NASA stand for?
755.   What acronym represents the U.S.-based long-range radar surveillance and control center for air defense?

Quiz 152

756.   What is the scientific name for memory loss?
757.   A wallaby is related to what common marsupial?
758.   What is the name for a group of ducks?
759.   What is the study of earthquakes called
760.   What do aardvarks eat?

Quiz 153

761.   What sea bird has a large red and yellow beak?
762.   What feature is smaller on the Indian elephant than the Asian elephant?
763.   If an animal is omnivorous, what does that mean?
764.   What flower is also known as the Lent Lily?
765.   Do blondes or brunettes have more hair follicles?

Quiz 154

766.   What does the Troy system measure?
767.   Is earth's gravity pull stronger over salt domes or the solid rock?
768.   The first cinema was opened in the late 1800s by who?
769.   True or False: most house dust is human skin.
770.   Each body cell contains how many chromosomes?

Nature & Science

Answers

Answers – Quiz 1

1. Northern Crown
2. Bones
3. Ivan Pavlov
4. Fokker
5. Aerodynamics

Answers – Quiz 2

6. Grizzly
7. The first bird domesticated by man was the goose.
8. The hummingbird
9. -273 Degrees C or Kelvin - 459 degrees F
10. Sea horse or pipe fish

Answers – Quiz 3

11. Pb
12. Cells
13. Sulphur & charcoal
14. Frank Whittle
15. International Air Transport Association

Answers – Quiz 4

16. Hymenoptera
17. Breathe and swallow at the same time
18. Bacteria
19. Supermarine
20. Reindeer

Answers – Quiz 5

21.   Velcro
22.   The banana
23.   Dolphin
24.   625
25.   A Hiccough

Answers – Quiz 6

26.   Hydroponics
27.   Queens
28.   Lemur
29.   1
30.   The Chinese, circa 200 A.D.

Answers – Quiz 7

31.   Photochromic
32.   80 years
33.   Formicary
34.   Dr. W. S. Halstead
35.   Equator

Answers – Quiz 8

36.   The Sun is at present, about 70% hydrogen and 28% helium by
        mass everything else amounts to less than 2%
37.   Rubella
38.   The Big Crunch
39.   The abominable snowman
40.   Uniform Resource Locater

Answers – Quiz 9

41.   Cattle
42.   Real & imaginary
43.   To combat disease and infection
44.   4 legs
45.   A backbone

Answers – Quiz 10

46.   Daedalus's
47.   Guinea
48.   The feet
49.   The earth is about 4.5 billion years old.
50.   Capacitance

Answers – Quiz 11

51.   In the neck
52.   Amphibians
53.   Sir Alexander Fleming
54.   The dark
55.   Anders Celsius

Answers – Quiz 12

56.   Barbary Ape, Gibraltar
57.   Adenosine triphosphate, the molecule that is used for energy by all cells
58.   Poupee
59.   Tongueprints, so no toes or fingers
60.   Menopause

Answers – Quiz 13

61.	PVC
62.	The frontal lobe
63.	Daddy Long Legs
64.	Flying reptiles related to dinosaurs
65.	Beryl Markham

Answers – Quiz 14

66.	Pygmy shrew
67.	Maggots
68.	Read Only Memory
69.	Beginners All Purpose Symbolic/Standard Instruction Code
70.	Jupiter is the fastest spinning planet in our solar system rotating on average once in just under 10 hours.

Answers – Quiz 15

71.	Head, thorax & abdomen
72.	Proxima Centauri (aka Alpha Centauri)
73.	Ambisexual
74.	Arctic whale
75.	Liquid Petroleum Gas

Answers – Quiz 16

76.	A rhombus
77.	In Germany in 1360
78.	Because of its size, hence Earth-shaking lizard
79.	Bees
80.	Ten

Answers – Quiz 17

81. Football field
82. Elephant
83. Sea snail
84. An ancient form of medicine which involved making holes in human skull to relieve pressure; don't try this at home!
85. The Pan-American Highway

Answers – Quiz 18

86. Longsighted
87. Vampire
88. 3000 degrees Celsius and 100,000 atmospheres. That's 10132500 kPA, at least 20,000 times more pressure than the pressure inside the average bike tire!
89. One hump
90. Morris Garages

Answers – Quiz 19

91. Body weight
92. Red And green
93. Canada, due to the number of northern islands.
94. Silicone
95. Asbestos

Answers – Quiz 20

96. The Peregrine falcon
97. Greek
98. 12 years
99. A bristlecone pine in California... it's about 4600 years old!
100. Central America Rainforest

Answers – Quiz 21

101.   Capetown, South Africa
102.   Ants & termites
103.   Barometer
104.   Sir Charles Babbage
105.   The first clone - Dolly the sheep was created

Answers – Quiz 22

106.   Alexander Graham Bell
107.   The Gramophone
108.   Buckminster Fuller
109.   The Milky Way is actually a giant, as its mass is probably
        between 750 billion and one trillion solar masses, and its
        diameter is about 100,000 light years.
110.   A leveret

Answers – Quiz 23

111.   Crow
112.   Barnes Wallis
113.   An orchid
114.   Palm
115.   Albert Einstein

Answers – Quiz 24

116.   Japan Black Enamel was the only paint that would dry quick
        enough to keep up with the assembly line
117.   Bolus
118.   Barrow
119.   Lactic acid
120.   Developed in New York & London

Answers – Quiz 25

121.	It stood 40 inches tall
122.	Heisenberg
123.	Bone
124.	Homing device
125.	The Milky Way is a spiral galaxy.

Answers – Quiz 26

126.	Sleeping sickness
127.	The move
128.	Gamma rays
129.	Bee hummingbird (2 grams)
130.	Shrew

Answers – Quiz 27

131.	Shrimp prawn
132.	The Ovum
133.	The Becquerel (Bq). 1 Bq = 1 disintegration per second
134.	Blood transfusion
135.	Desert sandstorm

Answers – Quiz 28

136.	3rd
137.	3 years
138.	Acidity or alkalinity
139.	The mosquito
140.	Female horse

Answers – Quiz 29

141.   3.141592
142.   Charged particles from solar wind
143.   Check its teeth
144.   Steven Hawkins
145.   The kneecap

Answers – Quiz 30

146.   Poisons
147.   Color blindness
148.   Osmosis
149.   Yes.
150.   About 10%

Answers – Quiz 31

151.   Capybara
152.   Jawbone
153.   Courage
154.   Earth, water, fire & air
155.   The braille system

Answers – Quiz 32

156.   Appendix
157.   A sonic boom
158.   Usually blue with a greenish tinge
159.   Triceratops
160.   Chlorophyll

Answers – Quiz 33

161.	Naval Lieutenant Jacques Cousteau & Engineer Emil Gagnan
162.	The Bristlecone Pine
163.	In the ear
164.	Venus, surface temperature 460oC
165.	Archimedes

Answers – Quiz 34

166.	Gall bladders
167.	20 months
168.	They don't close their eyes
169.	Up to three years
170.	Postpartum

Answers – Quiz 35

171.	Pregnant mother
172.	Aloe vera
173.	1_pint container.
174.	32
175.	Electrons

Answers – Quiz 36

176.	Pluto
177.	Halley
178.	Linus Yale
179.	To get insects below the bark
180.	Vredefort Ring in South Africa, 299km diameter

Answers – Quiz 37

181.	No. Now be honest, did you try?
182.	Taurids
183.	Shingles
184.	Conrad Röntgen
185.	Around 376 600 km.

Answers – Quiz 38

186.	The carburetor
187.	Fishermen
188.	Otto Hahn
189.	Albatrosses
190.	Copper and zinc

Answers – Quiz 39

191.	Pigmy shrew
192.	Five times
193.	The Menarche
194.	Oviraptor
195.	Ferdinand Porsche

Answers – Quiz 40

196.	Low blood sugar
197.	Extrasolar planets
198.	Sociable
199.	Anorexia Nervosa
200.	Roots

Answers – Quiz 41

201.   Onions, garlic, leek, shallot and chive
202.   Armadillo
203.   An isosceles triangle
204.   In Iran in the 7th century
205.   The Lapwing

Answers – Quiz 42

206.   Estrogen & Progesterone
207.   Mach
208.   Bateleur
209.   New shoes
210.   Plasma

Answers – Quiz 43

211.   Frown
212.   Cryogenics
213.   Diagonally
214.   Cranium
215.   The shoulder blade

Answers – Quiz 44

216.   Dachshunds
217.   Physiology and medicine
218.   Absolute zero
219.   Amplitude Modulation
220.   Rare earth metals

Answers – Quiz 45

221.   The Welcome Stranger
222.   An egg laying mammal
223.   Adrenaline
224.   Tuberculosis
225.   Insulin

Answers – Quiz 46

226.   It had a short head with a parrot-like beak
227.   Sacred animals
228.   6 feet
229.   Around 120 days.
230.   Jaw

Answers – Quiz 47

231.   Eohippus
232.   Polluted water
233.   A crash
234.   2nd full moon in 1 month
235.   Diuretic

Answers – Quiz 48

236.   The lotus
237.   Eddie Valiant, (Bob Hoskins)
238.   Beluga
239.   Hemoglobin
240.   Virtual Reality

Answers – Quiz 49

241.   Ferrum
242.   12 hours
243.   Grand Theft Auto
244.   Fifty percent
245.   Worm

Answers – Quiz 50

246.   An artificial body part
247.   Joint damage
248.   33 Vertibrae
249.   Blue-green algae from South Africa at 3.2 billion years old.
250.   A long tube of glass usually marked in 0.1mL units that's equipped with a stopcock for the controlled addition of a liquid to a receiving flask

Answers – Quiz 51

251.   Stegosaurus
252.   Poll
253.   The Earwig
254.   Spends most of its time underground
255.   Mammoth

Answers – Quiz 52

256.   Amethyst
257.   The pressure of a closed system.
258.   Tonic water
259.   The Ladybird/Ladybug
260.   Lead poisoning

Answers – Quiz 53

261.   Shells
262.   Acquired Immune Deficiency Syndrome
263.   -40
264.   An onion
265.   Benjamin Franklin

Answers – Quiz 54

266.   17%
267.   Karl Freidrich Benz
268.   Cartilage
269.   Rn
270.   Aspirin

Answers – Quiz 55

271.   Sonar
272.   If the Sun were a hollow ball, you could fit about one million
       Earths inside of it!
273.   Berenice's Hair
274.   Mercury
275.   Magnetron

Answers – Quiz 56

276.   Smell
277.   Seatbelt
278.   Its feet
279.   Aluminium
280.   Arm. The kinkajou has a prehensile (gripping) tail that
       it uses much like another arm.

Answers – Quiz 57

281. Goliath beetle
282. Astrophysics
283. A fruit.
284. Ohm's Law
285. Electroconvulsive Therapy

Answers – Quiz 58

286. A spinning propeller
287. Big bear
288. Ornithology
289. Captivity
290. Eucalyptus saligna

Answers – Quiz 59

291. Lye
292. 3M
293. Pac Man
294. Venus Flytrap
295. Hygrometer

Answers – Quiz 60

296. Grist
297. Love Apple
298. Birds
299. Listen to music
300. 1930's (1932)

Answers – Quiz 61

301.	Tooth enamel.
302.	1 Day/ 24 Hours
303.	A moth grub moving inside the bean
304.	Bullfrogs
305.	Cucumber

Answers – Quiz 62

306.	Vitamin B
307.	Laying eggs
308.	Aepyornis
309.	Teaspoon
310.	Circle / Ellipse

Answers – Quiz 63

311.	No. Tsunamis are caused by water displacement. Tidal waves are caused by the moon & Sun's gravitational pull.
312.	Minus forty celcius
313.	Kidney
314.	Herpetophobia
315.	Polar bear

Answers – Quiz 64

316.	2,400 meters
317.	Anti-freeze
318.	Porcine
319.	False. Sterling silver contains up to 7.5% copper.
320.	In Russia, at the Cherepovets Works

Answers – Quiz 65

321.	Radioactivity
322.	Spawning
323.	Lightning
324.	Mechanically Recovered Meat
325.	A capacitor

Answers – Quiz 66

326.	Traffic lights
327.	Ostriches
328.	Bird's mouth
329.	Zebras
330.	Black & Decker

Answers – Quiz 67

331.	Faster than light
332.	Ballistics
333.	Sunburned
334.	An Atom
335.	Orionids

Answers – Quiz 68

336.	Britain
337.	Hairless
338.	Model T Ford
339.	Hippocrates
340.	The Suez Canal

Answers – Quiz 69

341. The ant
342. The kidney
343. A Brief History Of Time
344. Single day
345. Astronomy

Answers – Quiz 70

346. Photons
347. Rotterdam, The Netherlands
348. Singularity
349. Le Figaro
350. Bamboo

Answers – Quiz 71

351. Electroencephalograph
352. Kodak
353. The Dog Star
354. Its remains were first discovered in Edmonton
355. Incisors, Canines, Premolars/Bicuspids & Molars

Answers – Quiz 72

356. Tooth decay
357. Gaggles or skeins
358. 24 ribs
359. The Cat's Eye
360. Automatic windshield wipers

Answers – Quiz 73

361. Lesser Lion
362. The Hoover Dam
363. Asteroid
364. Electrical Current
365. The Fontanelle

Answers – Quiz 74

366. An arc
367. Cataracts
368. White. Technically adding all colors of light together is called color addition.
369. Vitamin B1
370. First man to fly faster than sound

Answers – Quiz 75

371. Spider Plant
372. Mercury.
373. The Compact Disk / Player
374. Glides for distances
375. Antimatter.

Answers – Quiz 76

376. The Smallpox Vaccine
377. Alfred Nobel
378. Rattles
379. Red and white
380. The iris

Answers – Quiz 77

381. Trigonometry
382. ME
383. Lachrymal Glands
384. Curlew
385. Mulberry leaves

Answers – Quiz 78

386. Campanulate
387. 1.75kg (4lbs)
388. Fossils
389. Prairie dogs
390. The Atom Bomb

Answers – Quiz 79

391. Electric current
392. 64
393. The UK. Encephalartos Woodii at Kew Gardens
394. 25,000 feathers on its body.
395. Grow back

Answers – Quiz 80

396. John Walker in 1827
397. Protractor
398. O
399. Antelope
400. The Mountain Pygmy Possum

Answers – Quiz 81

401.   J Robert Oppenheimer
402.   Big Bang
403.   Fructose
404.   Red, green, blue
405.   Chalk

Answers – Quiz 82

406.   Almon Strowger
407.   0.5
408.   The Royal disease
409.   Pneumonic plague
410.   Schiaparelli

Answers – Quiz 83

411.   Chlorophyl
412.   The geese
413.   Ultraviolet light
414.   The eye's lens continues to grow throughout life, becoming thicker and less transparent.
415.   A Latin edition of The Bible

Answers – Quiz 84

416.   Valium
417.   Grass
418.   Golden
419.   Yes, the cartilage disks in your spine expand under zero gravity.
420.   Grooming

Answers – Quiz 85

421.	Igor Sikorsky
422.	Africa
423.	Au
424.	Serpent Bearer
425.	The armpit

Answers – Quiz 86

426.	Elk
427.	Meteorite.
428.	The nose
429.	Louis Daguerre in 1826
430.	A photon

Answers – Quiz 87

431.	Each day
432.	Ionian
433.	Together
434.	The first documented Conjoined twins
435.	Emulsify fats in the small intestine

Answers – Quiz 88

436.	Karyolymph
437.	Early morning
438.	The aorta
439.	5000000
440.	Bacillus of Calmette and Guerin

Answers – Quiz 89

441.   Keratin (Hair)
442.   In or around water
443.   The bumblebee
444.   Deciduous
445.   The badger

Answers – Quiz 90

446.   One millionth of a meter
447.   A form
448.   Igneous.
449.   Stalactites.
450.   People often favor one leg over the other. It is possible that over time the discrepancy between the two leg strides may indeed cause you to walk in circles.

Answers – Quiz 91

451.   A lizard
452.   Faces backwards
453.   1.5kg (3lbs)
454.   Bowhead whale
455.   Stork

Answers – Quiz 92

456.   Underground
457.   Shrinkage of neck muscles after death
458.   Albatross
459.   Acceleration
460.   A googol

Answers – Quiz 93

461.   Grafting
462.   Scut
463.   Neck & shoulder area
464.   Give milk
465.   Salyut

Answers – Quiz 94

466.   Count Alessandro Volta
467.   Anti-Clockwise
468.   An asp
469.   Its hump
470.   Electrocardiograph

Answers – Quiz 95

471.   AB negative. <1% of the population
472.   Ground
473.   Multiply by 9, divide by five and add 32
474.   Karl Benz
475.   Mini Cooper

Answers – Quiz 96

476.   2.5 Pints
477.   On its legs
478.   The hollow woody tissue in plants that carries water and
        minerals from the roots to throughout the entire plant
479.   Evolved
480.   98.6 F or 36.5C

Answers – Quiz 97

481. Laslo Biro
482. The female
483. Jellyfish
484. Young cat
485. The Death Cap

Answers – Quiz 98

486. Hoofs
487. Ambergris
488. Extending 50km above the troposphere
489. Keratin
490. Barcelona

Answers – Quiz 99

491. The cornea
492. Elisha Otis
493. A Mexican state
494. Fort Meyer, Virginia
495. 20 people

Answers – Quiz 100

496. David Brown (1 Time Owner)
497. Curdle
498. The back of your mouth
499. They spread overground
500. One quarter

Answers – Quiz 101

501.   Deciduous
502.   Around 250 grams.
503.   Avionics
504.   1 Month
505.   Fly backwards

Answers – Quiz 102

506.   Still waters
507.   Vultures
508.   The Universe is at least 15 billion years old, but probably not more than 20 billion years old.
509.   Migratory flight
510.   De Havilland (The Comet)

Answers – Quiz 103

511.   Dragonflies
512.   The Big Bang Theory
513.   Above
514.   Argon
515.   Snow Leopard

Answers – Quiz 104

516.   Measles
517.   A cancer-producing substance
518.   Neither. they missed each other by about 42 million years
519.   The structure of cells
520.   The Border Collie

Answers – Quiz 105

521.   Sir Christopher Cockeral
522.   The troposphere
523.   G8 (G8 Sumit)
524.   Graphite
525.   Bubonic plague

Answers – Quiz 106

526.   The Mountain Ash
527.   True. Some bones in infant's skulls have not yet fused together.
528.   Chewing gum
529.   Joey
530.   Seasonal Affective Disorder

Answers – Quiz 107

531.   The male sperm
532.   Candela
533.   Ringing in the ears
534.   The Tsetse fly
535.   372km/h over Mt Washington, New Hampshire on April 12, 1934.

Answers – Quiz 108

536.   Father of Andromeda
537.   Washing soda
538.   Tapetum
539.   The gums
540.   A substance that causes fever.

Answers – Quiz 109

541. Colt
542. Siamese
543. Marie Curie
544. Box jellyfish
545. Fulcrum

Answers – Quiz 110

546. The Giant Redwood Or California Sequoia
547. Rookery
548. In China in the 1200's
549. Morris
550. Amphibian

Answers – Quiz 111

551. A beetle
552. About every 80 births
553. Pi
554. Sea lion
555. Once every 120 years

Answers – Quiz 112

556. Brontosaurus
557. Anteater
558. The tongue
559. CPU / Processor
560. 150 pounds

Answers – Quiz 113

561.	Lithium
562.	Troposphere
563.	Joseph Lister
564.	Ag
565.	Isambard Kingdom

Answers – Quiz 114

566.	The energy of the Universe is constant; it can neither be created or destroyed but only transferred and transformed.
567.	Photosynthesis
568.	It maintains your balance
569.	Fresh water
570.	Western pacific

Answers – Quiz 115

571.	The heat of chilies
572.	Plankton
573.	Mendeleev
574.	270 degrees
575.	Stephen Hawking

Answers – Quiz 116

576.	1869
577.	Cooling
578.	Acoustics
579.	Gimpy
580.	Jurassic

Answers – Quiz 117

581.	5 billion years
582.	Top speed was 220
583.	Es
584.	James Hargreaves
585.	The leaves

Answers – Quiz 118

586.	Garfish
587.	Lamborghini
588.	European
589.	The Antartic
590.	The ostrich

Answers – Quiz 119

591.	Limb
592.	True. It dilates blood vessels.
593.	Cougar
594.	In Mesopotamia c.3000 Bc
595.	Sirius.Sirius is also known as Alpha Canis Majoris or the Dog Star

Answers – Quiz 120

596.	Nicolas Copernicus
597.	Bayer
598.	Turpentine; Syncarpia glomulifera
599.	To regulate growth & the metabolism
600.	Formic acid

Answers – Quiz 121

601.	Baking soda
602.	The Polaroid Camera
603.	The crayfish/crawfish
604.	The chest
605.	Navigation

Answers – Quiz 122

606.	It's hypotenuse
607.	Onager
608.	Vacuum
609.	A sphere
610.	A low body weight to wing ratio

Answers – Quiz 123

611.	Wood frogs
612.	25.4 mm
613.	Dry Ice
614.	Uranium (238)
615.	Nine months

Answers – Quiz 124

616.	Low blood pressure
617.	12 Pints
618.	Approximately 132 A.D.in China
619.	On the trunk of a tree
620.	1093

Answers – Quiz 125

621.　A perfect number
622.　An embolism
623.　The electric toaster
624.　Dr Beeching
625.　In the Alps at high altitude

Answers – Quiz 126

626.　Twice the speed of sound
627.　An American chemist named William H. Carothers
628.　Nutria
629.　No one knows.
630.　They are all Mollusks

Answers – Quiz 127

631.　The Bee Hummingbird
632.　A stethoscope
633.　Trans-Siberian Railway
634.　Alcholism
635.　Titmouse

Answers – Quiz 128

636.　Sett
637.　Willys
638.　Humans
639.　Fe
640.　Two

Answers – Quiz 129

641.   It's carnivorous
642.   C
643.   Microwave oven
644.   Virgil Grissom
645.   Active

Answers – Quiz 130

646.   The Blue Whale
647.   Poodle
648.   A Worm (mass mailing)
649.   Dudley East Midlands 1712
650.   The rattlesnake

Answers – Quiz 131

651.   The world's first nuclear power station
652.   Cloud
653.   Pall Mall London in 1807
654.   Meltdown
655.   Female

Answers – Quiz 132

656.   The dial telephone
657.   Google
658.   Thisbe
659.   Sound intensity
660.   First test tube baby

Answers – Quiz 133

661.   A particle small enough to be carried by air currents.
662.   Alligator
663.   Badgers
664.   Swan Upping
665.   Territorial behavior

Answers – Quiz 134

666.   Pewter
667.   Underground At CERN between France & Switzerland
668.   Ecdysis
669.   The White Rabbit
670.   The larynx

Answers – Quiz 135

671.   The Grand Canal In China
672.   Fawn
673.   John Logie Baird
674.   Penguins
675.   Friedrich Wilhelm Herschel

Answers – Quiz 136

676.   Bullets
677.   Daisy
678.   Solid Carbon Dioxide
679.   TNT
680.   Patrick Moore

Answers – Quiz 137

681.   The movements of the sunspots indicate that the Sun rotates once every 27 days at the equator, but only once in 31 days at the poles.
682.   Stockton & Darlington
683.   The nerve cell (neuron).
684.   Eta Aquarids
685.   Boeing

Answers – Quiz 138

686.   A cold
687.   Great horned owls, bald eagles, cottontail rabbits, and striped skunks
688.   He
689.   Bactrian
690.   Hg

Answers – Quiz 139

691.   A berry
692.   They get too dry from the surrounding air.
693.   Baldness
694.   Antarctic continent
695.   Be Back In A Minute

Answers – Quiz 140

696.   50
697.   Jupiter
698.   Dates
699.   Crow
700.   A Neutron Star

Answers – Quiz 141

701.   Paracetamol/Tylenol
702.   German Measles
703.   Evaporation
704.   Bamboo. Some species reach up to 39 meters in height.
705.   New Guinea

Answers – Quiz 142

706.   Vitamin D and calcium
707.   14 Legs
708.   Basenji
709.   Species
710.   The Thrush

Answers – Quiz 143

711.   Icebergs
712.   Experience
713.   It is Proxima Centauri, the nearest member of the Alpha
        Centauri triple star system.
714.   Steel
715.   Respiration

Answers – Quiz 144

716.   Roar like a lion
717.   Malignant
718.   Computer mouse
719.   It's your outer ear (the bit you see made out of cartilage)
720.   Pacman (The Ghosts)

Answers – Quiz 145

721. Bonsai
722. Dozing
723. Years
724. Zero
725. Liger

Answers – Quiz 146

726. A spider
727. Kinsey
728. Dyne
729. Walk on land
730. The asteroid belt

Answers – Quiz 147

731. Joule
732. Warm or sunny
733. Hydrochloric Acid
734. The male sex
735. Needle

Answers – Quiz 148

736. Females
737. Dmitry Ivanovich Mendeleyev
738. Marcos
739. Starve to death
740. Capsaicin

Answers – Quiz 149

741.   Floppy Disks
742.   Charioteer
743.   101 degrees Fahrenheit
744.   White gold is usually an alloy of gold and a white metal such as silver and palladium.
745.   Each ear

Answers – Quiz 150

746.   Gams or Pod
747.   The Great Barrier Reef, Australia
748.   Toucan
749.   The Eagle
750.   Dung

Answers – Quiz 151

751.   Linus Pauling
752.   Scottish. Kirkpatrick Macmillan 1840
753.   Gobble
754.   National Aeronautics and Space Administration
755.   AWACS

Answers – Quiz 152

756.   Amnesia
757.   Kangaroo
758.   A paddling
759.   Seismology
760.   Termites or ants

Answers – Quiz 153

761.   Atlantic Puffin
762.   The ears
763.   Feeds on any food
764.   The Daffodil
765.   Blondes.

Answers – Quiz 154

766.   Precious metals
767.   Salt domes
768.   The Lumiere Brothers
769.   False There's a common misconception that it's mostly human
        skin. Two thirds of the dust in your house comes from outside.
770.   46

Geography

TRIVIA

DID YOU KNOW?

2 MIN.

The shortest commercial flight lasts only 2 minutes.
It takes place between two islands in Scotland.

Quiz 1

1. Where is the Gumbo Limbo trail?
2. On which line of latitude would it be possible to sail around the world without ever touching land?
3. Which island country lies immediately to the west of Mauritius?
4. What is the national airline of Greece
5. What is the name of the river that runs through Paris, France?

Quiz 2

6. What navigation marker touches the mouth of the Amazon River and Lake Victoria?
7. Which is Europe's second largest country?
8. In which country is the Suez Canal located?
9. Which museum in London has a chamber of horrors?
10. Which country is located at the Eastern Caroline Islands in the northwest Pacific Ocean and is comprised of more than 40 volcanoes and 600 islands?

Quiz 3

11. In which country is the city of Plock?
12. In which county is Chequers, the PM's official residence?
13. What is South America's highest peak in the Andes, Argentina?
14. If you drove in a straight line from Moscow to Madrid how many countries would you drive through all together?
15. In which city is the Royal Mile?

Quiz 4

16. Name the sea north of Murmansk, Russia.
17. What is the name of the extinct volcano that rises above Edinburgh?
18. Which strait separates Alaska from Russia?
19. What is the name of Russia's national airline?
20. Who is credited for renaming the South Sea as the Pacific Ocean in the early 1500s?

Quiz 5

21. Name the large mountain chain in the eastern U.S.A.
22. If a section of shallow ocean water is separated from deeper waters by a coral reef or sand bar, what term would describe it?
23. To the nearest 100 million years, how old is the Earth?
24. What island is Pearl Harbor on?
25. Where is Notre Dame?

Quiz 6

26. What bridge in London was previously named William Pitt Bridge?
27. Gore is also known as the Brown Trout Capital of the world and New Zealand's _____?
28. What mountain peak in Mexico is the second tallest?
29. In what island group is Corregidor?
30. What was the highest mountain in the world before the discovery of Everest?

Quiz 7

31. _____ is derived from the Indian word Bhotanta, meaning "the edge of Tibet." It is located in Asia near the southern fringes of the eastern Himalayas.
32. In what country is Mandalay?
33. Which country has the most countries bordering it?
34. In which ocean is Greenland located?
35. What English city boasts the first iron bridge?

Quiz 8

36.   If its 4:00pm in Seattle, Washington what time is it in Portland, Oregon?

37.   What term describes the deepest part of the ocean?

38.   What is the name of the largest sea on earth?

39.   Who is regarded as the most influential monarch of Russian Romanov Dynasty?

40.   How many countries have a population over 130 million?

Quiz 9

41.   From 1835 - 1843 14,000 Dutch Boers moved inland to set up new colonies, what was this journey called?

42.   What museum, located in France, is the largest in the world?

43.   What Venetian bridge got its name from prisoners who would be overwhelmed by its beauty?

44.   Cairo, Egypt and Fez, Morocco are home to the oldest _____.

45.   Which European country has a name that literally means lower lands?

Quiz 10

46.   Who hired Henry Staley to establish an arm of the Belgian empire in Central America?

47.   The only national airline that has never had a crash or a forced landing?

48.   In what mountain range is Kicking Horse Pass?

49.   What's the highest mountain in the 48 contiguous U.S. states?

50.   Where in the United States was the original London Bridge relocated?

Quiz 11

51. What is the nearest town to the Lightwater Valley Theme Park?
52. Which 4 countries are located in The Alps (PFE)?
53. What does Copenhagen mean in English?
54. Can you give me the two former names of the modern Turkish capital of Istanbul?
55. Which Scottish Loch is the deepest?

Quiz 12

56. What lake is the largest among the British Isles?
57. What is the name of the largest desert in the world?
58. Which Islands were the subject of a war between Argentina and Britain in 1982?
59. Into what body of water does the Yukon River flow?
60. The Great Pyramid presides over which plateau on the outskirts of Cairo?

Quiz 13

61. Into where does the Volga (Europe's longest river) flow?
62. Denmark, Norway and Sweden combine to make what?
63. Which city is the farthest south: Seattle, Bordeaux, or Toronto?
64. What formation separates Spain and Morocco?
65. Which sea separates Turkey from Greece?

Quiz 14

66. Can you give me the capital of the following three countries: Syria, Morocco and Libya?
67. Which county is Basingstoke in?
68. What is the name of the largest lake in Europe?
69. What is Iran's capital city?
70. The northernmost U.S. state capital is _____.

Quiz 15

71. Name the desert located in southeast California.
72. Which famous cocktail was invented at the Raffles Hotel in the Far East around 1910?
73. Which group of islands is known as The Friendly Islands?
74. The most southern point of Great Britain boasts the name of an animal; what is it?
75. Which city in New Zealand is known both as the City of the Plains and the Garden City?

Quiz 16

76. What tourist attraction is wearing away at a rate of 5 feet per year?
77. In what province is Dublin?
78. What European country is the smallest independent state on the map?
79. Ouagadougou is the capital of _____?
80. _____, previously known as Aden, is a country located in the south Arabian Peninsula.

Quiz 17

81. Where is Mount Kennedy?
82. What is the Beaufort scale?
83. Which German federal state surrounds the city of Berlin?
84. The Monegasque natives of _____ _ constitute only about 16 percent of the nation's population.
85. What body of water is fed by the Danube River?

Quiz 18

86.   The planner of the city of _____ was French
      architect Pierre L'Enfant. In 1791, it was known as Federal City.
87.   Is the Tropic of Capricorn North or South of the equator?
88.   What English lake measures 258' deep?
89.   _____, in Russia, is the largest city north of the
      Arctic Circle.
90.   Where is Broadway?

Quiz 19

91.   What country produces the original Edam cheese?
92.   "Honolulu" means _____.
93.   Van Gogh's ear was cut off during the holiday season of 1888
      after he finished painting what bridge?
94.   Why did builders choose International Orange as the color of
      the Golden Gate Bridge?
95.   Where is the world's busiest international airport?

Quiz 20

96.   The smallest island with country status is _____ in
      Polynesia, at just 1.75 square miles (4.53 sq. km).
97.   What is the port city serving Tokyo?
98.   _____ has official state neckwear -- the bolo tie.
99.   Which bridge was the first major suspension bridge in the
      world?
100. Which American bridge has people who will drive you across if
      you're afraid to drive yourself?

Quiz 21

101.   Which borough is northeast of and adjacent to Manhattan?
102.   Linz, Austria is a leading port on which river?
103.   What capitol city is the farthest south on the globe?
104.   Which rocky island group off the Northumberland coast is associated with Grace Darling and St Cuthbert?
105.   Which 2 countries occupy The Iberian Peninsula?

Quiz 22

106.   In which English county is the town of Crook?
107.   What is the name of the sea located between China and Korea?
108.   What two US states are rectangular?
109.   What mountain peak is the windiest place on the earth?
110.   Which South American capital city is also the name for a variety of bean?

Quiz 23

111.   Which gulf lies between Iran and Saudi Arabia?
112.   What is the Sirocco?
113.   Who paid for Christopher Columbus 's first voyage across the Atlantic
114.   What was the former name of Manhattan's Park Avenue?
115.   Approximately what percentage of the Earth's surface is covered in water?

Quiz 24

116.   This section of Manhattan is noted for its Negro and Latin American residents.
117.   Mount Victoria is the highest peak of this island country.
118.   Who was the first European woman to visit Gabon in the late 1800s?
119.   What divides the American North from the South?
120.   Name the capital of Brazil.

Quiz 25

121. Tourists who are eager to visit recently erupted volcanoes while on vacation should take heed. Volcanic ash has been known to remain hot for a period of nearly _____.
122. Madrid and Lisbon are both located near this river.
123. What Arab country lacks a desert?
124. Who is James Clavell's novel Shogun based on?
125. The Arctic ocean is the smallest and _____

Quiz 26

126. What city is home to the Leaning Tower of Pisa?
127. Which city is the world's most densely populated?
128. In which European capital is the famous Mankin Pis?
129. Which is the world's second highest mountain?
130. Which Palace was the principal home of the Monarchy prior to 1837 when Buckingham Palace became the Monarch's address?

Quiz 27

131. Who employed Henry Hudson to search for the Northwest Passage?
132. What is the world's longest concrete dam?
133. What was the capital of East Germany?
134. Which famous Egyptian queen ordered the expedition to Punt & insisted on dressing as a king while wearing a false beard?
135. Which Ancient Egyptian burial monuments built during the Old & Middle Kingdom periods have associations with Royal Solar & Stellar Cults?

Quiz 28

136.   Which Carthaginian navigator founded 6 colonies along the
        African coast & reached The Bight Of Benin?
137.   This is the longest suspension bridge in the U.S.A.
138.   Where is Sugarloaf Mountain?
139.   The northernmost point in mainland Australia is on this
        geographic feature.
140.   What is the name of the highest mountain in Japan?

Quiz 29

141.   How tall is Everest to the nearest thousand feet?
142.   What state in the USA is smaller than the rest?
143.   What was so special about the Brooklyn Bridge?
144.   What explorer sailed around the Cape of Good Hope in the mid-
        1400s on accident?
145.   Which county is Maidstone in?

Quiz 30

146.   What country is home to the tallest building on earth?
147.   What is the second biggest lake in the United States?
148.   Which British land owner owns the largest amount of acreage?
149.   For centuries, Spain's _____ has been and still is
        one of the world's largest.
150.   The birthplace of Napoleon, also the capital of Corsica, is?

Quiz 31

151.   What was David Livingstone's purpose for travelling to Africa?
152.   What island group contains Jersey, Guernsey, Sark and Her?
153.   Where is the internet domain .me located?
154.   Name 2 of the 3 South American countries through which the
        equator passes?
155.   What is the capitol city of the African country The
        Gambia?

Quiz 32

156.   Which three countries border Luxembourg?
157.   Where in Britain is Ronaldsway Airport?
158.   Where is the Golden Gate Bridge?
159.   What is the basic unit of currency for Kazakhstan?
160.   In which sea is the country of Cuba located?

Quiz 33

161.   In what year did Captain Cook reach New Zealand?
162.   Which Pacific Nation gained independence from New Zealand In
        1962?
163.   Which mountain range lies in the North of Spain, west of The
        Pyrenees?
164.   Kampuchea was previously known as _____.
165.   How many countries have an area less than 10 square miles?

Quiz 34

166.   What does the river Seine empty into?
167.   What river separates the city of Florence?
168.   How did Henry Stanley carry his boat The Lady Alice, overland?
169.   Where do tangerines grow?
170.   What sea is between Italy and Yugoslavia?

Quiz 35

171.   What city boasts the highest population out of all capital cities?
172.   What is significant about the Oresund Bridge?
173.   What bridge serves as a link between Asia and Europe?
174.   What is the date and purpose of the largest national holiday of
        Australia?
175.   The largest city on the Mississippi River is
        _____

Quiz 36

176.   Which country uses the Lek as a unit of currency?
177.   Which island was born near Iceland in 1963?
178.   What mountains are located on the border of Tennessee &
       North Carolina?
179.   What is the name of the large natural landmark in northern
       Australia also known as Uluru?
180.   What country's flag has only one color (Green)?

Quiz 37

181.   What city is the capitol of Louisiana?
182.   What are Switzerland's three officially recognized languages?
183.   What city is the capitol of Estonia?
184.   Which motorway connects London with Cardiff?
185.   In what country is Taipei?

Quiz 38

186.   To the nearest 500 million, how many people are alive today?
187.   What is Rhodesia now called?
188.   What is common to The Republic of Ireland, Northern Ireland,
       Scotland, Wales, Monaco, Denmark & Portugal?
189.   What is the common name for the chemical symbol EU?
190.   What is the unit of currency in India

Quiz 39

191.   Where is the original London Bridge now located?
192.   Which islands were named after Prince Philip of Spain?
193.   What do you call a narrow strip connecting 2 land masses?
194.   Which of the 7 oceans is the largest?
195.   Name the second most-spoken language in Germany.

Quiz 40

196.   What is another name for the South Pole?
197.   What Central American country has a name that means The Savior when it is translated into English?
198.   The Thatcher Ferry Bridge crosses what canal?
199.   What country is the largest country on earth?
200.   What's the opposite of the Orient?

Quiz 41

201.   What city is the oldest populated city on the globe?
202.   Who were the first Europeans to reach Mount Kilimanjaro in Tanzania?
203.   What does PKN stand for in a fertilizer?
204.   The name of which Scandinavian capital starts and ends with the same letter?
205.   Where in the Baja Peninsula was once favored by pirates because of its safe harbors?

Quiz 42

206.   Which two countries have square flags?
207.   Near which river is the Temple of Karnak?
208.   What is the tallest North American waterfall?
209.   What country in Central America means many fish when translated into English?
210.   An archipelago is what?

Quiz 43

211.   Which continent is the smallest on earth?
212.   What is the largest lake in England?
213.   The poster for the movie Manhattan features what famous bridge?
214.   What is the native language of the country of Bogota?
215.   What North American state has the fewest people?

Quiz 44

216.   Which Scottish bridge replaced the much-loved ferry at the Kyle Of Lochalsh?
217.   By what name was the river Zaire formerly known as?
218.   What is the name of the longest river in the Western hemisphere?
219.   What is the capitol of Rhode Island?
220.   He invented the most common projection for world maps.

Quiz 45

221.   In which county is Stratford-upon-Avon?
222.   What is the most common shop on the Ponte Vecchio?
223.   In which country is the basic monetary unit the tala?
224.   A sextant is a tool that measures _____.
225.   Belgium, the Netherlands, and Luxembourg are part of a union called _____.

Quiz 46

226.   What do dotted lines mean on ordinance survey maps?
227.   Before the euro, what was the Sweden's currency?
228.   In which US state is the city of Chicago?
229.   What is the name of the sea north of Australia below New Zealand?
230.   What name do the Falkland Islands go by in Argentina?

Quiz 47

231.   In Kyrgyzstan, what is the basic unit of currency?
232.   Which Sicilian port shares a name with a city in New York State?
233.   How many degrees is the variation between true north to Britain's magnetic north?
234.   Between which two countries would you find Lake Olirid?
235.   Which Icelandic Viking chief founded the Norse colonies on Greenland?

Quiz 48

236.   There are _____ South American countries.
237.   What was the first artificial flavoring, created in Germany in 1897?
238.   The Mackenzie River flows into which sea?
239.   What percentage of Earth's water is drinkable?
240.   Indonesia's basic unit currency is called what?

Quiz 49

241.   Which US state capital is also colloquially known as the Mile High City due to its elevation above sea level?
242.   In 1847, which US city did the Mormons establish as their headquarters?
243.   What is the scientific name for the northern lights?
244.   Australia's highest mountain is named after which Polish general?
245.   Where was the world's fair held in 1939?

Quiz 50

246.	Which Australian town is situated nearest the country's geographic center?

247.	What is the name for the longest British river?

248.	Concord is the capital city of which US state?

249.	In Nottinghamshire, which famous country park surrounds the village of Edwinstowe?

250.	With about 865 people per square mile, which island is one of Europe's most densely populated regions?

Quiz 51

251.	List the world's four oceans in alphabetical order.

252.	_____ is an English village known for barracks and racehorses.

253.	What word is used to denote the letter "Q" in NATO's phonetic alphabet?

254.	Which three components form the earth?

255.	The Suez Canal is which country?

Quiz 52

256.	What is the name shared by mountain ranges in both Australia and Scotland?

257.	The Atlas Mountains are located in which country?

258.	What nationality was the first explorer who sailed through the Bering Strait in Canada?

259.	What sea is located north of Africa and is the third largest sea on earth?

260.	In County Cork, Ireland, which is the most famous castle?

Quiz 53

261.   What is an Isthmus?
262.   Which river is known as China's sorrow?
263.   What nationality was the European explorer Vasco Da Gama?
264.   Which city is served by Tempelhof airport?
265.   Hamilton is the capital of which island?

Quiz 54

266.   In the British Isles, what town is located farther north than any other?
267.   In 2006, what country boasted the globe's tallest building?
268.   St. Petersburg, Russia, has _____ bridges.
269.   Which famous ship belonged to Sir Francis Drake?
270.   Which is England and Wales' highest peak?

Quiz 55

271.   What is the tallest Appalachian mountain?
272.   What city is the farthest above sea level?
273.   What river is only shorter than the Nile?
274.   The intensity of an earthquake is measure by which scale?
275.   The Kennedy Space Center is in which US state?

Quiz 56

276.   Where do meridians converge?
277.   What is the name of the administrative center of East Sussex?
278.   An anthracite is a what?
279.   Where was Henry Stanley when he said the phrase Dr. Livingstone, I presume?
280.   In Brazil, what is the first language?

Quiz 57

281.   What was considered the tallest mountain in the world before the discovery of Mount Everest?

282.   Which continent has no reptiles or snakes?

283.   Which station on the London underground has a different name on two of its platforms?

284.   Which European capital city is nicknamed the City of a Hundred Spires?

285.   Where is Cape Horn?

Quiz 58

286.   What capital city in Europe's mainland is the farthest west?

287.   What is the straight between the two main islands of New Zealand?

288.   What famous ranch is visible from Ranch Road 1 in southern Texas?

289.   Which sea has the highest salt content?

290.   What prison island once lay off the coast of French Guiana?

Quiz 59

291.   Which nation located in the Atlantic Ocean has no minerals except salt and pozzolana?

292.   Where is Dogger Bank?

293.   What is the 2nd Lake Ponchartrain Causeway known for?

294.   There are approximately 320,000 floating _____ in the world.

295.   By which name was Sri Lanka previously known?

Quiz 60

296.   Seismology is the study of which subject?
297.   What is the name of Australia's longest river?
298.   What capital city is farthest north on a globe?
299.   What is the name of the world's largest cathedral?
300.   What mountain chain separates most of Spain from France?

Quiz 61

301.   Which Chinese river is commonly known as the Yellow River?
302.   Though part of Britain, which island is not bound by British law unless it chooses to be?
303.   What the largest park in London?
304.   What is the sea called between Asia Minor and Greece?
305.   Which country is the third most populous on earth?

Quiz 62

306.   Which seaport handles the most cargo tonnage?
307.   Who visited Australia and New Zealand, before surveying the pacific coast of North America?
308.   Which mountain is the highest in the Alps?
309.   What is the name of the most western part of England?
310.   By which name was Iran formerly known?

Quiz 63

311.   At what height might you find a cumulonimbus cloud at?
312.   Which mountains lie between Europe and Asia?
313.   What country begins with the letter A, but does not end with it?
314.   What is the general geographic location of the Yolla Bolly Mountains?
315.   What city is home to the world-renowned Taj Mahal?

Quiz 64

316.	Name the city at Lake Superior's west end.
317.	Dhaka is the capital of which country?
318.	Which explorer convinced many African leaders to cede power to France?
319.	Which island lies at the UK's most southwesterly point?
320.	What natural resource do Oxford, Reading, Windsor, and London have in common?

Quiz 65

321.	What is the highest mountain peak in Africa?
322.	The only borough of New York City that is not on an island is called what?
323.	Between which two countries does the Palk Strait run?
324.	Criminals were beheaded in England, and their heads were placed on spikes on a gate above what famous landmark?
325.	What bridge is less-commonly known as the dancing bridge?

Quiz 66

326.	What is the southernmost point in the 48 American states (excluding Alaska and Hawaii)?
327.	The Black, or inhospitable, sea is bordered by _____ countries.
328.	What famous bridge is known by locals as The Coathanger?
329.	The Plain Dealer is a newspaper in which city?
330.	In which continent is the Amur River?

Quiz 67

331.   This Canadian island is the fifth largest in the world.
332.   The Arc De Triomphe in Paris is the central point of how many avenues?
333.   What state in Australia has the largest land mass?
334.   How long did it take to complete the earth's first circumnavigation by air?
335.   In which city are Copacabana Beach and Ipanema?

Quiz 68

336.   What is the second highest peak in Africa?
337.   What is Hawaii's capital city?
338.   In which UK County is Broadmoor Hospital?
339.   What language is the only official spoken language of the nation of Israel?
340.   The Ganges River flows in which bay?

Quiz 69

341.   Who is credited with discovering the actual source of the Nile River?
342.   Spain and Portugal are located on which peninsula?
343.   What is the name of the bridge connecting Tibet to Nepal?
344.   What bridge connected the four main islands of Japan in the late 1900s?
345.   Bridgetown is the capital of which country?

Quiz 70

346.   What is Israel's basic unit of currency?
347.   What country claims "Waltzing Matilda" as its theme?
348.   When was the first propeller-driven Atlantic crossing
349.   From which two countries do Tyroleans originate?
350.   In 1990, how many times did the British raise Tower Bridge?

Quiz 71

351.   Which is the third most widely spoken language?
352.   Which southern US city was named for King Charles ii?
353.   What is the sea west of Alaska called?
354.   What is the name of the longest mountain range in the world?
355.   The Elbe River flows into which sea?

Quiz 72

356.   What famous capitol city resides on the Potomac River?
357.   What is the name of the island in the Philippine's with the largest land mass?
358.   The capitol megacity of _____ is Kinshasa.
359.   What 18th-century bridge was built in Cambridge without a single nail?
360.   Which is Luxembourg's main airline?

Quiz 73

361.   Which U.S. state is home to Bridgeport?
362.   In 1904 the Sargasso Sea was found to be the breeding ground of which fish?
363.   What is the name of the first suspension bridge in London, England?
364.   Where are the Pyrenees Mountains?
365.   Name the countries divided by the 49th parallel.

Quiz 74

366.   What is Haiti's capital city?
367.   What's the name of the tunnel connecting France to Italy?
368.   What is the most aged crossing of the river Thames in London?
369.   Where in England is Glenveagh National Park?
370.   Continental drift is explained by which theory?

Quiz 75

371.   In 1955 which town in Strathclyde was newly created?
372.   What is the name of Poland's capital city?
373.   What are the three Baltic republics?
374.   What country is the source of the Thames River in Europe?
375.   Built in 1897, which building contains 327 miles of bookshelves?

Quiz 76

376.   What country uses the EAK international car registration codes?
377.   Two countries gave coastlines on the Bay of Biscay. Name them.
378.   What sea is referred to as the graveyard of the Atlantic?
379.   By area, which is the largest sea?
380.   The currency for Latvia is called what?

Quiz 77

381.   What building now stands on the Earl of Shrewsbury's former home?
382.   What is the name of the oldest capital city in North, Central, and South America?
383.   What is the world's smallest ocean, mostly covered by ice?

Geography TRIVIA Answers

Answers – Quiz 1

1. Everglades National Park
2. 60 Degrees South
3. Réunion
4. Olympic Airways
5. The Seine

Answers – Quiz 2

6. The Equator
7. Ukraine
8. Egypt
9. Madame Tussaud's
10. Federated States of Micronesia

Answers – Quiz 3

11. Poland
12. Buckinghamshire
13. Aconcagua
14. Eight (Russia, Belarus, Poland, Czech Republic, Germany, Switzerland, France & Spain
15. Edinburgh

Answers – Quiz 4

16. Barents
17. Arthur's Seat
18. The Bering Strait
19. Maya Island Air
20. Ferdinand Magellan

Answers – Quiz 5

21. The Appalachians
22. A lagoon
23. 4,540 million years
24. Ohau
25. Paris

Answers – Quiz 6

26. Blackfriars Bridge London
27. Country music capital
28. Popocatepetl
29. The Philippines
30. Mount Everest

Answers – Quiz 7

31. Bhutan
32. Myanmar (or Burma)
33. China (16)
34. Arctic
35. Ironbridge, near Telford in Shropshire, England

Answers – Quiz 8

36. 4:00pm
37. Abyss
38. The South China Sea
39. Peter I or Peter the Great
40. Seven (Pakistan, Russia, Brazil, Indonesia, United States, India and China)

Answers – Quiz 9

41. The Great Trek
42. The Louvre
43. The Bridge Of Sighs (St Johns College)
44. University
45. Netherlands

Answers – Quiz 10

46. King Leopold II of Belgium
47. Qantas
48. Rockies
49. Mount Whitney
50. Lake Havasu, Arizona

Answers – Quiz 11

51. Ripon
52. France , Italy , Switzerland , Austria
53. Merchants' Haven or Merchants' Harbour
54. Constantinople, Byzantium
55. Loch Ness

Answers – Quiz 12

56. Lough Neagh in Northern Ireland
57. The Sahara
58. Falklands
59. Bering sea
60. Giza

Answers – Quiz 13

61.   The Caspain Sea
62.   Scandinavia
63.   Toronto
64.   The Straits of Gibraltar
65.   Aegean sea

Answers – Quiz 14

66.   Damascus, Rabat, Tripoli
67.   Hampshire
68.   Lake Lagoda
69.   Teheran
70.   Juneau, Alaska

Answers – Quiz 15

71.   Mojave
72.   The Singapore Sling
73.   The Tonga Islands
74.   Lizard Point
75.   Christchurch

Answers – Quiz 16

76.   Niagara Falls
77.   Leinster
78.   Vatican
79.   Burkina Faso
80.   Yemen

Answers – Quiz 17

81.   Yukon
82.   It measures wind speeds
83.   Bradenburg
84.   Monoco
85.   Black Sea

Answers – Quiz 18

86.   Washington D.C.
87.   South
88.   Wastwater
89.   Murmansk
90.   New York City, USA.

Answers – Quiz 19

91.   The Netherlands
92.   Sheltered harbor
93.   The Lanlois Bridge In Arles
94.   The color was easy to see through the fog
95.   London, Heathrow

Answers – Quiz 20

96.   Pitcairn
97.   Yokohama
98.   Arizona
99.   The Menai Strait Bridge
100.   The Mackinac Bridge over Lake Michigan

Answers – Quiz 21

101.	The Bronx
102.	Danube
103.	Wellington, New Zealand
104.	The Farne Isles
105.	Spain & Portugal

Answers – Quiz 22

106.	Durham
107.	The Yellow Sea
108.	Colorado and Wyoming
109.	Mount Washington, New Hampshire
110.	Lima

Answers – Quiz 23

111.	Persian Gulf
112.	A wind
113.	Ferdinand & Isabella Of Spain
114.	Fourth Avenue
115.	71%

Answers – Quiz 24

116.	Harlem
117.	Fiji
118.	Mary Kingsley
119.	The Mason-Dixon Line
120.	Brazilia

Answers – Quiz 25

121.	100 years
122.	Tagus
123.	Lebanon
124.	Will Adams, an Elizabethan adventurer
125.	Shallowest

Answers – Quiz 26

126.	Pisa, Italy.
127.	Macau
128.	Brussels
129.	K2
130.	St James Palace

Answers – Quiz 27

131.	The Dutch East India Company
132.	Grand Coulee Dam
133.	East Berlin
134.	Hatshepsut
135.	Pyramids

Answers – Quiz 28

136.	Admiral Hanno, who set sail in 425 BC
137.	Verrazano-Narrows
138.	Rio De Janeiro
139.	Cape York
140.	Mount Fujiyama Or Mount Fuji

Answers – Quiz 29

141.   29,000 Feet
142.   Rhode Island
143.   It was the world's first steel suspension bridge
144.   Bartolomeu Dias
145.   Kent

Answers – Quiz 30

146.   Burj Khalifa of Dubai
147.   Huron
148.   The Forestry Commision
149.   Fishing fleet
150.   Ajaccio

Answers – Quiz 31

151.   He was a missionary
152.   The Channel Islands
153.   Montenegro
154.   Brazil, Equador, Columbia
155.   Banjul

Answers – Quiz 32

156.   France, Belgium and Germany
157.   The Isle Of Man
158.   San Francisco, California, USA.
159.   Tenge
160.   Caribbean

Answers – Quiz 33

161.	1769
162.	Western Samoa
163.	The Cantabrian Mountains
164.	Cambodia
165.	Four (Vatican City, Monaco, Nauru and Tuvalu)

Answers – Quiz 34

166.	The English Channel
167.	Arno
168.	He divided it into 8 sections
169.	Tangier, Morocco
170.	Adriatic

Answers – Quiz 35

171.	Tokyo (c. 34 million)
172.	It was the first permanent link between Europe & the Swedish peninsula
173.	The Galata Bridge over the Bosporus in Istanbul
174.	Australia Day
175.	Memphis, Tennessee

Answers – Quiz 36

176.	Albania
177.	Surtsey
178.	Smokey Mountains
179.	Ayers Rock
180.	Libya

Answers – Quiz 37

181. Baton Rouge
182. French, German, Italian
183. Tallin
184. The M4
185. Taiwan

Answers – Quiz 38

186. 5,5 Billion People
187. Zimbabwe
188. They all have a coastline and a land border with only 1 other country
189. Europium
190. The Rupee

Answers – Quiz 39

191. Lake Havasu, Arizona
192. The Philippines
193. An isthmus
194. The Pacific Ocean
195. Turkish

Answers – Quiz 40

196. Amundsen Scott Station
197. El Salvador
198. The Panama Canal
199. Russia
200. The occident

Answers – Quiz 41

201.	Damascus, Syria
202.	2 Germans , Johannes Rebmann & Ludwig Krapf
203.	Phosphorus, Potash & Nitrogeon
204.	Oslo
205.	Los Cabos

Answers – Quiz 42

206.	Switzerland and the Vatican
207.	The Nile
208.	Yosemite
209.	Panama
210.	A group of islands

Answers – Quiz 43

211.	Oceania
212.	Windermere
213.	Queensboro Bridge
214.	Spanish
215.	Wyoming

Answers – Quiz 44

216.	The Skye Bridge
217.	The Congo
218.	The Amazon
219.	Providence
220.	Mercator

Answers – Quiz 45

221.	Warwickshire
222.	Jewellers
223.	Western samoa
224.	The angle of the sun or stars above a horizon
225.	Benelux

Answers – Quiz 46

226.	Footpaths
227.	Krona
228.	Illinois
229.	Tasman
230.	The Malvinas

Answers – Quiz 47

231.	Som
232.	Syracuse
233.	8 Degrees West
234.	Albania & Macedonia
235.	Erik The Red

Answers – Quiz 48

236.	Thirteen
237.	Vanilla essence
238.	Beaufort
239.	1%
240.	Rupiah

Answers – Quiz 49

241.	Denver
242.	Salt Lake city
243.	Aurora Borealis
244.	Tadeusz Kościuszko
245.	New York City

Answers – Quiz 50

246.	Alice Springs
247.	The Severn
248.	New Hampshire
249.	Sherwood Forest
250.	Madeira

Answers – Quiz 51

251.	Arctic, Atlantic, Indian and Pacific
252.	Catterick
253.	Quebec
254.	Core, Mantle, Crust
255.	Egypt

Answers – Quiz 52

256.	Grampians
257.	Algeria
258.	Norwegian Roald Amundsen
259.	Mediterranean
260.	Blarney Castle

Answers – Quiz 53

261.   A narrow sliver of land that connects two larger pieces of land
262.   The Yellow River
263.   Portugese
264.   Berlin
265.   Bermuda

Answers – Quiz 54

266.   Lerwick
267.   Taiwan (Tapei 101)
268.   365
269.   The Golden Hind
270.   Mount Snowdon

Answers – Quiz 55

271.   Mt. Mitchell
272.   Lhasa, Tibet
273.   Amazon
274.   The Richter Scale
275.   Florida

Answers – Quiz 56

276.   Pole s
277.   Lewes
278.   A type of coal
279.   Ujiji on the shores of Lake Tanganyika
280.   Portuguese

Answer – Quiz 57

281.   Mount Everest
282.   Antarctica
283.   Bank and Monument
284.   Prague
285.   Bottom of South America

Answer – Quiz 58

286.   Lisbon (Portugal)
287.   Cook Strait
288.   The LBJ ranch
289.   The Dead Sea
290.   Devil's Island

Answer – Quiz 59

291.   Cape Verde
292.   The North Sea
293.   It is the longest bridge in the world
294.   Icebergs
295.   Ceylon

Answer – Quiz 60

296.   The study of earthquakes
297.   Darling
298.   Reykjavik (Iceland)
299.   St. Peter's
300.   Pyrenees

Answers – Quiz 61

301.   Hwang Ho
302.   Isle of Man
303.   Hyde Park
304.   Aegean
305.   The Usa

Answers – Quiz 62

306.   Rotterdam
307.   George Vancouver
308.   Mont Blanc
309.   Land's End
310.   Persia

Answers – Quiz 63

311.   20,000 - 30,000 Feet
312.   The Ural Mountains
313.   Afghanistan
314.   USA, California
315.   Agra

Answers – Quiz 64

316.   Duluth
317.   Bangladesh
318.   Pierre Ne Brazza
319.   Bishop Rock
320.   The River Thames

Answers – Quiz 65

321. Mt. Kilimanjaro
322. The Bronx
323. India and Sri Lanka
324. London Bridge
325. Le Pont D'Avignon

Answers – Quiz 66

326. Key West
327. Six - Turkey, Georgia, Russia, Ukraine, Romania and Bulgaria
328. Sydney Harbour Bridge
329. Cleveland
330. Asia

Answers – Quiz 67

331. Baffin
332. Twelve
333. Western Australia
334. 175 Days
335. Rio

Answers – Quiz 68

336. Mt. Kenya
337. Honolulu
338. Berkshire
339. Hebrew
340. Bengal

Answers – Quiz 69

341. Sir Richard Burton & John Speke
342. The Iberian Peninsula
343. The Friendship Bridge
344. The Seto Ohashi Bridge
345. Barbados

Answers – Quiz 70

346. Sheqel
347. Australia
348. 1845
349. Austria and Italy
350. 460 Times

Answers – Quiz 71

351. Russian
352. Charleston
353. Bering
354. Andes
355. North Sea

Answers – Quiz 72

356. Washington D.C.
357. Luzon
358. Democratic Republic of the Congo
359. The Mathematical Bridge (Queens College)
360. Luxair

Answers – Quiz 73

361.	Connecticut
362.	European eel
363.	Hammersmith Bridge
364.	Between Spain and France.
365.	The Usa & Canada

Answers – Quiz 74

366.	Port au Prince
367.	Mont Blanc Tunnel
368.	Richmond Bridge
369.	County Donegal, Ireland
370.	Plate Tectonics

Answers – Quiz 75

371.	Cumbernauld
372.	Warsaw
373.	Estonia, Latvia, Lithuania
374.	Gloucestershire
375.	The Library of Congress

Answers – Quiz 76

376.	Kenya
377.	France & Spain
378.	Sable Island
379.	South China Sea
380.	Lats

381. Alton Towers
382. Mexico City
383. Arctic Ocean

History

TRIVIA

DID YOU KNOW?

THE FIRST WEBCAM EVER WATCHED A COFFEE POT.

Quiz 1

1. What favorite toy of the 1980s was associated with Xavier Roberts?
2. Which character of the "Bloom County" comic strip ran for president even though he was dead at the time?
3. 1789 marked the beginning of which revolution?
4. Who was the first democratically elected President of Russia?
5. Near what falls did Jimmy Angel crash his plane in 1937?

Quiz 2

6. Who ordered troops to seize the Suez Canal in the mid-1900s?
7. Which languages did Thomas Jefferson know?
8. To signal a rebellion against the state, what did Julius Caesar cross?
9. In the US, how many states did Nixon carry in year 1972?
10. What was the first city to reach a population of one million?

Quiz 3

11. Which British coin was introduced in place of the ten shilling note in 1968?
12. 'Devils Dancing Hour' refers to which time of day?
13. What were the Choctaw Indians' police force called?
14. Which actor died in a car crash on their way to a race?
15. Henry Shrapnel invented what?

Quiz 4

16. Music record discs are made of which material?
17. What famous general was once attacked by rabbits?
18. For how many years did the 30 Years War last? 27, 30 or 36?
19. Which empire had no written language?
20. What treaty, signed in 1713, ended the War of the Spanish Succession?

Quiz 5

21. When John F Kennedy was assassinated, how old was he?
22. What year was the character of Rudolph the Red-Nosed Reindeer created in?
23. Which star sign is assigned to someone born on Halloween?
24. In early 2011, Donald Trump began to publicly question two things about President Barack Obama; what were they?
25. Boadicea was the leader of which Celtic tribe?

Quiz 6

26. What is Myrrh?
27. A memo originating in New York was circulated in early 2013 suggesting Donald Trump run for which political position?
28. What is the more common name for the American M4 tank?
29. A Roman Legion was made up of how many men?
30. In British TV, which war drama was first seen in October 1972?

Quiz 7

31. The U.S. began direct military involvement in Vietnam in what year?
32. In 1803, the land that would come to be known as Oklahoma was part of the what?
33. Karen, Richard and Joseph all have what in common?
34. The Magna Carta was issued by which English king in 1215?
35. In Scotland, the 1692 McDonald massacre took place where?

Quiz 8

36. Name the U.S. President, Chester Alan _____.
37. Portland Place, London, became the new headquarters for which corporation in May 1932?
38. In 1958, which toy was launched by Danish toymakers Ole and Godtfred Kristiansen?
39. Which fictional radio presenter was created by Steve Coogan?
40. What type of food was shown in Claymation dancing to "Heard it Through the Grapevine?"

Quiz 9

41. Which Belgian noble woman received a death sentence for bathing in the blood of murdered servant girls to preserve her youth?
42. In which ocean was the Battle of Midway fought?
43. When do archaeologists believe the Rosetta stone was written?
44. How old was Catherine of Aragon when she was betrothed to Prince Arthur?
45. What is a caribou?

Quiz 10

46. The Falklands conflict began in which year?
47. How was the Anglo-Chinese war of 1839-1842 more commonly known?
48. Who did Spartacus fight against in the Third Servile War?
49. What Halloween decoration is the most common?
50. How many WrestleMania events has Donald Trump hosted?

Quiz 11

51. What female pilot flew from England to Australia in the early 1900s?
52. Which horse was the winner of the 1964 Epsom Derby?
53. Who was Sir Henry Morgan?
54. When Donald Trump changed his party affiliation in 2009, what did he change it to?
55. Roman statues were made with a certain detachable body part, so that one could be removed and replaced by another. What was the body part?

Quiz 12

56. In what year was the Democratic Party labeled, "The party of communism, corruption, and Korea?"
57. L. Halliday and B. Guy won Victoria Crosses for their actions in which military campaign?
58. Which famous US author published President Grant's autobiography?
59. In Medieval England what was the name given to the area controlled by a lord?
60. What Soviet satellite was the first to be launched into space in 1957?

Quiz 13

61. What German R&B duo lost their Grammy for Best New Artist in the 1980s?
62. What subject and in what year was the first British Referendum held?
63. Actor Mercedes McCambridge made what contribution to Linda Blair's performance in The Exorcist
64. Which seaside resort became England's first nudist beach?
65. In what year did Napoleon Bonaparte's reign as Emperor of France begin?

66. What kind of transport was used by the British police for the first time in 1967?
67. In 1955, what reference book went on sale for the first time?
68. What did the classical architect Jefferson design?
69. What was the name of the ancient emperor married to Roxana?
70. 200,000 British troops fled from which French port on June 4th 1940?

Quiz 15

71. The Roman's First Colony in England was where?
72. In 1789, The 14th of July marked the start of what?
73. Where in France did Joan of Arc die?
74. Who designed the White House?
75. Men conscripted to work in mines during World War Two were usually known as what?

Quiz 16

76. In music, "Jiles P Richardson" is more commonly known by which name?
77. In what century was The War of the Roses fought?
78. Which German city received the heaviest bombing of WWII in early 1945?
79. What relation was Louis XV to his predecessor, Louis XIV of France?
80. 'Little Boy' and 'Fat Man' were names for what?

Quiz 17

81. Which long-lasting western made its debut on TV on Sept. 12th 1959, and ran until Jan 17 1973?
82. Sir Howard Carter discovered what in 1922?
83. What was the original name for the presidential retreat, Camp David??
84. What was the name of the place also known as the 'Isle of Apples', where Christ and Joseph of Arimathea are supposed to have travelled?
85. What 1960s actress was attacked by anti-bodies on film?

Quiz 18

86. In the 1970s, Richard John Bingham made the news for what reason?
87. Which famous Giant Panda died in 1972 at London Zoo?
88. What was Donald Trump's original campaign slogan?
89. What process is used for dating ancient organic objects?
90. What famous serial killer was less-commonly known as the Whitechapel Murderer?

Quiz 19

91. Who was the Roman Emperor who followed Claudius?
92. Which comedian ended up on the front page of The Sun in March 1986 for allegedly eating a hamster?
93. In Europe, on the 23rd of August 1939, which two leaders signed a non-aggression pact?
94. In the TV show, Emu's World, what was the name of the witch, Grotbag's pet?
95. In 1960, what British coin was no longer recognized as legal tender?

Quiz 20

96.   During the 80s, what was the affordable designer watch of choice for teens?

97.   In New York City, on May 1st 1931, the world's tallest building for the time was opened. What was it called?

98.   In order not to appear scared, which king wore two shirts to his execution?

99.   What were the last words of Frosty the Snowman?

100.   A Ballista was a what type of what?

Quiz 21

101.   Which protest movement was Biko involved with?

102.   What item of clothing was first seen worn on the 10th October 1886?

103.   In A Mutinous Roman Cohort, what name was given to the killing of every tenth man?

104.   Which 'unready' king ruled England from 978-1016?

105.   Where did Richard Wagner, the composer, die?

Quiz 22

106.   What late-night TV show was replaced by The Tomorrow Show?

107.   What was the name of the final port of call for the Titanic?

108.   There are more man-made _____ in Oklahoma than in any other North American state.

109.   What is the name of the winged horse of Greek mythology?

110.   Which gangster died on the 25th of January 1947?

111. When was the law allowing witches to be burned finally abolished in Great Britain?
112. The Acropolis buildings are made up of the Propylaea, the Erechtheion, and the _____.
113. What battle did William Wallace fight and win to defeat the English?
114. In cricket, which Australian scored a then-world record first-class innings of 452 not out?
115. In France, which King was also known as the Sun King?

Quiz 24

116. What Middle-Eastern country had the most troops during Operation Desert Storm?
117. When was the storming of the Bastille?
118. Which magician was an advisor to King Arthur
119. Which one of Santa's 8 reindeer is also the name of a mythological god of love?
120. The first atomic bomb exploded where?

Quiz 25

121. In Qumran, Jordon, what was discovered by a shepherd boy in 1947?
122. Who was one of MTV's first female VeeJays?
123. What was the name of MTV's first game show?
124. Where did Queen Guinevere go to die?
125. What age was James Dean when he died?

Quiz 26

126. Which type of shoes were once preferred by skateboarders?
127. Who were the First Reich?
128. What company built the first color arcade video game?
129. Before her music stardom, what was Samantha Fox in the tabloids for?
130. Who was the father of Ramses III?

Quiz 27

131. What famous Portuguese explorer was the first to successfully cross the Pacific Ocean?
132. Which vehicle designed by Ferdinand Porsche, started to be mass produced in 1936?
133. What rock-n-roll magazine debuted in the 80s and is now Rolling Stone's biggest competitor?
134. In 1955, what opened in Anaheim, California?
135. What position was John Masefield appointed to in May 1930?

Quiz 28

136. Matthew Broderick played Dr. Niko Tatopoulos in which 1998 remake?
137. What didn't President Buchanan have?
138. When Oklahoma joined the United States in 1907, which number state was it?
139. Which French designer created the New Look in 1950?
140. Which ocean was Amelia Earhart flying over before she vanished?

141.   In 1931, the New Party was formed by which former Labour MP?
142.   In December 1967 Louis Washkansky became the first person to undergo which type of surgery?
143.   Pol Pot ruled over which country?
144.   In the TV show, Emu's World, who played Grotbags?
145.   What was the famous route taken by the Cherokee Indians to Oklahoma during their relocation?

Quiz 30

146.   What country is known as the originator of gift giving?
147.   Where was President John F Kennedy assassinated?
148.   The character of Dracula comes from which country?
149.   Which three rock stars died in a plane crash on Feb 3rd 1959?
150.   A group of Angels is known as a what?

Quiz 31

151.   One in four people were killed by what disease in fourteenth century In Europe?
152.   The first newspaper produced in the US was called what?
153.   What did Mars and Murrie create in 1941?
154.   King Tut's tomb was robbed how many times?
155.   Which words are commonly inscribed on a Victoria Cross?

Quiz 32

156.   What is the approximate number of children Ramses II had?
157.   Thomas Nast used a cartoon to link the Democratic Party to what symbol?
158.   The earliest known peace treaty was between Egypt and what other people group?
159.   Which word did Frederico Fellini use for the first time in La Dolce Vita?
160.   How many countries joined the United Nations when it was first created?

Quiz 33

161. A Sopwith Camel was a what?
162. Elvis Presley died in 1977. Where exactly was he when he died?
163. In the Russian War of 1855, what means of transport was used for Torpedoes?
164. Maurice Gibb of The Bee Gees married which pop singer in 1969?
165. What is the more common name of the Great Rising?

Quiz 34

166. What sitcom featured Judd Hirsch, Andy Kaufman, Tony Danza and Danny DeVito?
167. Which famous London building was ruined by fire in November 1936?
168. Which was the first town liberated by the Allies on D-Day?
169. Which 60's singing duo divorced after being married for over a decade?
170. What would happen if a person looked a gorgon in the eye?

Quiz 35

171. Napoleon Bonaparte was born where?
172. When did the Torrey Canyon oil tanker come aground near Land's End?
173. What disease killed 1 in every 100 people worldwide in 1918?
174. Where does the phrase 'Yeah, That's The Ticket' come from?
175. In the Bible, who is credited with raising the spirit of Samuel at King Saul's request?

176.   What type of animal is commonly depicted as a witch's familiar?
177.   What was the purpose of press men in the early 1900s in the UK?
178.   What famous event took place at Max Yasgur's Dairy Farm in New York State in August 1969?
179.   Which shop in Regent St is the world's biggest toy store?
180.   The Romans built which wall to keep out the Scots?

Quiz 37

181.   What was the name of the Olympics' sister ship?
182.   What became the tallest building in England in October 1965
183.   In 1832 in Glasgow, thousands of people died from what deadly disease?
184.   Which human organ was the first to be successfully transplanted?
185.   When did the United Kingdom give Korea to China?

Quiz 38

186.   Which famous futuristic novel was published in1932?
187.   What is the name of the journey made by Mao to Northwest China after Chiang Kai-Shek drove his forces out of the South and the East?
188.   What card appeared in the UK for the first time in 1963?
189.   According to tradition, which wise man brought the gift of gold for baby Jesus?
190.   What was the first adhesive postage stamp called?

Quiz 39

191.   What was Edward III's eldest son better known as?
192.   In March 1979, a big nuclear accident occurred where?
193.   What employment did Patricia Hearst claim when booked
194.   Oklahoma is also known by which nickname?
195.   What wrestling event did Donald Trump host at his Taj Mahal in Atlantic City?

196.   What did Washington's marriage to Martha make him?
197.   Which French Ruler was defeated in 1815?
198.   Which was the last of the 5 civilized tribes to arrive in Oklahoma?
199.   Which war claims the Battle of Rorke's Drift?
200.   Oklahoma comes from two Choctaw words, okla and humma, which translates as what?

Quiz 41

201.   Upon his marriage, George Washington acquired approximately how many children?
202.   Which torture instrument was a hinged case full of spikes?
203.   Which 1950s film took place on Altair-4 in the year 2280?
204.   What is the name of the telescope that was placed in orbit in the 1980s?
205.   What happened to The Apollo I spacecraft in January 1967?

Quiz 42

206.   The name Axl Rose is an anagram for what?
207.   What highly successful store chain opened its doors in California in 1954?
208.   What did the Indians call the black soldiers that were fighting against them in the late 19th century?
209.   In which film does the character of Leatherface first appear?
210.   In 1719, Charles VI created what principality?

Quiz 43

211.   Which epic battle featured the Charge of the Light Brigade?
212.   What Pope died 33 days after his election?
213.   In the movie E.T., what is the alien's favorite candy?
214.   What did Reagan do to the striking air traffic controllers?
215.   What historical festival was the ancient origin of many Halloween activities?

Quiz 44

216.   Which school was founded by Plato?
217.   Which kind of men's jacket had its name on the breast pocket, and epaulets on the shoulders?
218.   When was the battle of Trafalgar?
219.   Who was President during the Civil War?
220.   Between 1347 and 1558, which French port belonged to England?

Quiz 45

221.   In WWII, what were Mulberries?
222.   What were President Washington's dentures made of?
223.   Which of the following was not a present given by a magi? (Diamonds, Gold, Frankincense, or Myrrh)
224.   After the Iranian Hostage takeover, what TV shows soared in popularity?
225.   What did pre-Christian pagans call the winter solstice?

Quiz 46

226.   In the movie Knight Rider, what is the name of David Hasslehoff's vehicle?
227.   Name the only national spectator sport originating in the US.
228.   For the very first time in 1791, what did the Bank of England issue?
229.   In 70's CB radio slang, what is referred to by the term "Smokie?"
230.   The Great Fire of London happened during which king's reign?

Quiz 47

231.   In the game Pac Man, what are the names of the ghosts?
232.   What popular toy first went on sale in 1959 for the price of just $3?
233.   Which country was the first to offer a pension program for employees who had retired due to old age?
234.   What U.S. city was home to the 1962 World Fair?
235.   Which Egyptian pharaoh is credited with determining that the month of August was the 8th month of the year?

236.   What comic strip character debuted in 1931?

237.   In which year was The Berlin Wall constructed?

238.   How did Michael Milken get rich and famous?

239.   How many foreign models did Donald Trump's modeling agency bring to the United States since 2000?

240.   What should you remove after kissing someone under the mistletoe?

Quiz 49

241.   What does LL Cool J.'s name stand for?

242.   Ozzy Osborne sang about which witch in 1980?

243.   Which rock star died when the mini car he was in crashed into a tree?

244.   What US state opened the first Disneyland?

245.   In the late 1980s, Budweiser's mascot was a party dog called what?

Quiz 50

246.   What height was George Washington?

247.   Which of these is NOT a reindeer of Santa's? (Donner, Dixon, Comet, Dasher)

248.   Which comedic Canadian sketch show helped kickstart John Candy's career?

249.   Which chapter of the 'Phantasm' series was titled 'Oblivion'

250.   When was the Chinese Republic Established?

Quiz 51

251.   What global organization was formed in 1945?

252.   What was the 20th state to become part of the U.S.?

253.   Lady Godiva lived in which century?

254.   Which pharaoh has the most statues still surviving today?

255.   What are the funerary figurines called that are placed in tombs to act as servants for the deceased?

256.　What TV show was geared towards adults over the age of 29?

257.　What is the sailor Sir Francis Beaufort best remembered for?

258.　When was the first complete English translation of the Bible finished?

259.　What was the name of the nuclear missile defense system proposed by US President Reagan?

260.　Which famous painting by Edward Munch was the mask in the film Scream based on?

Quiz 53

261.　Which Chinese Dynasty ran from 1368 until 1644?

262.　In Egypt, where is The Tomb of Tutankhamun?

263.　Spencer Perceval, the only British Prime Minister to be assassinated, was killed where?

264.　Who was defeated at the Battle of Little Bighorn?

265.　From what form of improvisatory theatre did the characters Harlequin, Pantalone, Il Capitano originate?

Quiz 54

266.　Who was King Tut's wife?

267.　In the US, what unpopular law came to an end in December 1933?

268.　The Jimi Hendrix Experience's record producer/manager Chas Chadler made his name with which band?

269.　What was the 'big con' called, that Paul Newman and Robert Redford carried out in The Sting?

270.　What is a domestic turkey's natural lifespan

271.   What was the largest real estate deal in U.S. history?
272.   Those buried at sea are said to be in which resting place?
273.   Which eighties board game contained six categories of questions and small pie shaped pieces to collect?
274.   Which US candy fell into a pool in Caddyshack, causing a mass exodus?
275.   Where was Hannibal from?

Quiz 56

276.   The conquering of England by William the Conqueror is commemorated by which tapestry?
277.   Who landed in America in 1620?
278.   Thomas Jefferson founded which university?
279.   Where was 'ALF' from?
280.   Who described himself as a 'stable genius'?

Quiz 57

281.   What line did Ronald Reagan borrow from Harry Callahan to motivate tax increasers?
282.   What work is Anne Frank known for?
283.   What was the mistake made by Coca-Cola in 1985?
284.   When did the Titanic famously sink?
285.   Which medication was launched in 1960 & was linked with the sexual attitudes of the era?

Quiz 58

286.   What was said in the first transatlantic radio message?
287.   Who was the legendary fire fighter sent to extinguish the oilfields of Kuwait in 1991?
288.   What country's Prime Minister was assassinated on the way home from the movies with his wife?
289.   What war took place on a Caribbean island in the 1980s?
290.   In China of 1949, which political party rose to power?

Quiz 59

291. Name the person who was the primary instigator of France's The Reign of Terror.
292. Alanis Morrisette appeared on the ironic 1980s TV show _____.
293. What Disney movie uses the well-known address of 17 Cherry Tree Lane?
294. What 9th century city boasted several thousand bookstores?
295. When was King Tut's tomb discovered?

Quiz 60

296. What was the name of the coding machine used by Germany in World War II?
297. Eileen Collins was the first woman in space to be a _____.
298. King Edward II was supposedly murdered in which castle in Gloucestershire?
299. How long is the period between the signing of the Magna Carta and that of the American Declaration of Independence?
300. What two words finish this famous line from The Longest Day, "The long sobs of autumn's violins wound my heart with _____ _____."

Quiz 61

301. What famous battle was fought in 1346?
302. According to superstition, what does wearing socks inside out protect you from?
303. Who was the first Catholic Pope?
304. What is Sri Lanka's original name?
305. Where was The Magna Carta signed by King John?

306.   What was the name of the road that attached Exeter to Lincoln with a 220-mile stretch?

307.   Mikhail Gorbachev became leader of The Soviet Union in which year?

308.   The first men on the moon were with which Apollo space mission?

309.   What are most pumpkins used for?

310.   What was the name of the military nobility of medieval Japan?

Quiz 63

311.   What does 'Mince Pies" mean in Cockney rhyming slang?

312.   What 2 things about Mr. T's appearance made him instantly recognizable?

313.   Argentina and the UK fought over what?

314.   Who starred as the columnist "Jane Lucas" in the sitcom agony?

315.   Dr. Christian Barnard performed the first surgery of its kind in South Africa in 1967. What was it?

Quiz 64

316.   18 British Art Galleries and museums began to do what in 1974?

317.   In Stephen King's Carrie, what does Carrie's mother warn her about regarding the prom?

318.   The French Government that collaborated with the Nazis was referred to by what name?

319.   What did America pay Russia for the land now known as Alaska?

320.   On what date did America gain its independence?

321. Henry VIII's wives, Anne Boleyn and Catherine Howard, were both executed where?
322. What was Frosty the Snow man's nose made from?
323. Ramses III was the pharaoh of which Egyptian dynasty?
324. Some ghosts are known make noises. What are they known as?
325. Which notorious event happened on the 24th October 1929?

Quiz 66

326. Which singer/pianist married his bass player's 13 year old daughter?
327. Who was the first confirmed female pharaoh?
328. What does Dorothy steal from the Wicked Witch in The Wizard of Oz?
329. What living thing does Beetlejuice eat when he reaches from his scale model grave?
330. Under which pharaoh did the first known labor strike happen?

Quiz 67

331. In the 1980s, what pain-reliever had a PR scare?
332. Which Nazi leader had his six children poisoned before his own death?
333. Which record company did Berry Gordy Jr. begin in 1959?
334. In which war was the Battle of Balaclava fought?
335. 144 people were killed in 1966 in a land slide in which Welsh town?

Quiz 68

336. What 'CE' does Adam call his wife on December 24th?
337. What was the name of Charles Lindberg's airplane?
338. How long was the American Civil War?
339. What do the five rings on the Olympic flag mean?
340. Adam Faith played Ronald Bird in which 1971 television show?

341.   Andrew Johnson was US president through which years?
342.   Where were the Nazi troops most famously encircled during WWII?
343.   Prior to his solo career, of which band was Rod Stewart a member?
344.   Which company made the "unsinkable" Titanic?
345.   On May 28th 1588, something left Lisbon and did not return intact. What was it?

Quiz 70

346.   When was the film "Dirty Dancing" released?
347.   In 1985, The Greenpeace flagship Rainbow Warrior was sunk in which city?
348.   Henry The 8th had a bit of a bad rep when it comes to his wives but he only executed 2. Which ones?
349.   After gaining independence from Great Britain in 1957, The Gold Coast Britain renamed itself what?
350.   What toy created an instant craze among children upon its release in 1957?

Quiz 71

351.   Who was given the name Robins in Victorian England?
352.   What soccer player was sent home for illegal substance abuse in the late 1970s?
353.   What sort of building did Plato and Aristotle teach in?
354.   When did Great Britain gain control of Hong Kong?
355.   Which universe was replaced by the Copernican universe?

356. By what name is the stock market collapse of October 1929 more commonly known?
357. What country has a Near Year's tradition of stuffing a doll with clothing and lighting it on fire?
358. "Take a black cat and sit it on your shoulder" is a line from which T-Rex hit?
359. Which notorious murderer who was hanged in July 1953, was the film Ten Rillington Place about?
360. What did George Washington and his wife Martha never have?

Quiz 73

361. What is the common name for Muscivora forficata, the state bird of Oklahoma?
362. What name was given to the Allied invasion of North Africa in 1942?
363. When visiting Finland, Santa leaves his sleigh behind and rides on what?
364. What started in 1848 when gold was discovered at Sutter's Mill?
365. What historic event does the nursery rhyme "Ring around the Rosie" commemorate?

Quiz 74

366. What monarch reigned during Shakespeare's' lifetime?
367. What did New Zealand abolish in 1961?
368. Gaston Leroux wrote a famous horror novel titled _____.
369. What does ALF stand for?
370. What disaster struck London in 1666?

371.　What was the name of the company that the characters on Taxi worked for?

372.　What was the name of the government newspaper in ancient Rome?

373.　Which band was dropped by their label EMI due to unacceptable behavior?

374.　What was the predecessor of the United Nations?

375.　How did George Gershwin die?

Quiz 76

376.　What year was the old-age pension introduced in the United Kingdom?

377.　What German building burned down in 1933?

378.　Henry McCarty became what famous Wild West character?

379.　What is the popular name for little baked sausages wrapped in biscuit dough?

380.　What famous criminal started a soup kitchen in 1931?

Quiz 77

381.　What was the name of the space shuttle that exploded in January, 1986?

382.　Which University is currently the oldest in the USA?

383.　"Book of Love" was a one hit wonder by which group?

384.　Which Indian group ruled in early Peru?

385.　"Expletive Deleted" came into fashion due to which transcript publication?

386.   What was the name of the atom bomb dropped on Hiroshima?
387.   Oliver Cromwell was part of which government?
388.   In its first edition, what encyclopedia described California as part of the West Indies?
389.   Who was Hitler's favorite dog?
390.   New York's John F. Kennedy Airport was previously called what?

Quiz 79

391.   What product was the first to be advertised on TV?
392.   What was the name of the vehicle in which Sir Malcom Campbell broke the 300 mph barrier in 1935?
393.   In the 1970s, what was Charlie Rich looking for?
394.   What movie was based on Robert Stroud?
395.   Who played Emma Peel in The Avengers?

Quiz 80

396.   Where was Thomas Becket murdered?
397.   Which eighties fashion accessory was made up of a safety pin and beads?
398.   How many children did King Tut have?
399.   If an Italian gave you a gift of Smeg, what would the gift be?
400.   A group of witches is called a what?

Quiz 81

401.   "The Taxman's Taken All My Dough" is the opening line of which 60s hit?
402.   In 1692, where did the US witch trials begin?
403.   Six farm hands were arrested for forming a trade union. What were they collectively known as??
404.   Jet fighters first fought each other in which war?
405.   Oklahoma's four   include the Ouachitas, Arbuckles, Wichitas, and the Kiamichis.

406.   What is Abraham Zapruder famous for?

407.   From where did the bayonet originate?

408.   Pierre Francois Bouchard discovered what famous piece of archaeological history?

409.   Which eighties song sold over 20 million copies and featured Vincent Price?

410.   What is the old Celtic name for Halloween?

Quiz 83

411.   In 1934, which great ocean liner was first launched?

412.   Which English Queen became known as Bloody Mary?

413.   In which city did Crocket and Tubbs spend most of their time?

414.   Which star is Paul Anka's "Puppy Love" written about?

415.   At the end of WWI, where was German fleet defeated?

Quiz 84

416.   What did the vanity plates on the Back to the Future vehicle spell out?

417.   Name the New York night club that assisted in launching the careers of several early new wave groups?

418.   Who was Alexander the Great's teacher?

419.   People took to the streets in Britain in 1936. What was the protest known as?

420.   Which disgraced US vice president's yearbook quote was; "An ounce of wit is worth a pound of sorrow?"

Quiz 85

421. Blanchard and Jeffries became the first to cross the English Channel via what form of transportation in 1785?
422. In Roman numerals, write the number 69.
423. What was the Roman name for Scotland?
424. What is a commonly used name for male witches?
425. In 1978, three Americans flew a balloon across the Atlantic Ocean. What was the balloon called?

Quiz 86

426. Where did John Lennon and Yoko Ono begin their honeymoon?
427. What will keep vampires away if worn around the neck?
428. In order to commemorate his triumphs, what did Napoleon have built?
429. Where does Santa Claus live?
430. Is a pumpkin a fruit or vegetable?

Quiz 87

431. "It's the Great Pumpkin, Charlie Brown" was written by who?
432. At the Nuremburg trials, Rudolf Hess was sentenced to what?
433. Which nation was founded by Moshoeshoe?
434. When did the Battle of Hastings occur?
435. The US boycotted which Olympics??

Quiz 88

436. Which is an icicle? A stalagmite or a stalactite?
437. In "The Great Space Coaster," what was Gary Gnu's catch phrase?
438. What family lives at 1313 Cemetery Lane?
439. By what name was Ghana known during the Colonial era?
440. On Halloween, ringing a bell is said to do what?

441. Who won the first European Winner's Cup?
442. In the Bible, What was Joseph of Arimathea's job?
443. Who was the son of Cleopatra and Julius Caesar?
444. Who sang "So You Win Again?"
445. Which household cleaning product was launched at the Savoy Hotel In 1960?

Quiz 90

446. Which act commonly known as The Cat & Mouse Act gave people temporary release from prison to prevent starvation in 1913?
447. If a Viet Minh crossed into South Vietnam, what were they called?
448. How many total gold rings are given to the "true love" of the famous Christmas song?
449. This U.S. Secretary of State won the Nobel Peace Prize in 1973.
450. What automotive flop was named for Henry Ford's only son?

Quiz 91

451. With its name coming from the Latin word for knowledge and a Greek word meaning branch of learning, which California-founded church moved its headquarters to Sussex in 1959?
452. In 1980, what was Mark David Chapman famous for?
453. Which popular toy was hard to come by for the 1983 Christmas season?
454. What tax began in England and Wales in the late 1600s, and was repealed 150 years later?
455. What 1980s TV show showed the lives of performing arts students in high school?

456. What children's bike model had a gear shifter on the frame?
457. House of Wax was the first movie by a major studio to be made in what manner?
458. How did UN secretary General Dag Hammarskjöld die?
459. By what name was the British city of Winchester known to the Romans?
460. In what year was NASA founded?

Quiz 93

461. Where were the Hanging Gardens?
462. Santa has how many reindeer?
463. Transformers are what artifacts in disguise?
464. How does Good King Wenceslas like to eat his pizza?
465. What California suburb has the nickname "Surf City?"

Quiz 94

466. What is the name of Adrienne Barbeau's character in The Fog?
467. "Hell no, we won't go!" Began in reference to what?
468. What war followed the shot heard round the world?
469. When was Queen Elizabeth I born?
470. What was George A. Custer's horses' name?

Quiz 95

471. Who sang with Donna Summer on the track No More Tears?
472. What series of of natural disasters hit the American Midwest in 1935?
473. Which age came between the stone and the iron ages?
474. Who was the Spanish king who sent an armada against the English in the late 1500s?
475. What was the only state George McGovern carried in the 1972 Presidential election?

Quiz 96

476. What year marked the beginning of the French Revolution?
477. In Halloween, Michael Meyers wore a Halloween mask of what famous character?
478. What did presidents Madison, Monroe, Polk, and Garfield have in common?
479. What do you call a quiet armor wearer?
480. In 1922, Lord Carnavon and Howard Carter made what fascinating discovery?

Quiz 97

481. Which war involving the United Kingdom began in 1982?
482. Which new country was formed in 1971 at the end of the Pakistan / India conflict?
483. Who was Elizabeth I's birth mother?
484. The Greek army under Leonidas was annihilated here by the Persians in 480BC.
485. Which country did Britain fight in the War of Jenkins's Ear?

Quiz 98

486. What North Carolina explorer was never able to finish his book due to being banished to the Tower of London?
487. What iconic revolutionary was assassinated on October 9th, 1967?
488. In the TV show 'Til Death Do Us Part, what football team was Alf a fan of?
489. Where did Napoleon Bonaparte live during his exile?
490. Which daughter of Russian Czar Nicholas II was believed to have escaped death in the revolution?
491. Who was the 19th-century Railroad King?

History

TRIVIA

Answers

Answers – Quiz 1

1. Cabbage Patch Kids
2. Bill the Cat
3. The French Revolution
4. Boris Yeltsin
5. Angel Falls

Answers – Quiz 2

6. President Nassar
7. French, Greek, Italian, Latin, and Spanish.
8. Rubikon
9. Forty-nine
10. Ancient Rome

Answers – Quiz 3

11. 50 pence piece
12. Midnight
13. Lighthorsemen
14. James Dean
15. The exploding shell

Answers – Quiz 4

16. Vinyl
17. Napoleon Bonaparte
18. 30 Years
19. The Incan Empire
20. Treaty of Utrecht

Answers – Quiz 5

21.	46
22.	A=1939
23.	Scorpio
24.	Citizenship and eligibility to serve as President.
25.	The Iceni

Answers – Quiz 6

26.	Gum resin, used as a perfume, anointing oil, incense, and medicine
27.	Governor of the state in 2014.
28.	The Sherman tank
29.	4000 - 6000
30.	Colditz

Answers – Quiz 7

31.	1964
32.	Louisiana purchase.
33.	All Carpenters
34.	King John
35.	Glencoe

Answers – Quiz 8

36.	Arthur
37.	The BBC
38.	Lego
39.	Alan Partridge
40.	Raisins

Answers – Quiz 9

41.   Countess Elizabeth Bathory
42.   Pacific Ocean
43.   196 BC, in Memphis, Egypt
44.   She was three
45.   A reindeer

Answers – Quiz 10

46.   1982
47.   The Opium War
48.   The Roman Republic
49.   Jack-o-Lantern
50.   Two.

Answers – Quiz 11

51.   Amy Johnson
52.   Santa Claus
53.   A Buccaneer/Pirate
54.   Republican.
55.   Heads

Answers – Quiz 12

56.   1952, by Dwight Eisenhower
57.   The Boxer Rebellion
58.   Mark Twain
59.   Manor
60.   Sputnik

Answers – Quiz 13

61. Milli Vanilli
62. 1975, Membership Of The EEC
63. Provided the Devil's voice
64. Brighton
65. 1804

Answers – Quiz 14

66. Helicopters
67. Guinness Book Of Records
68. Monticello and other notable buildings.
69. Alexander the Great
70. Dunkirk

Answers – Quiz 15

71. Colchester
72. French Revolution
73. Rouen
74. James Hoban
75. Bevin Boys

Answers – Quiz 16

76. The Big Bopper
77. 15th Century
78. Dresden
79. Great-grandson
80. Atom Bombs

Answers – Quiz 17

82. Bonanza
83. Tutankhamun's Tomb
84. Shangri-La
85. Avalon
86. Rachel Welch

Answers – Quiz 18

87. As Lord Lucan, he disappeared after his wife was murdered, and has never been found.
88. Chi Chi
89. "Make America Great Again."
90. Radiocarbon Dating
91. Jack the Ripper

Answers – Quiz 19

92. Nero
93. Freddie Star
94. Hitler & Stalin
95. Croc
96. Farthing

Answers – Quiz 20

97. Swatch
98. Empire States Building
99. Charles I
100. I'll Be Back Again Someday
101. An ancient siege machine, a giant catapult or crossbow

Answers – Quiz 21

102.	Apartheid
103.	Tuxedo
104.	Decimate
105.	Ethelred
106.	Venice

Answers – Quiz 22

107.	David Letterman
108.	Queenstown
109.	Lakes
110.	Pegasus
111.	Al Capone

Answers – Quiz 23

112.	1735
113.	Parthenon
114.	Battle of Stirling Bridge
115.	Donald Bradman
116.	Louis XIV

Answers – Quiz 24

117.	Saudi Arabia.
118.	July 14th, 1789
119.	Merlin
120.	Cupid
121.	Trinity site, New Mexico

Answers – Quiz 25

122.   The Dead Sea Scrolls
123.   Martha Quinn
124.   Remote Control
125.   Amesbury Abbey
126.   24

Answers – Quiz 26

127.   Vans
128.   The Holy Roman Empire
129.   Atari
130.   She was a page three girl
131.   Setnakhte

Answers – Quiz 27

132.   Ferdinand Magellan
133.   The Volkswagen
134.   Spin
135.   Disneyland
136.   Poet Laureate

Answers – Quiz 28

137.   Godzilla'
138.   A wife
139.   46th
140.   Chriatian Dior
141.   The Pacific

Answers – Quiz 29

142.	Sir Oswald Mosley
143.	A heart transplant
144.	Cambodia (Kampuchea)
145.	Carol Lee Scott
146.	Trail of Tears

Answers – Quiz 30

147.	Italy (Romans)
148.	Dallas / Texas
149.	Transylvania
150.	Buddy Holly, Big Bopper, Richie Valens
151.	A Host, or flight (Shakespeare)

Answers – Quiz 31

152.	The Black Death or Bubonic Plague
153.	Publick Occurrences
154.	M & Ms
155.	2 times
156.	For Valour

Answers – Quiz 32

157.	160
158.	A donkey.
159.	The Hittites
160.	Paparazzi
161.	51

Answers – Quiz 33

162. A single-seater armed biplane used in WWI
163. On the toilet
164. Kites
165. Lulu
166. The Peasants' Revolt

Answers – Quiz 34

167. Taxi
168. The Crystal Palace
169. Sainte-Mère-Église
170. Sonny and Cher
171. You turned to stone

Answers – Quiz 35

172. Ajaccio, France in the region of Corsica
173. 1967
174. Spanish Flu
175. William Shakespeare
176. Witch of Endor

Answers – Quiz 36

177. A Black Cat
178. To impress men into the Royal Navy
179. Woodstock Festival
180. Hamley's
181. Hadrian's Wall

Answers – Quiz 37

182.	The Titanic
183.	Post Office Tower
184.	Cholera
185.	A kidney
186.	1997 (June 30th)

Answers – Quiz 38

187.	Brave New World
188.	The Long March
189.	The American Express card
190.	Melchior
191.	Penny Black

Answers – Quiz 39

192.	The Black Prince
193.	Three Mile Island (in Pennsylvania)
194.	Urban guerrilla
195.	The Sooner state
196.	The 1991 WBF Championship.

Answers – Quiz 40

197.	One of the ten wealthiest planters in Virginia
198.	Napoleon
199.	Seminole
200.	Zulu Wars
201.	Red people

Answers – Quiz 41

202. Two step-children, a boy and a girl.
203. The Iron Maiden
204. Forbidden Planet
205. The Hubble
206. Caught fire on the launch pad killing all 3 crew

Answers – Quiz 42

207. Oral Sex
208. FedMart
209. Buffalo soldiers
210. Texas Chainsaw Massacre
211. Lichtenstein

Answers – Quiz 43

212. Balaclava
213. John Paul I
214. Reese's Pieces
215. Fired them
216. Samhain

Answers – Quiz 44

217. Academy
218. Members Only
219. 1805
220. Abraham Lincoln
221. Calais

Answers – Quiz 45

222.	Floating harbors used on D-Day
223.	Ivory and human teeth
224.	Diamonds
225.	Nightline
226.	Yule

Answers – Quiz 46

227.	Kitt
228.	Rodeos
229.	Banknotes
230.	A Policeman
231.	Charles II

Answers – Quiz 47

232.	Inky Pinky Blinky & Clyde
233.	Barbie
234.	Germany (1891)
235.	Seattle
236.	Augustus Caesar

Answers – Quiz 48

237.	Dick Tracy
238.	1961
239.	Junk Bonds
240.	About 250.
241.	One of the berries (for good luck)

Answers – Quiz 49

242. Ladies Love Cool James
243. Aleister Crowley
244. Marc Bolan
245. California (Annaheim)
246. Spuds McKenzie

Answers – Quiz 50

247. Six feet.
248. Dixon
249. SCtv
250. Phantasm 4
251. 1911

Answers – Quiz 51

252. United Nations
253. Mississippi
254. 11th Century
255. Amenhotep III
256. Shabti dolls

Answers – Quiz 52

257. Thirty-something
258. His system of wind force indicators
259. In 1388, the Wycliff Bible translation was finished after his death
260. Star Wars
261. The Scream

Answers – Quiz 53

262.   Ming
263.   Valley Of The Kings, Luxor
264.   The Lobby Of The House Of Commons
265.   General Custer
266.   Commedia dell'Arte

Answers – Quiz 54

267.   Ankhesenamun
268.   Prohibition
269.   The Animals
270.   The Wire
271.   12 Years

Answers – Quiz 55

272.   Louisiana purchase
273.   Davey Jones' Locker
274.   Trivial Pursuit
275.   A Baby Ruth candy bar
276.   Carthage

Answers – Quiz 56

277.   Bayeux Tapestry
278.   The Pilgrims/Puritans
279.   The University of Virginia.
280.   Melmac
281.   Donald Trump.

Answers – Quiz 57

282.   "Go ahead, make my day".
283.   A diary about her life in hiding from the Germans in WW2
284.   New Coke
285.   1912
286.   The Birth Control Pill

Answers – Quiz 58

287.   S in Morse code
288.   Red Adair
289.   Sweden (Olof Palme)
290.   Grenada
291.   The Communists

Answers – Quiz 59

292.   Maximilien Robespierre
293.   You Can't Do that On Television
294.   Mary Poppins
295.   Baghdad
296.   1922

Answers – Quiz 60

297.   Enigma
298.   Commander of a space shuttle.
299.   Berkeley castle
300.   561 years
301.   Monotonous langour

Answers – Quiz 61

302.	Crecy
303.	Witches
304.	Peter
305.	Ceylon
306.	Runnymede

Answers – Quiz 62

307.	Fosse Way
308.	1985
309.	Apollo 11
310.	Halloween decoration, as in the US, many people are too lazy to carve them any more
311.	The samurai

Answers – Quiz 63

312.	Eyes
313.	His mohawk haircut and extensive gold jewelry
314.	Falkland Islands
315.	Maureen Lipman
316.	Heart transplant

Answers – Quiz 64

317.	Charge admission
318.	"They are all going laugh at you."
319.	Vichy
320.	7.2 Million
321.	July 4th, 1776

Answers – Quiz 65

322. The Tower Of London
323. Button
324. The Twentieth Dynasty
325. Poltergeists
326. The Wall Street Crash or (Black Thursday)

Answers – Quiz 66

327. Jerry Lee Lewis
328. Sobekneferu
329. Her broomstick
330. A fly
331. Rameses III

Answers – Quiz 67

332. Tylenol, which had been laced with cyanide, caused several murders.
333. Joseph Goebbels
334. Motown
335. The Crimean
336. Aberfan

Answers – Quiz 68

337. Christmas Eve
338. Spirit of St Louis (achieved in 1927)
339. Four years
340. 5 continents
341. Budgie

Answers – Quiz 69

342.	1865 to 1869.
343.	Stalingrad
344.	The Faces
345.	Harland & Wolff
346.	The Spanish Armada

Answers – Quiz 70

347.	1987
348.	Auckland
349.	Anne Boleyn, Katheryn Howard
350.	Ghana
351.	The Hula Hoop

Answers – Quiz 71

352.	Postmen
353.	Willie Johnston
354.	Gymnasium
355.	1842
356.	Ptolemaic

Answers – Quiz 72

357.	Black Thursday
358.	Colombia
359.	Ride a white swan
360.	John Reginald Christie
361.	Children of their own. Martha already had two children when she married him.

Answers – Quiz 73

362.   Scissor-tailed flycatcher
363.   Operation Torch
364.   A Goat named Ukko
365.   The California Gold Rush
366.   The Great Plague/Black Death/Bubonic Plague

Answers – Quiz 74

367.   Elizabeth I & James I
368.   The death penalty
369.   The Phantom Of the Opera
370.   Alien Life Form
371.   The Great Fire

Answers – Quiz 75

372.   Sunshine Cab Company
373.   Acta Diurna (Daily Happenings)
374.   The Sex Pistols
375.   League of Nations
376.   Brain tumor

Answers – Quiz 76

377.   1908
378.   The Reichstag (German Parliament)
379.   Billy the Kid, alias William H Bonney
380.   Pigs in blankets
381.   Al Capone

Answers – Quiz 77

382.	Challenger
383.	Harvard (founded 1636, in Cambridge Massachusetts)
384.	The Monotones
385.	Inca
386.	The Watergate Tapes

Answers – Quiz 78

387.	Fat Man
388.	The Commenwealth Goverment
389.	Encyclopedia Britannica's.
390.	Blondi, a German Shepherd
391.	Idlewind

Answers – Quiz 79

392.	Bulova watch
393.	Bluebird
394.	Freedom
395.	The Birdman of Alcatraz
396.	Diana Rigg

Answers – Quiz 80

397.	Canterbury Cathedral
398.	Friendship pins
399.	Two
400.	A Kitchen Appliance
401.	A Coven

Answers – Quiz 81

402. Kinks/Sunny Afternoon
403. Salem, Massachusetts
404. The Tolpuddle Martyrs
405. The Korean War
406. Mountain ranges

Answers – Quiz 82

407. He filmed John F. Kennedy's assassination
408. Bayonne, France
409. The Rosetta Stone
410. Thriller
411. Samhain (pron) sow-en

Answers – Quiz 83

412. The Queen Mary
413. Mary I
414. Miami Vice
415. Annette Funicello
416. Scapa Flow

Answers – Quiz 84

417. OUTATIME
418. CBGB
419. Aristotle
420. The Jarrow March
421. Spiro Agnew.

Answers – Quiz 85

422.   Balloon
423.   LXIX
424.   Caledonia
425.   Warlocks
426.   The Double Eagle II

Answers – Quiz 86

427.   Holland/Amsterdam
428.   Garlic
429.   Arc de Triomphe
430.   Rovaniemi
431.   A fruit that grows on vines

Answers – Quiz 87

432.   Charles M. Schultz
433.   Life imprisonment
434.   Basotho
435.   1066
436.   1980

Answers – Quiz 88

437.   Stalagtite
438.   No Gnus is Good Gnus
439.   The Addams Family
440.   Gold Coast
441.   Scare evil spirits

Answers – Quiz 89

442. Tottenham (Spurs)
443. Carpenter
444. Caesarion
445. Hot chocolate
446. Fairy liquid

Answers – Quiz 90

447. The Prisoners Act
448. The Viet Cong.
449. 40 (5x8=40)
450. Kissinger
451. The Edsel

Answers – Quiz 91

452. Church of Scientology
453. Shooting John Lennon
454. Cabbage Patch Kid
455. Window tax
456. Fame

Answers – Quiz 92

457. The Chopper
458. It was the first movie from a major motion-picture studio to be shot using the three-dimensional, or stereoscopic, film process
459. In an air crash
460. Venta Bulgarum
461. 1958

Answers – Quiz 93

462.   Babylon
463.   8 / (9 With Rudolph)
464.   Robots
465.   Deep, pan crisp and even
466.   Santa Cruz

Answers – Quiz 94

467.   Stevie Wayne
468.   The Vietnam War
469.   The War of American Independence
470.   1533
471.   Comanche

Answers – Quiz 95

472.   Barbara Streisand
473.   Dust storms
474.   The Bronze Age
475.   Philip II
476.   Massachusetts

Answers – Quiz 96

477.   1789
478.   Captain Kirk mask
479.   The first name "James"
480.   A Silent Knight
481.   The Tomb Of Tutankhamun

Answers – Quiz 97

482.   The Falklands War
483.   Bangladesh
484.   Anne Boleyn.
485.   Thermopylae
486.   Spain

Answers – Quiz 98

487.   Sir Walter Raleigh.
488.   Che Guevara
489.   West Ham
490.   His first Exile: Elba, his second: St Helena
491.   Anastasia
492.   The financier George Hudson

People & Places

TRIVIA

DID YOU KNOW?

THE LONGEST MOUSTACHE EVER IS 4.29m (14 FT) LONG AND BELONGS TO AN INDIAN MAN.

Quiz 1

1. What is the name of Fidel Castro's brother?
2. Who were Balthazar, Melchior and Gaspar?
3. In 2007, which celebrity launched a perfume line called 'M' for Christmas?
4. By what name was mistletoe known by the Vikings who discovered it?
5. In the film, Halloween, what is Michael Myers's middle name?

Quiz 2

6. Who was the Captain of the Titanic when it sank?
7. Who is Joley Richardson's mother?
8. Who held the post of The Archbishop Of Canterbury in 1995
9. What was Eric Morecambes partner's real name?
10. In 1979, who bought Paris' Ritz Hotel?

Quiz 3

11. According to superstition, if a girl places letters of the alphabet face down in water, how will she know who she will marry?
12. Who was the first female Prime Minister of the United Kingdom?
13. Who first said the lines "They think it's all over, it is now?"
14. Which King is famous for supposedly trying to turn back the sea?
15. Who released an album in the 1970s called "Physical Graffiti?"

Quiz 4

16. Who was the first in the British Royal Family to graduate from a University?
17. Deva was the name given by the Romans to which British city?
18. Which Hollywood actor was arrested at Sydney airport in 2006 for smuggling banned hormones into the country in his suitcase?
19. Name the founder of Playboy magazine.
20. In 2003, who did Mervyn King succeed as Governor of the Bank of England?

Quiz 5

21. Who wrote the fictional novel Frankenstein?
22. Which ex-TV detective turned crooner sang "Silver Lady?"
23. Who was the author of "The Witching Hour?"
24. Who released an album in The 1970's called "The Grand Tour?"
25. During a visit to Wales in 1991, which politician punched a protestor after being egged?

Quiz 6

26. What was the name of the German who landed his plane in Red Square?
27. Whose real name is "Cherilyn Sarkisian La Pierre?"
28. Who ran against Reagan in 1984 and lost?
29. Who released an album called "Cosmo's Factory" in the 1970s?
30. The first British Labour Government was formed by who?

Quiz 7

31. Of what nationality Was Hans Christian Andersen?
32. Which publisher was known by the name "Cap' N Bob?"
33. Which famous author Had A "Fatwa" issued against him in 1989?
34. Who is Allan Stewart Konigsberg more commonly known as?
35. Who won a Guinness Record for writing 26 books in 1983?

Quiz 8

36. Name the person who led the Million Man March on Washington.
37. Who was killed by Indians at the battle of Little Big Horn?
38. Whose birth name is Farouk Bulsara?
39. In cricket, which Australian wicket keeper bet against his own team at 500-1 and won?
40. Name the last British Viceroy of India.

Quiz 9

41. Who became president following the assassination of Abraham Lincoln?
42. Where was Mike Tyson born?
43. To whom is the actress Charlotte Rampling married?
44. After being described as "Boring," who sued for libel?
45. "Here's another fine mess you've gotten me into." was who's catchphrase?

Quiz 10

46. Who released Blood On The Tracks?
47. Which eighties group was named after the radio inventor?
48. Who was the Australian actor who advertised Foster's Lager in a television advertising campaign in the 1980s?
49. Where is the National Horseracing Museum located in Britain?
50. What is Bob Dylan's real name?

Quiz 11

51. Which Zoologist authored Man Watching?
52. What were the 1920s called in the United States?
53. Which US President was previously a peanut farmer?
54. Who released The 1970's album "The Stranger?"
55. Which rock band released the 1970's album "Exile on Main Street?"

Quiz 12

56. Who was the first woman to officially become a billionaire in the US?
57. Whose US Election campaign slogan was "You've Never Had It So Good?"
58. Who was titled Miss Hungary in 1936?
59. When Uncle Sam first got a beard, who was president of the U.S?
60. Name the person awarded with the only Nobel Peace Prize given during WWI?

Quiz 13

61. In a 60s film, who was the bravest of them all?
62. Who directed the movie Eyes Wide Shut?
63. In Irish mythology, what is the spirit whose wailing foretells death called?
64. Who won Eurovision in 1999?
65. Name the First Director General of the BBC?

Quiz 14

66. Who hosted a breakaway World Series Cricket match for his Australian TV network?
67. Who played bowls before engaging The Spanish Armada?
68. Who bought one of Leonardo Da Vinci's notebooks in 1994 for more than 19 million British pounds?
69. Three of Santa's reindeers names begin with D. Dasher, Dancer and _____.
70. Who was the German Officer who rescued Mussolini and lived and died in Madrid?

Quiz 15

71. Who holds the title of the heaviest person to have ever sat in Parliament
72. Which candidate did the LA times endorse in the 1964 US presidential election?
73. What important event happened on July 20, 1969 for the first time?
74. Who released a 1970's Album named "déjà vu?"
75. Who released the album, "The Pleasure Principle" in the 1970s?

76.   Who did Bobby Darin marry in 1960?

77.   By what name is Meg Lake more commonly known?

78.   Who was Ronald Regan's first wife?

79.   Who beat Floyd Patterson to win the world heavyweight boxing title in 1962?

80.   In 1955, who made headlines after refusing to give up her seat to a white person?

Quiz 17

81.   Who voiced Charlie in the show "Charlie's Angels?"

82.   Which Tomorrow's World presenter married Keith Chegwin?

83.   Who made the first non-stop transatlantic crossing in an airplane?

84.   Who was the first person to sing in the Band Aid single of 1984?

85.   In the 1970s, who released the album "New Boots and Panties?"

Quiz 18

86.   While in prison, who did Hitler dictate Mein Kampf to?

87.   In the UK, who was elected Conservative MP for Henley in 2001?

88.   Who did Harold Wilson succeed as Prime Minister?

89.   What was Princess Diana's family name before marrying Prince Charles?

90.   Who did Queen Victoria succeed to the throne?

Quiz 19

91.   Who was the host of the Nickelodeon show Double Dare?

92.   Who started London's first birth control clinic?

93.   In the 2000 season, which footballer was sent off in both of the opening premiership games?

94.   Who released the 70's album "Electric Warrior?"

95.   Which cricketer is also known as "The Cat?"

96.   Washington was a commander who emphasized _____ above all.
97.   Who released the album "John Barleycorn Must Die?"
98.   Who was the leader of the British Fascist Party who started out as a Tory before becoming a Labour MP?
99.   What part of Betty Grable's body was insured for over a million dollars
100. In 1769, who was the inventor of The Spinning Frame?

Quiz 21

101. What the Titanic's sister ship called?
102. Who was the C.I.A's director from 1976 to 1977?
103. Whose name was originally "Arthur Stanley Jefferson?"
104. Who is the lead singer of the Smiths?
105. What was Madam Tussaud's first name?

Quiz 22

106. What was Judge Jefferies' nickname?
107. What English football manager was fired in 1964?
108. In music, who released "Machine Gun Etiquette?"
109. In the Bible, who is Jesus's father?
110. Which two famous TV presenters were once MP's?

Quiz 23

111. In music, which band released the 70's album "Destroyer?"
112. Which group released the 1970's music album named "Trafalgar?"
113. In 2002, which famous actress was convicted for shoplifting?
114. Name the first (and last) Catholic president of the US?
115. Who led child workers in a 125 mile march to President Theodore Roosevelt's home on Long Island?

Quiz 24

116. Who was the only American to hold the titles of vice president and president after the president resigned?
117. In the film "The Santa Clause" which actor plays Santa?
118. Which singer released the 1970's album "Blue?"
119. Who was the final president of the Soviet Union?
120. Who was the lead vocalist of the Cure?

Quiz 25

121. Who was the character on the first Garbage Pail Kids Pack?
122. Who designed London's Regent's Park in the early 19th century?
123. Who was Australian Outlaw famous for wearing metal body armor?
124. What British jockey was imprisoned for tax evasion?
125. Which Monaco ruler married actress Grace Kelly in 1956?

Quiz 26

126. What is Peter Roget Famous for?
127. Which former member of The Goodies enjoys bird watching?
128. Who was the first woman to fly solo across the Atlantic?
129. What do you call a poor American holy man?
130. King Richard I is sometimes referred to by what name?

Quiz 27

131. Who was Maradona playing for when first caught taking cocaine
132. Who batted with a bat made from aluminum?
133. Name the last British monarch who was born overseas?
134. What was Jackie Kennedy's maiden name?
135. Who was Molly Pitcher?

136.   Who was the second wife of Henry VIII?
137.   Who released the album "All Mod Cons?"
138.   Who was Jeremy Thorpe found not guilty of plotting to murder in 1979?
139.   Which MP was elected for Belfast West in 1997?
140.   Which British Labour MP tried to fake his disappearance?

Quiz 29

141.   In what is often thought of as the first live televised murder, who killed who?
142.   Who were the stars of The Goon Show
143.   Who was the first female US astronaut?
144.   Who led the Alamo attack?
145.   What did Churchill, Cromwell, and Catherine of Aragon have in common?

Quiz 30

146.   In 2000, what was the most common girls' name?
147.   What was Sir Roger Hollis the leader of?
148.   In music, who released "Here Come the Warm Jets?"
149.   Who authored The Guns Of Navarone?
150.   What was the Duchess of Windsor's name before she became the Duchess?

Quiz 31

151.   In the pantomime Aladdin by Henry James Byron, what is the surname of the comic foil to Aladdin?
152.   Name the 17th President of the United States.
153.   Which MP & former leader of the GLC is known for keeping salamanders
154.   In music, who released the album "Out of the Blue?"
155.   Who became Poet Laureate in 1999?

Quiz 32

156. Who was the last Apache warrior chief?
157. In music, who released the 70's album "Slayed?"
158. What is Robert Mugabe's middle name?
159. When the now British Conservative Party were officially called the Tories, what were their main opponents called?
160. Who was the second man to walk on the moon?

Quiz 33

161. From what did Al Capone die?
162. Who came up with an 86-letter syllabary for the Cherokee language in the US?
163. Who did Jason Hatch disguise himself as in order to break into Buckingham Palace?
164. Who helps Santa in his workshop?
165. Which "family man" was convicted of masterminding the Helter Skelter murders?

Quiz 34

166. Which 80s child actor gave evidence at Michael Jackson's trial?
167. Who did Pocahontas marry?
168. What was the maiden name of Wallis Simpson, whom Edward VIII abdicated the throne for in the 1930s?
169. Who sang "No More Heroes?"
170. Which actor played young Scrooge in the classic film featuring Alistair Sim?

Quiz 35

171. Who was leader of the British labor party before Neil Kinnock?
172. Who was known as "The Elephant Man?"
173. What establishments have no windows or clocks?
174. Who was the manager of The Beatles?
175. Which older woman did Ashton Kutcher marry?

Quiz 36

176. What was Punky Brewster's dog called?
177. Who led the British Expeditionary Force in WWI?
178. Who gifted John F. Kennedy Pushinka the dog?
179. Who sang "Amityville House On The Hill" in 1986
180. Which politician is also known as Tarzan

Quiz 37

181. Who succeeded Churchill as the British Prime Minister?
182. Who first said the phrase "Turn on Tune In, Drop Out?"
183. What is the real name of "Paul Hewson?"
184. Who was the singer of "El Condor Pasa" (If I Could)?
185. What was the name of the woman thought to be the last full blooded Tasmanian aborigine, who died in 1876?

Quiz 38

186. The album "For Your Pleasure" was released by who in the 70s?
187. What social butterfly stole over 8 million pounds' worth of artwork in 1974, but only served 8 years in prison?
188. Which controversial comedian from Manchester died in June 2007 at the age of 76?
189. What is the link between Eric Clapton, Marilyn Monroe, and Larry Grayson?
190. Who had a 1970 No 1 hit with "I Hear You Knockin'?"

Quiz 39

191. Who was the cult leader of the Branch Davidians?
192. Who met in Yalta in 1945?
193. In music, who released the album "Abraxas?"
194. Whose 1938 radio reading of War Of The Worlds caused panic in America?
195. Who was made London's Mayor in 1397, 1398, 1406 and 1419?

Quiz 40

196.   Who played Cleopatra in the 1963 film of the same name?

197.   Who are Lloyd Bridges' two sons?

198.   Who was sued for not acting in "Boxing Helena?"

199.   Who is one of the most well-known female icons of WWII?

200.   In Star Wars, Who was the sidekick of C3PO?

Quiz 41

201.   What is commonly associated with Rod Hull?

202.   In music, who released the 1970's album "Broken English?"

203.   Who did US President Eisenhower say "I just will not, I refuse to get into the gutter with that guy," about?

204.   Who helped organize England's rigged match scandal?

205.   Who was filmed kissing the Duchess of York's toes?

Quiz 42

206.   Who assassinated Robert Kennedy?

207.   Who was the character acted By Anne Bancroft In "The Graduate?"

208.   In music who released the 1970's album "Fun House?"

209.   What those campaigning for social reform in England between 1836 & 1858 called?

210.   The license plate "COM1C" famously belongs to who?

Quiz 43

211.   Which radio show did Roy Plomley create?

212.   Which president had a child born on July 4th?

213.   Who released the album "My Aim is True?"

214.   Who was Norman Bates played by in the 1998 remake of "Psycho?"

215.   Name the last person to sit on the Peacock throne?

Quiz 44

216.   Who directed the film "Billy Budd" starring Terrance Stamp in 1962?
217.   In 1978, the British police launched a major manhunt to find the murderer of what newspaper boy?
218.   By what name was UK Labour cabinet minister and social reformer Frank Pakenham more commonly known as?
219.   Which name belongs to a main character in the witchcraft movie, "The Craft?" Is It Bonnie, Mary, Sally, or Penny?
220.   Which British man famously broke into the Queen's bedroom for a chat?

Quiz 45

221.   The phrase "You're Fired," is most commonly associated with which 2 people?
222.   Name the Romanian tennis player famous for throwing tantrums?
223.   What year did the California Gold Rush start?
224.   Where is the commemoration statue of Sherlock Holmes located?
225.   Who wrote the lyrics to "Auld Lange Syne?"

Quiz 46

226.   In music, who released "Sticky Fingers?"
227.   Who was the man who came up with a new method of freezing food?
228.   What was the name the ruler of the USSR from 1917 to 1922?
229.   Name the last English player to be sent off in the 2006 World Cup?
230.   Corazon Aquino was ousted by whom in 1986?

Quiz 47

231.   Name the only British Pope?
232.   Who was President of the USA in 1952?
233.   Who founded Live Aid?
234.   Who did Eric Sykes play on Screen Sister?
235.   What was the more common name of Charles I, who ruled the Franks and united most of Western Europe in the Middle Ages

Quiz 48

236.   Who was the first African-American female to win a Wimbledon Tennis event? In both 1957 And 1958.
237.   What is the nickname of Paul Gascoigne's friend, James Gardner?
238.   Who was the teenage showgirl who caused the resignation of British MP John Profumo?
239.   How Did Damon Hill's father die?
240.   What did Marilyn Monroe wear in bed?

Quiz 49

241.   Which aviator was Time's first Man of the Year?
242.   In music, who released the album "Tonight's the Night?"
243.   Who denounced Stalin?
244.   Who made a controversial speech about "Rivers Of Blood?"
245.   Name the 1995 Director General of The BBC

Quiz 50

246.   Name The Everly Bros.
247.   In Dallas, Texas, who was assassinated on November 22, 1963?
248.   What is Tony Adams biography called?
249.   Who was the founder of the Salvation Army in London in the 19th century?
250.   Charlene Tilton played Lucy Ewing on the hit TV drama Dallas; what was her nickname?

Quiz 51

251.   According to tradition, who were The 3 Wise Men that brought gifts to the baby Jesus?
252.   Who became the first elected female prime minister in an Islamic country?
253.   Who discovered the vaccination against smallpox in the late 18th century?
254.   Who had chart success with the song "Greased Lightning?"
255.   Who succeeded President Kennedy after his assassination?

Quiz 52

256.   What military award was established during the Civil War?
257.   Name the playwright whose date of both birth and death was the 23rd of April.
258.   Who released the album "Grievous Angel?"
259.   Which former British ambassador to the US later became Chief Financial Editor of the BBC?
260.   With which letter do most British names begin?

Quiz 53

261.   Who was famous for "Pomes?"
262.   Who received the nickname "Hanoi Jane" due to her propaganda broadcasts over the radio in Vietnam?
263.   Who Released the Transformer Album of the 70's?
264.   What was the nickname of President Duvalier of Haiti, who died in 1971?
265.   Which Norwegian explorer had ships called Fram and Maud?

Quiz 54

266.   Who was Dita Beard's employer?
267.   In the movie Bridget Jones Diary, who played Bridget Jones?
268.   Who released the 1970's album "Next?"
269.   Who was the first to make it to the North Pole?
270.   Which 16th century seer was famous for his predictions?

Quiz 55

271. Which comedian's real given name is Bob Davies?
272. Which engineer's statue is placed at London's Paddington Station?
273. Name the first woman shot by the FBI?
274. Name Garfield's vet?
275. What is Meatloaf's real name?

Quiz 56

276. Name the famous artist who painted the most paintings?
277. Who was first elected to the Aviation Hall of Fame?
278. Who did Germany, Italy & The USSR ban in The 1930's
279. Who outlawed gladiator sports in Rome?
280. Whose car did Mary Jo Kopechne die in?

Quiz 57

281. Who sacked her manager, Jonathon Shallit in 2000?
282. What was Air Chief Marshall Arthur Harris also known as?
283. Which sportsman was also known as Hurricane?
284. Who was the first incumbent President to survive a gunshot?
285. Which political party was banned in Italy after WWII?

Quiz 58

286. Who became Archbishop of Canterbury in 1980?
287. Which fraternal music duo released "Kimono my House?"
288. What popular fall party game originated as a fun way to determine who would be the next person to marry?
289. Who does Jamie Lee Curtis play in Halloween 20 years Later (H20)?
290. Who was the first man on the Moon?

291.   What is Andrew Lloyd Webber's brother named?
292.   Who is Norm's wife in Cheers?
293.   Who led an unsuccessful revolt by the gladiators against Rome?
294.   Name the cartoon where messages on the characters' clothes expressed their feelings.
295.   Which Liberal leader was acquitted of attempted murder?

Quiz 60

296.   What did Charles Dawson find out on Piltdown Common?
297.   Who plays Chris Kringle in the 1994 film "Miracle On 34th Street?"
298.   By what name is Nigel Benn Known in the ring?
299.   Who invented the potato crisp in the 19th century?
300.   What is the link between Cleopatra, Margaret Thatcher, & Mia Farrow?

Quiz 61

301.   Who released "Toys in the Attic?"
302.   Who resigned after his affair with Christine Keeler?
303.   Whose epitaph reads, "Free at last, free at last; thank God almighty, I'm free at last?"
304.   Who invented the thermometer
305.   Who became the South African president in 1989?

Quiz 62

306.   Who is the killer in the film, "A Nightmare on Elm Street?"
307.   Name the First Christian Emperor Of Rome.
308.   Which pop stars renamed themselves Sharon & Phyllis?
309.   Who was Henry VIII's fourth wife?
310.   What is Paddy Ashdown's given first name?

Quiz 63

311. By what title was Joseph Merrick more commonly known?
312. What should you call someone who lives in Newcastle?
313. Who was the last queen of the House of Hanover?
314. Who is the top scorer in the Arsenals history?
315. Where are Sinhalese people from?

Quiz 64

316. Elton John's middle name is what?
317. Jane Caine was the first person to do what?
318. Who succeeded Stalin as leader of the USSR?
319. Who first presented The UK National Lottery Draw
320. Who was the first to die from King Tut's curse?

Quiz 65

321. Who was Henry Bolingbroke's father
322. What was George VI's "real" first name; David - Albert - Louis - Edward – George?
323. Who was Margaret Thatcher?
324. Who was England's football manager in the 1970 finals of the World Cup?
325. Name the daughter of a lighthouse keeper who rescued survivors from a shipwreck?

Quiz 66

326. Name hinge's partner
327. Name the youngest man to chair the Joint Chiefs of Staff?
328. Which tennis player was Jimmy Connors engaged to?
329. Who was the English king during The Battle of Agincourt?
330. Who was the first American chess champion?

331.	Who was the first monarch of the House of Windsor in the UK?
332.	Who was the first King of Scotland?
333.	Who released the album "Legalize It?"
334.	Who killed Lee Harvey Oswald?
335.	Who did British Princess Anne marry in 1992?

Quiz 68

336.	Who was the crook's Daniel Stern's partner in the 1990 film "Home Alone?"
337.	What is the name of the first President of the U.S.?
338.	Who was the Queen of the Iceni tribe of England who led an uprising against the Romans?
339.	What were Bonnie & Clyde's surnames?
340.	Who was the apostle of Northumbria?

Quiz 69

341.	Whose children are Trixiebell, Little Pixie, & Peaches?
342.	Who played the policeman in The Blue Lamp?
343.	What bridge between Sweden and Denmaek starts over water and ends under it?

People & Places

TRIVIA

Answers

Answers – Quiz 1

1. Raoul
2. The 3 Wise Men
3. Mariah Carey
4. Dung on a stick
5. Audrey

Answers – Quiz 2

6. Edward J. Smith
7. Vanessa Redgrave
8. George Carey
9. Ernest Wiseman
10. Mohammed Al Fayed

Answers – Quiz 3

11. His initials will be face up the next day
12. Marget Thatcher
13. Kenneth Wolstenholme
14. King Canute
15. Led Zeppelin

Answers – Quiz 4

16. Prince Charles
17. Chester
18. Sylvester Stallone
19. Hugh Hefner
20. Eddie George

Answers – Quiz 5

21.   Mary Shelley
22.   David Soul
23.   Anne Rice
24.   George Jones
25.   John Prescott

Answers – Quiz 6

26.   Mathias Rust
27.   Cher
28.   Walter Mondale
29.   Creedence Clearwater Revival
30.   Ramsey MacDonald, 1924

Answers – Quiz 7

31.   Danish
32.   Robert Maxwell
33.   Salman Rushdie
34.   Woody Allen
35.   Barbara Cartland

Answers – Quiz 8

36.   Louis Farrakhan.
37.   General Custer
38.   Freddie Mercury
39.   Rodney Marsh
40.   Lord Louis Mountbatten

Answers – Quiz 9

41.   Andrew Johnson
42.   Brooklyn
43.   Jean Michelle Jarre
44.   William Roache (Ken Barlow)
45.   Oliver Hardy

Answers – Quiz 10

46.   Bob Dylan
47.   Tesla
48.   Paul Hogan
49.   Newmarket
50.   Robert Zimmerman

Answers – Quiz 11

51.   Demond Morris
52.   The Roaring Twenties
53.   Jimmy Carter
54.   Billy Joel
55.   The Rolling Stones

Answers – Quiz 12

56.   Oprah Winfrey
57.   Harold Macmillian, 1959
58.   Zsa-Zsa Gabor
59.   Abraham Lincoln.
60.   International Red Cross

Answers – Quiz 13

61.   The Man Who Shot Liberty Valance (Gene Pitney)
62.   Stanley Kubrick
63.   Banshee
64.   Charlotte Nilsson
65.   Marmaduke Hussey

Answers – Quiz 14

66.   Kerry Packer
67.   Sir Francis Drake
68.   Bill Gates
69.   Donner
70.   Otto Skorzeny

Answers – Quiz 15

71.   Cyril Smith
72.   Barry Goldwater
73.   Apollo 11 landed on the moon.
74.   CSNY
75.   Gary Newman

Answers – Quiz 16

76.   Sandra Dee
77.   Mystic Meg
78.   Jane Wyman
79.   Sonny Liston
80.   Rosa Parks

Answers – Quiz 17

81.	John Forsythe
82.	Maggie Philpin
83.	Alcock & Brown
84.	Paul Young
85.	Ian Dury

Answers – Quiz 18

86.	Rudolf Hess.
87.	Boris Johnson
88.	Sir Alec Douglas Home
89.	Spencer
90.	William IV

Answers – Quiz 19

91.	Mark Summers
92.	Marie Stoppes
93.	Patrick Vieira
94.	T. Rex
95.	Phil Tuffnel

Answers – Quiz 20

96.	Training.
97.	Traffic
98.	Oswald Mosley
99.	Her legs
100.	Sir Richard Arkwright

Answers – Quiz 21

101.	Olympic
102.	George Bush
103.	Stan Laurel
104.	Morrisey
105.	Marie

Answers – Quiz 22

106.	The Hanging Judge
107.	Alf Ramsey
108.	The Damned
109.	God
110.	Brian Walden, Robert Kilroy Silk

Answers – Quiz 23

111.	KISS
112.	Bee Gees
113.	Winona Ryder
114.	John Fitzerald Kennedy
115.	Mary Harris Jones

Answers – Quiz 24

116.	Gerald Ford.
117.	Tim Allen
118.	Joni Mitchell
119.	Mikhail Gorbachev.
120.	Robert Smith

Answers – Quiz 25

121. Blasted Billy or Adam Bomb
122. John Nash
123. Ned Kelly
124. Lester Piggot
125. Prince Ranier

Answers – Quiz 26

126. His thesaurus of words
127. Bill Oddie
128. Amelia Earheart
129. Saint Nickle-Less
130. Richard The Lionheart

Answers – Quiz 27

131. Napoli
132. Dennis Lillee
133. King George II
134. Jacqueline Bouvier
135. Mary Ludwig Hays. She took water to the soldiers at the Battle of Monmouth in June 1778.

Answers – Quiz 28

136. Anne Boleyn
137. The Jam
138. Norman Scott
139. Gerry Adams
140. John Stonehouse

Answers – Quiz 29

141.   Jack Ruby killed Lee Harvey Oswald
142.   Michael Bentine, Peter Sellers, Spike Milligan, Harry Secombe
143.   Sally Ride
144.   Santa Anna
145.   They all had Red hair

Answers – Quiz 30

146.   In the US, it was Emily, and in England and Wales it was Chloe as nr.1, and Emily as nr.2
147.   MI5
148.   Eno
149.   Alistair McClaine
150.   Wallace Simpson

Answers – Quiz 31

151.   Twankey
152.   Andrew Johnson.
153.   Ken Livingstone
154.   ELO
155.   Andrew Motion

Answers – Quiz 32

156.   Geronimo
157.   Slade
158.   Gabriel
159.   The Whigs
160.   Buzz Aldrin

Answers – Quiz 33

161. Cardiac arrest, he also had Syphilis.
162. Sequoyah
163. Batman
164. Elves
165. Charles Manson

Answers – Quiz 34

166. Corey Feldman
167. John Rolfe
168. Warfield
169. The Stranglers
170. George Cole

Answers – Quiz 35

171. Michael Foot
172. Joseph Merrick
173. Casinos
174. Brian Epstein
175. Demi Moore

Answers – Quiz 36

176. Brandon
177. Field Marshal Douglas Haig
178. Nikita Khrushchev
179. Lovebug Starski
180. Micheal Hestletine

Answers – Quiz 37

181. Clement Attlee, the first time and Anthony Eden, the second time
182. Timothy Leary
183. Bono
184. Simon & Garfunkel
185. Truganini

Answers – Quiz 38

186. Roxy Music
187. Dr Bridget Rose Dugdale
188. Bernard Manning
189. They all are or were illegitimate
190. Dave Edmunds

Answers – Quiz 39

191. David Koresh
192. Churchill, Roosevelt, Stalin
193. Santana
194. Orson Welles
195. Richard (Dick) Whittington

Answers – Quiz 40

196. Elizabeth Taylor
197. Jeff & Beau
198. Kim Bassinger
199. Rosie the Riveter
200. R2D2

Answers – Quiz 41

201. Emu
202. Marianne Faithfull
203. Senator Joseph McCarthy
204. Hansie Cronje
205. John Bryan

Answers – Quiz 42

206. Sirhan Bishara Sirhan
207. Mrs Robinson
208. The Stooges
209. The Chartists
210. Jimmy Tarbuck

Answers – Quiz 43

211. Desert Island Discs
212. Barack Obama
213. Elvis Costello
214. Vince Vaughn
215. Shah Mohammed Reza Pahlavi

Answers – Quiz 44

216. Peter Ustinov
217. Carl Bridgewater
218. Lord Longford (7th Earl of Longford)
219. Bonnie
220. Micheal Fagan

Answers – Quiz 45

221.	Alan Sugar & Donald Trump
222.	Ilie Nastase
223.	1848
224.	Baker Street, London
225.	Robert Burns

Answers – Quiz 46

226.	Rolling Stones
227.	Clarence Birdseye
228.	Vladimir Lenin
229.	Wayne Rooney
230.	Ferdinand Marcos

Answers – Quiz 47

231.	Adrian IV
232.	Harry Truman
233.	Bob Geldof
234.	Hattie Jaques
235.	Charlemagne

Answers – Quiz 48

236.	Althea Gibson
237.	Five Bellies
238.	Christine Keeler
239.	In a plane crash
240.	Chanel No. 5

Answers – Quiz 49

241.	Charles Lindbergh
242.	Neil Young
243.	Nikita Khrushchev
244.	Enoch Powell
245.	Lord Reith

Answers – Quiz 50

246.	Don & Phil
247.	President John F. Kennedy
248.	Addicted
249.	William Booth
250.	Poison Dwarf

Answers – Quiz 51

251.	Gaspar, Melchior, Balthasar
252.	Benazir Bhutto
253.	Edward Jenner
254.	John Travolta
255.	Lyndon B Johnson

Answers – Quiz 52

256.	The Medal of Honor
257.	Shakespeare
258.	Gram Parsons
259.	Peter Jay
260.	B

Answers – Quiz 53

261.   Pam Ayers
262.   Jane Fonda
263.   Lou Reed
264.   Papa Doc
265.   Roald Amundsen

Answers – Quiz 54

266.   Itt
267.   Renée Zellweger
268.   The Sensational Alex Harvey Band
269.   Robert Edwin Peary
270.   Nostradamus

Answers – Quiz 55

271.   Jasper Carrott
272.   Isambard Kingdom Brunel
273.   Bonnie Parker (of Bonnie and Clyde fame)
274.   Liz
275.   Marvin Lee Aday

Answers – Quiz 56

276.   Picasso
277.   The Wright Brothers
278.   Mickey Mouse
279.   Caesar
280.   Edward Kennedy

Answers – Quiz 57

281. Charlotte Church
282. Bomber Harris
283. Alex Higgins
284. Ronald Reagan
285. The National Fascist Party

Answers – Quiz 58

286. Robert Runcie
287. Sparks
288. Bobbing for apples.
289. Kere Tate
290. Neil Armstrong

Answers – Quiz 59

291. Julian
292. Vera
293. Spartacus
294. Shirt Tales
295. Jeremy Thorpe

Answers – Quiz 60

296. The Missing link
297. Richard Attenborough
298. The Dark Destroyer
299. George Crumb
300. They all had twins

301. Aerosmith
302. John Profumo
303. Martin Luther King Jr.
304. Galileo, however the Italian, Santorio Santorio (1561-1636) is generally credited with having applied a scale to an air thermoscope at least as early as 1612 and thus is thought to be the inventor of the thermometer as a temperature measuring device
305. F.W. de Klerk

Answers – Quiz 62

306. Freddy Krueger
307. Constantine The Great
308. Elton John & Rod Stewart
309. Anne Of Cleeves
310. Jeremy

Answers – Quiz 63

311. The Elephant Man
312. A Novocastrian
313. Queen Victoria
314. Ian Wright
315. Sri Lanka

Answers – Quiz 64

316. Hercules
317. Speaking Clock Voice
318. Khrushchev.
319. Noel Edmonds
320. Lord Carnarvon

Answers – Quiz 65

321.   John Of Gaunt (The Duke Of Lancaster)
322.   Albert
323.   Prime Minister of Great Britan
324.   Sir Alf Ramsey
325.   Grace Darling

Answers – Quiz 66

326.   Bracket
327.   Colin Powell.
328.   Chirs Evet
329.   Henry V
330.   Bobby Fischer

Answers – Quiz 67

331.   George V (reigned 1910-1936)
332.   Kenneth (Cináed mac Ailpín)
333.   Peter Tosh
334.   Jack Ruby
335.   Tim Lawrence

Answers – Quiz 68

336.   Joe Pesci
337.   George Washington
338.   Boudicca
339.   Clyde Barrow & Bonnie Parker
340.   St Aidan

Answers – Quiz 69

341.   Bob Geldof & Paula Yates
342.   Jack Warner
343.   The Øresund Bridge

Religion & Mythology

TRIVIA

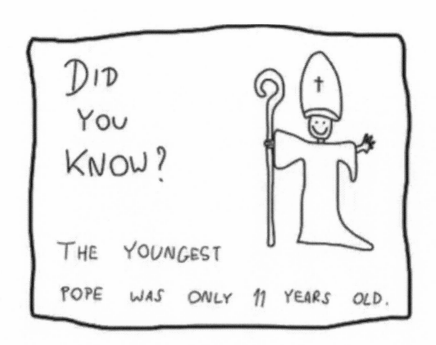

DID
YOU
KNOW?

THE YOUNGEST
POPE WAS ONLY 11 YEARS OLD.

Quiz 1

1. What is Islam's holy book?
2. The oldest route to Santiago de Compostela, first taken in the 9th century, is referred to as the Original Way or Camino Primitivo, and begins where?
3. Which religion uses the Avesta texts?
4. Shintoism is associated with what geographical region?
5. If travelling the Way of St. James pilgrimage on a bike, what distance needs to be travelled to receive a certificate of accomplishment?

Quiz 2

6. What is the name of a Muslim male's yearly pilgrimage to Mecca?
7. What is the 1st book of the Hindu scripture?
8. Who is the Greek equivalent of the Roman god Mars?
9. Who killed a dragon in the 12th century, in ancient mythology?
10. Which religion worships Vishnu and Brahma?

Quiz 3

11. In theology, the study of final things such as death, judgment and the end of the world is called what?
12. In Greek mythology, who was the son of Peleus and Thetis?
13. What Chinese religion was founded by Lao-zi?
14. Which book of the Bible was written by King David?
15. What are the 7 Deadly Sins?

Quiz 4

16. Who is the current Archbishop of Canterbury in 2020?
17. Whose teaching consisted of four "Noble Truths?"
18. Who was the ancient Egyptian moon god?
19. This Roman soldier pierced the crucified Christ in His side with his spear.
20. Shia is a term used to denote a branch of which major religion?

Quiz 5

21. Which two books in the Old Testament list the Ten Commandments? (In order of appearance)?
22. What day has the Catholic Church determined to be the day Christ rose from the dead?
23. Who led the Mormons to Utah?
24. What is Islam's holy month?
25. According to the Bible, who were the brothers of Jesus?

Quiz 6

26. How many animals of each kind did Moses take onto the ark?
27. In what city does a certain church forbid burping or sneezing?
28. In Greek mythology who did Athena turn into a spider?
29. Who is the Greek god of war?
30. What religion is Joseph Smith associated with?

Quiz 7

31. How many Popes have been of Spanish origin?
32. How long did it take God to create the Universe?
33. Where was Mother Theresa born?
34. According to the Bible, how many years did Methuselah live?
35. What has no reflection, no shadow, and can't stand the smell of garlic?

Quiz 8

36.   He was the father of Zeus.
37.   What is the Hindu festival of lights?
38.   Which religious group produces the magazine The Watchtower?
39.   Where was Methodism founded?
40.   How many Pillars does Islam have?

Quiz 9

41.   The "Harmandir Sahib" belongs to which religion?
42.   Which Roman God was the equivalent of the Greek God Dionysus?
43.   What belief system does the Dalai Lama hold?
44.   Geographically, where did Chondoism originate?
45.   How old is a Jewish boy when he becomes a man?

Quiz 10

46.   In Egyptian mythology, who is known as the god of the desert?
47.   According to popular belief brides walk to the what in the church? (not the aisle)
48.   Part of what mollusk is generally regarded as a symbol of the Camino de Santiago?
49.   What popular hymn features these lyrics: "I fear no foe, with Thee at hand to bless, Ills have no weight and tears no bitterness."
50.   In what country is the Islamic holy city of Mecca?

Quiz 11

51.   Apollo was the Greek god of _____?
52.   In what year did 400k people report their religion as Jedi on their census forms?
53.   Who was Ancient Egyptian goddess of fertility, love and beauty?
54.   Who is the Roman goddess of destiny?
55.   What is the date of St. James's Day?

56. What two biblical cities did God destroy with fire and brimstone?
57. Candomble is the major religion of which African country?
58. How many pilgrims travelled to Santiago in 2016?
59. What did Pandora release when she opened the box?
60. This pilgrimage is located in Ireland, can be completed barefoot, and traces the steps of which saint?

Quiz 13

61. Who was the ancient Egyptian goddess of the sky and queen of heaven?
62. What book is the holiest for devout Jews?
63. What religion has the most global followers?
64. Egyptian Ibis-headed god?
65. The goal of all Buddhists is to be free from all suffering, which is known as _____.

Quiz 14

66. How many books are in the protestant Christian Bible?
67. Where did Taoism originate?
68. What religion was founded by Lao-tzu?
69. In 1985, the route of the Way of St. James pilgrimage was named one of UNESCO's what?
70. A Pilgrim's Mass is held where?

Quiz 15

71. "O Lord, my God, when I in awesome wonder consider all the world Thy hands have made..." These are the opening words of which Christian hymn?
72. What is the name given to the supreme reality in Hinduism?
73. In China why were kites flown on the ninth day of every month?
74. Where did the Bahai religion originate?
75. Which ancient continent is said to be submerged?

76. What was the first sign shown to Moses by God according to the Bible?

77. When a female Sikh is baptized, she receives the surname Kaur, which means _____ in English.

78. What was the town that ancient Greeks believed to be the center of the world, and was the home of a famous oracle?

Religion & Mythology

TRIVIA

Answers

Answers – Quiz 1

1. Koran
2. Oviedo
3. Zoroastrianism
4. Japan
5. 200km

Answers – Quiz 2

6. Hajj
7. Rig Veda
8. Ares
9. St. George
10. Hinduism

Answers – Quiz 3

11. Eschatology
12. Achilles
13. Taoism
14. Psalms
15. Pride, greed, lust, envy, gluttony, wrath and sloth.

Answers – Quiz 4

16. Justin Welby (Correct as of 4/13/2020)
17. Buddha
18. Khonsu
19. Longinus
20. Islam

Answers – Quiz 5

21.   Exodus and Deuteronomy
22.   Easter Sunday
23.   Young
24.   Ramadan
25.   James, Joseph, Judas/Jude and Simon

Answers – Quiz 6

26.   None (It was Noah, not Moses)
27.   Omaha, Nebraska
28.   Arachne
29.   Ares
30.   Mormonism and the Latter Day Saint movement

Answers – Quiz 7

31.   Two – Pope Alexander VI and Pope Callixtus III
32.   Six days - he rested on the seventh
33.   Republic of Macedonia
34.   969
35.   Vampires

Answers – Quiz 8

36.   Cronus
37.   Diwali (or Deepavali)
38.   Jehovah's Witnesses
39.   Oxford University
40.   Five

Answers – Quiz 9

41. Sikhism (translates as "Golden Temple")
42. Bacchus
43. Buddhist
44. Korea (now divided into North and South Korea)
45. Thirteen

Answers – Quiz 10

46. Ash
47. The nave of the church
48. Scallop shell
49. Abide With Me
50. Saudi Arabia

Answers – Quiz 11

51. Music, poetry, light, prophecy, and medicine
52. 2001
53. Bastet
54. Fortuna
55. 25th July

Answers – Quiz 12

56. Sodom and Gomorrah
57. Brazil
58. 277,915
59. Misery and evil
60. St. Patrick's Steps

Answers – Quiz 13

61.   Hathor
62.   The Torah
63.   Christianity
64.   Thoth
65.   Nirvana

Answers – Quiz 14

66.   66
67.   China
68.   Taoism
69.   World Heritage Sites
70.   Cathedral of Santiago de Compostela

Answers – Quiz 15

71.   How Great Thou Art
72.   Brahman
73.   To banish evil
74.   Iran
75.   Atlantis

Answers – Quiz 16

76.   Burning bush
77.   Princess
78.   Delphi

Holidays

TRIVIA

DID YOU KNOW?

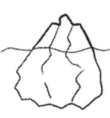

Titanic crew had no binoculars. They were inside a locker and the key was lost.

Quiz 1

1. Who was the first ghost to appear to Scrooge in the Dickens classic A Christmas Carol?
2. What is the next line "Christmas is coming the goose is getting fat ...?"
3. Who was declared dead on New Year's Day 1953 at the age of 29?
4. Which U.S. President was the first to have a Christmas tree in the White House?
5. Which 1996 TV Christmas special saw two of its stars dress as Batman and Robin for a fancy dress party?

Quiz 2

6. Halloween originated from a festival celebrated by what ancient European tribe?
7. Which singer's Christmas favorite is having his "nuts roasting on an open fire___?"
8. Which holiday takes place on March 26th?
9. By what name is St Sylvester's Day otherwise known?
10. What's "Stir-Up Sunday?"

Quiz 3

11. Who invented the Christmas Cracker?
12. Two groups have had three consecutive Christmas No 1's; the first was the Beatles, in 1963-64-65, name the second.
13. What is the connection between "Comet," "Cupid" and "Vixen?"
14. What Christian holiday is celebrated immediately after Halloween?
15. When was the date of the Christian festival Easter fixed by the Council of Nicaea?

16.   Why do we use holly at Christmas?

17.   Which U. S. President disregarded health and safety and insisted on putting lit candles on the White House Christmas tree?

18.   Who first celebrated what we've come to know as Halloween

19.   Which reindeer isn't featured in the poem The Night before Christmas?

20.   Which comedy trio made a "Daft Noise for Christmas?"

Quiz 5

21.   Beginning in the 1820s, who were relocated to what is now called "Indian territory?"

22.   What do you do with Swedish glogg?

23.   What is the link between Kenny Everett, Annie Lennox, and Isaac Newton?

24.   What was given on the eighth day of Christmas?

25.   Where did the tradition of Christmas trees originate?

Quiz 6

26.   What Christmas delicacy has blue veins and tastes cheesy?

27.   Who "sat in the corner eating a Christmas Pie?"

28.   Who was the Spirit of Christmas played by in "Blackadder's Christmas Carol?"

29.   When is the "Feast of Stephen?"

30.   What was called Armistice Day in the US until 1954?

Quiz 7

31. In British television, what was the name of Jean Alexander's Coronation street character?
32. Which American tycoon was born on Christmas Day and created one of the world's biggest hotel chains.
33. A lot of men end up in the hospital at Christmas for which decoration of their nether regions?
34. Which date marks the Christian Epiphany, when Jesus, Mary and Joseph met the Three Wise Men?
35. Who died on Christmas day 2006 and was nicknamed the Godfather of Soul?

Quiz 8

36. In British television, who was the first X Factor winner to gain a Christmas Number One?
37. In A Christmas Carol, which "CP" is one of the ghosts?
38. Which Christmas Carol tells about a 10th Century Bohemian Duke?
39. Who was crowned King of England on Christmas day 1066?
40. Who sang "I Believe in Father Christmas?"

Quiz 9

41. Which 3 Singers have sung the opening line "Do They Know Its Christmas?"
42. Why is the 26th of December known as Boxing Day?
43. When is St. Patrick's Day?
44. Who had a Christmas No 1 with "Lilly The Pink?"
45. According to some legends, which holiday tradition is attributed to spiders?

Quiz 10

46. Which native Mexican flower is also known as the Christmas flower?
47. Which pie has its origins in medieval Christmas time?
48. Which U.S. President moved Thanksgiving up a week to lengthen the holiday shopping season?
49. Which bank holiday was celebrated for the first time in the UK in 1978?
50. From what phrase does the word Halloween come from

Quiz 11

51. In the Ukraine what does it mean if you find a spider web in your house Christmas morning?
52. When is the Feast of St. Nicholas? Dec 6th, Dec 18th, Dec 25th, or Dec 27th?
53. On what day do children in Italy and Spain traditionally get their Christmas presents?
54. What does Santa do in his gardens?
55. Which Saint's Day is held on Boxing Day

Quiz 12

56. Which English Monarch used radio to begin the tradition of The Christmas Broadcast?
57. What seasonal name was given to Bart Simpson's dog?
58. Which city is known as "The Gingerbread Capital of the World?"
59. Which entertainer famous for the one liner "My little chickadee" died on Christmas Day 1946?
60. In 1840 London sweet maker Tom Smith came up with an invention that is still hugely popular today. What was it?

Quiz 13

61.   Who left their role as Russian Premier on Christmas Day 1991?

62.   Brenda Lee was doing what doing around the Christmas tree in 1958

63.   Which river did George Washington cross on Christmas night in 1776 during the American Revolutionary War?

64.   When is St Stephen's Day?

65.   In the carol "Away in a Manger" what was the little Lord Jesus sleeping on?

Quiz 14

66.   When was D-day?

67.   What does Michael Fish say to his wife when the Heavens open on Christmas?

68.   Where in the UK is "Uphelia" celebrated?

69.   What holiday became popular after it was featured on the TV show Seinfeld?

70.   Complete the verse – "'Twas the night before Christmas, when all through the house, not a creature was stirring not even a _____."

Quiz 15

71.   What did Rudolph the Red-nosed Reindeer never get to join in?

72.   Who are the four ghosts in Charles Dickens' novel A Christmas Carol?

73.   Name the English King crowned on Christmas Day.

74.   Who did Tom Cruise get married to on Christmas Eve of 1990?

75.   When did "Good King Wenceslas" look out?

76. Presepe in Italy refers to which Christmas tradition?
77. Where do people traditionally swim in Hyde Park on Christmas Day
78. By what name was the American comedian and actor William Claude, who died on Christmas day, better known?
79. On which date is Epiphany celebrated in the traditional Western calendar?
80. Name the former dictator executed by firing squad on Christmas Day of 1999

Quiz 17

81. What is the line in the song after "I'm dreaming of a white Christmas?"
82. In music, who had a Christmas hit with "There's No-One Quite Like Grandma?"
83. Michael Myers is the serial killer in which series of films?
84. How is Irving Berlin famously linked to Christmas?
85. Who had 3 Christmas number ones in a row from 1996 to 1998?

Quiz 18

86. In A Christmas Carol, what is Tiny Tim's surname?
87. Name the original eight reindeer from the poem, 'Twas the night Before Christmas.
88. How did the tradition of the Christmas turkey begin?
89. Halloween is celebrated on the eve of which Christian holiday?
90. What do salt and pepper say to one another at Christmas?

91.   Which word comes from a Greek word that means "we can act anything?"

92.   If someone handed you a frumenty at Christmas what would you do with it?

93.   What Christmas item was introduced by Henry Cole in the 1840s?

94.   Which band had a UK Christmas no 1 In December 1979?

Holidays TRIVIA Answers

Answers – Quiz 1

1. Marley's Ghost
2. Please put a penny in the old man's hat
3. Hank Williams
4. Franklin Pierce (1853-1857)
5. Only fools & horses

Answers – Quiz 2

6. The Celts
7. Nat King Cole
8. Make up you own holiday day
9. New Years Eve
10. The day to make Christmas Pudding

Answers – Quiz 3

11. Thomas Smith
12. The Spice Girls (1996-97-98)
13. All names of Santa's reindeer
14. All Saints Day
15. 325 AD

Answers – Quiz 4

16. Represents the crown of thorns worn by Jesus
17. Franklin Delano Roosevelt
18. The Druids, The Celts
19. Rudolph
20. The Goodies

Answers – Quiz 5

21.   The five civilized tribes
22.   Drink it, it's a hot spiced drink made from wine or spirits
23.   Born On Christmas Day
24.   Eight Maids-a-milking
25.   Germany (5th Century)

Answers – Quiz 6

26.   Stilton Cheese
27.   Little Jack Horner
28.   Robbie Coltrane
29.   December 26th
30.   Veterans Day

Answers – Quiz 7

31.   Hilda Ogden
32.   Conrad Hilton
33.   Sprigs of Holly
34.   January 6th
35.   James Brown

Answers – Quiz 8

36.   Shayne Ward
37.   Christmas Present / Past
38.   Good King Wenceslas
39.   William The Conqueror
40.   Greg Lake

Answers – Quiz 19

41.   Paul Young, Kylie Minogue, Chris Martin
42.   The rich gave presents to the poor, the masters gave presents to the servants
43.   March 17th
44.   The scaffold
45.   Tinsel

Answers – Quiz 10

46.   The poinsettia
47.   Mince Pie
48.   Franklin Delano Roosevelt
49.   1st May
50.   All Hallows Eve

Answers – Quiz 11

51.   Good luck
52.   Dec 6th
53.   January 5th
54.   Ho, Ho, Ho
55.   St Stephen

Answers – Quiz 12

56.   George V (1932)
57.   Santa's Little Helper
58.   Nuremburg
59.   W.C. Fields
60.   The Christmas Cracker

Answers – Quiz 13

61. Mikhail Gorbachev
62. Rocking
63. Delaware
64. 26th December
65. The Hay

Answers – Quiz 14

66. June 6th, 1944
67. It's Reindeer
68. Shetland Isles
69. Festivus
70. Mouse

Answers – Quiz 15

71. All the other reindeer games
72. Christmas Past, Present, Yet to Come, and Jacob Marley
73. William the Conqueror (1066)
74. Nicole Kidman
75. Feast Of Stephen

Answers – Quiz 16

76. Nativity scene (literally meaning crib)
77. The Serpentine
78. WC Fields
79. 6th January
80. Nicolae Ceausescu, (Romania)

Answers – Quiz 17

81.   Just like the ones I used to know
82.   St Winifred School Choir
83.   The Halloween series of films
84.   He wrote White Christmas
85.   The Spice Girls

Answers – Quiz 18

86.   Cratchett
87.   Comet, Cupid, Dasher, Dancer, Prancer, Vixen, Donner, Blitzen (or Dunder and Blixem)
88.   The Americans introduced turkey to England in 1526. In America, turkeys were preferred originally, because the farmers needed chickens for eggs, and cows for milk, thus turkeys were cheaper.
89.   All Saints Day
90.   Seasons Greetings

Answers – Quiz 19

91.   Pantomime
92.   Eat it (It's a spiced porridge)
93.   The Christmas Card
94.   Pink Floyd / Wall

Art & Literature

TRIVIA

DID YOU KNOW?

ZEBRAS ARE ACTUALLY BLACK WITH WHITE STRIPES, NOT WHITE WITH BLACK STRIPES.

Quiz 1

1. Which author described World War One as the War to End All Wars?
2. Who Wrote The Famous Book A Brief History Of Time in 1988?
3. American artist who became famous in the 1960s for painting iconic American objects?
4. Which European movement between 1800 and 1890 focused on expression and emotion rather than reason?
5. Which group of French painters active in the 1890s worked in a subjective, often mystical style, highlighting flat areas of color and pattern?

Quiz 2

6. Who wrote the novel The Silence of the Lambs?
7. In 2007 who topped the best seller's non-fiction list with Born to Be Riled?
8. What term did Roger Fry create to refer to artists who disliked impressionism?
9. Which famous book begins with the line "Marley was dead, to begin with. There was no doubt about that?"
10. Which writer, archaeologist & soldier joined the RAF after the First World War & changed his name to Shaw in 1927?

Quiz 3

11. Which author created the character of Tarzan
12. Who co-wrote Yeoman Of The Guard and Lolanthe and the Mikado?
13. Which Shakespearean play takes place in The Forest Of Arden?
14. Name the author of Robinson Crusoe?
15. What is the term for a painting or drawing executed in a single color?

Quiz 4

16. Which French impressionist created the piece "After the Bath, Woman drying herself?"
17. "When a man is tired of London he is tired of life" was a phrase coined by who?
18. The 1925 short story collection, In Our Time, was written by who?
19. Douglas Adams is famous for which book?
20. Who wrote Angela's Ashes and won a Pulitzer Prize?

Quiz 5

21. What was the sequel to Louisa May Alcott's Little Women?
22. What famous novel covers only one day, and is set in Dublin in June, 1904?
23. In The Rime of the Ancient Mariner which bird is shot?
24. What is a term that describes an early 1900s movement in France to explore the unconscious mind?
25. How old was the character Adrian Mole when he began writing his Secret Diary?

Quiz 6

26. Duke Leto Atreidea & The Harkonnens are characters in what popular sci-fi novel?
27. Which school did Billy Bunter attend?
28. Who is the author of the Harry Potter series?
29. What literary character said, "Neither a borrower nor lender be"?
30. What is a term to describe the erotic, decorative art movement of 1890-1910, using sinuous, florid lines, often derived from plants and flowers?

Quiz 7

31.   Which science fiction story centers on alien children in a village?

32.   What is the term for a 19th-century art movement that refers to objective representation?

33.   Homer wrote this account of the Trojan War.

34.   Which poet wrote no verse during his time as Poet Laureate?

35.   Who wrote The Dark Eyes Of London, Four Just Men & Sanders Of The River?

Quiz 8

36.   What was the famous novel written in jail by John Bunyan?

37.   What 11th-century European art style is characterized by an ornamental, complex sculpture?

38.   In A Christmas Carol, what was the name of the miser?

39.   What is the name of the Tibetan mountain retreat in the novel Lost Horizon?

40.   What recent artistic movement emphasizes the idea of art over the art itself?

Quiz 9

41.   What is the term for cutting into a solid material to make a sculpture?

42.   What novel features the fireman burning books?

43.   The three main types of Greek columns are Doric, Ionic, and _____.

44.   Which celebration of the arts is held in Wales?

45.   In Wuthering Heights, what is Cathy's surname?

Quiz 10

46. Who wrote Ender's Game?
47. Name the author of The Catcher in the Rye?
48. Rembrandt van Rijn famously painted - The Militia Company of Captain Frans Banning Cocq, by what name is it better known?
49. Who is the author of Rendezvous with Rama?
50. What is the name of the bird in the Peanuts comic strip?

Quiz 11

51. Who wrote Psycho?
52. Who is Karen Blixen better known as?
53. What do you call a picture that is made of various materials stuck together?
54. The technique of producing printed designs through various methods of incising on wood or metal blocks, which are then inked and printed.
55. French impressionist Claude _____

Quiz 12

56. Which US clarinetist player's real name was Arthur Jacob Shaw?
57. In Joel Chandler Harris' book, who told stories about Brer Rabbit & Brer Fox?
58. Ground chalk or plaster mixed with glue, used as a base coat for tempera and oil painting.
59. Which author wrote The Spy That Came in from the Cold?
60. Who drew drawings of absurd mechanical contrivances?

Quiz 13

61. What does JK of JK Rowling stand for?
62. Who wrote The Sound & The Fury, and As I Lay Dying?
63. A flat board used by a painter to mix and hold colors is known as a what?
64. Paint applied very thickly, often projecting from the surface, is called what?
65. Name the decorative style popular in the 1920's & 1930's?

Quiz 14

66. Who painted the "Scene d'ete?"
67. What American painting and sculpting movement emphasized strict, systematic compositions?
68. Which Sherlock Holmes novel was most famous?
69. What is an Onomatopoeia?
70. Name Shakespeare's last finished play?

Quiz 15

71. Name the British artist known for his paintings of horses?
72. Which book was used as evidence in Oscar Wilde's sodomy trial?
73. Water-soluble paint made from pigments and a plastic binder...?
74. Name the former jockey who specializes in writing horse racing novels?
75. Who was the group of American painters who united to oppose academic standards in the early twentieth century?

Quiz 16

76. The Scream was created by which artist?
77. What is the term for choice and arrangement of words and phrases or vocabulary, in a literary work?
78. Name the second best-selling book of all time?
79. In which Shakespeare play does the line "If music be the food of love play on" feature?
80. Spinning on one foot is known as what in ballet?

81. Who wrote The Wind in the Willows?
82. Who was the group of early 1900s American artists who focused on urban realism?
83. An artwork humorously exaggerating the qualities, defects, or peculiarities of a person or idea.
84. From whom did Bilbo obtain The One Ring?
85. What is the name given to the painting medium involving egg yolks?

Quiz 18

86. Who wrote the vampire series that featured Lestat as the main character?
87. Women's magazine launched by New York in the 70's.
88. Who wrote Mason & Dixon?
89. Which book begins with the famous line: "On January 6, 1482, the people of Paris were awakened by the tumultuous clanging of all the bells in the city?"
90. Frodo is chosen to deliver The One Ring into the heart of what?

Quiz 19

91. What was the Russian artistic movement of the early 1900s that focused on the simplicity of form?
92. Which literary character had a dog called Bull's Eye?
93. Who wrote the novels About a Boy, How to Be Good and High Fidelity?
94. Which character created by Dodie Smith drove a black & white car & wore a black & white fur coat?
95. What is the term for amateur paintings with a simple style and bold colors?

Quiz 20

96. Tilly Trotter, Hannah Massey and Maggie Rowan are all characters created by which novelist?
97. Which artist's name literally means Little Barrel?
98. This magazine used to boast a circulation of 7,777,777.
99. Who painted The Last Supper?
100. In what field of study would you find "flying buttresses?"

Quiz 21

101. Where would you find Poet's Corner?
102. Who wrote the opera The Flying Dutchman?
103. What is the term for a painting that is worked in multiple panels?
104. In sculpture, the building up of form using a soft medium such as clay or wax, as distinguished from carving. In painting and drawing, using color and lighting variations to produce a three-dimensional effect.
105. What painting technique developed in the 50s, and featured large areas of color?

Quiz 22

106. Which British artist is known for his paintings of Californian swimming pools, including a work titled, A Bigger Splash.
107. Which playwright wrote Hay Fever?
108. Which novel features the character of Perks The Station Porter?
109. The HAL 9000 appears in which famous film?
110. Name Colin Dexter's famous fictional detective?

111. On a represented form, what is the point of most intense light?
112. The attribution of human feelings and responses to inanimate things or animals, especially in art and literature, is known as what?
113. What is the most famous traditional Russian ballet company?
114. Who did Hitler call the Prophet of Right Wing Authoritarianism?
115. Robert Jordan wrote which series?

Quiz 24

116. What artistic movement began in the 1950s, and played with optical patterns?
117. Who wrote Gulliver's Travels?
118. Which painting concept is named "fool the eye" in French?
119. Who was William Shakespeare married to?
120. "Mr. & Mrs. Dursley of number 4 Privet Drive were proud to say that they were perfectly normal" is a line from which children's book?

Quiz 25

121. Scheherazade is a story teller in which literary work?
122. Which American author Wrote Roots?
123. Name the character who invariably misused words?
124. Many impressionists were said to have painted "en plein air," which translated means what?
125. Representation of either human or animal form.

Quiz 26

126. What book beings: "It is a truth universally acknowledged that a single man in possession of a good fortune must be in want of a wife?"
127. An etching technique where a solution of asphalt or resin is used, producing prints of rich, gray tones.
128. Name the Antipodean opera singer who sang at Charles and Diana's wedding.
129. The Royal Opera House in London is also home to which other art?
130. Name the Dutch artist who created Cafe Terrace at Night?

Quiz 27

131. Slaughterhouse Five and Breakfast Of Champions were penned by which author?
132. Which Michael Crichton novel was a best seller in 1993?
133. Which movement spanned the 17th century to the mid- 18th?
134. What was Shakespeare's first name?
135. Who Wrote Emma?

Quiz 28

136. Name the 3 Brontë sisters
137. Who wrote Black Beauty?
138. What is Gulliver's profession in Gulliver's Travels?
139. Name the merchant in Shakespeare's The Merchant Of Venice
140. What was Michelangelo's forename?

Quiz 29

141. What was George Elliot's real name?
142. What is the name of the 7th and final book in the Harry Potter series
143. Principally, of what nationality were the impressionist painters?
144. He penned the founding novel of the genre named for it, Utopia.
145. Which color followed Picasso's Blue Period?

146.	Which Jane Austen novel was published posthumously
147.	Who wrote The Dragonriders Of Pern?
148.	Jules Verne's Around The World In 80 Days featured which character?
149.	Who created Adrian Mole
150.	"Wamyouruijoshou" was the first book to coin which word?

Quiz 31

151.	What movement was Salvador Dali associated with?
152.	What term refers to the creative work of a culture that reflects their regional traditions?
153.	Which American artist is famous for painting a portrait of his mother?
154.	What was Picasso's forename?
155.	Jack Kerouac, William S. Burroughs and Allen Ginsburg were all part of which generation?

Quiz 32

156.	Which British landscape painter is most famous for The Hay Wain.
157.	Who is most noted for his paintings of the Moulin Rouge?
158.	Who wrote the Disc World series?
159.	Which painter is known for allegedly cutting off his own ear?
160.	What style began in Italy in the early 1400s, and grew through to the 1600s as it stressed a realistic representation of the world?

Quiz 33

161.	Who penned The Belgariad?
162.	Who author wrote The Strange Case of Dr. Jekyll and Mr. Hyde?
163.	Whose ghost materializes at the dinner table in Macbeth?
164.	Who penned the Tin Tin Stories?
165.	Who told us that "Full many a flower is born to blush unseen / And waste its sweetness on the desert air?"

166.   Who wrote the character of Horton the elephant?
167.   Which author wrote The Hunt For Red October and Clear And Present Danger?
168.   What does Captain Ahab grow obsessed with?
169.   What book tells that "Once Upon A Time There Was A Little Chimney Sweep And His Name Was Tom?"
170.   Distorting to show three-dimensional space as perceived by the eye.

Quiz 35

171.   Who released A Guide To Child Care in 1946?
172.   By what name is Mrs. William Heelis better known?
173.   The TV series "All Creatures Great & Small" was based on novels by which author?
174.   Name the protagonist in Milton's Paradise Lost?
175.   A thin layer of translucent color used in painting.

Quiz 36

176.   By what name is Dickens' Jack Dawkins otherwise known?
177.   Name William Wordworth's sister.
178.   Vienna is most associated with which dance?
179.   What is the term for the rendering of light and shade in painting?
180.   Brave New World was written by which author?

Quiz 37

181.   Which Algerian-born French author's works included L'Etranger & La Peste?
182.   What rank was Biggles?
183.   What is the most performed opera in the UK?
184.   JK Rowling created an official word; what was it?
185.   Which famous book contains the line "It was the best of times, it was the worst of times, it was the age of wisdom...?"

Quiz 38

186.   Who wrote Old Possum's Book of Practical Cats?

187.   Which famous book begins with the line "Not long ago, there lived in London a young married couple of Dalmatian dogs named Pongo and Missis Pongo?"

188.   What European artistic movement featured strong, emotional, dramatic artwork?

189.   Which novel was originally going to be titled Elinor and Marianne?

190.   What artistic style of the early 1900s featured slim lines and a geometric style?

Quiz 39

191.   What did H.G. Wells refer to Adolf Hitler as?

192.   Who created Horatio Hornblower?

193.   An engraving technique, using a sharp needle, that results in a print with soft, velvety lines.

194.   Who composed the opera Oedipus Rex?

195.   Who wrote Lady Chatterley's Lover?

Quiz 40

196.   Boris Pasternak declined a Nobel Prize in 1958. For which novel was it to be awarded?

197.   In The Lord of the Rings books, who deceived the King of Rohan for many years?

198.   What 18th-century French artistic style was considered refined, elegant, and decorative?

199.   John Donne was part of which school of poets?

200.   Who created Winnie the Pooh?

Quiz 41

201.   What is the earliest known drawing medium?
202.   Whose works, The Ballad Of Reading Gaol & De Profundis, were written from his experiences in prison
203.   In what opera would you find Lt. Pinkerton?
204.   What artistic style featured contorted poses, harsh lighting, and a crowded canvas?
205.   Who wrote The Threepenny Opera?

Quiz 42

206.   Who Is Pip's Benefactor In Great Expectations
207.   James Matthew Barrie created which famous character?
208.   Which author penned the Father Brown crime stories?
209.   Name Allen Lane's London publishing company founded in 1935?
210.   What is Dame Margot Fonteyn most famous for?

Quiz 43

211.   Who did Bob Kane create?
212.   Who wrote The 1999 Autobiography Managing My Life?
213.   Who penned The children's Noddy Stories?
214.   Who Composed the Ballet version of Romeo & Juliet?
215.   Who is noted for his Nonsense Verse?

Quiz 44

216.   Who is the author of Brave New World?
217.   What was Hector Hugh Munro's pseudonym?
218.   What is the name of Gandalf's horse in The Lord of the Rings series?
219.   Which French Author wrote Germinal?
220.   What were the tree-like creatures in The Lord of the Rings called?

221.   What Italian movement attempted to integrate the machine age into art?
222.   Which Em Forster novel features The Schlegal Sisters?
223.   Who painted Flatford Mill?
224.   What type of animal is Rupert the Bear's best friend Bill?
225.   What are the March Sisters' names in Louisa May Alcott's Little Women?

Quiz 46

226.   In one of Donald Horne's novels, what was Australia dubbed?
227.   Whose autobiography was entitled Dear Me?
228.   Who wrote the short story "The Birds"?
229.   What was Shakespeare's first play?
230.   Who wrote the gothic novel Dracula?

Quiz 47

231.   What word is Isaac Asimov famous for coining?
232.   Which characters were the longest running in the comic The Beano?
233.   What is the term for the figurative movement that emerged in the U.S. and Britain and can be called superrealism?
234.   A soft, subdued color; a drawing stick made of ground pigments, chalk, and gum water.
235.   A European style of the late eighteenth and early nineteenth centuries. Its elegant, balanced works revived the order and harmony of ancient Greek and Roman art.

Quiz 48

236. What Welsh poet died from alcohol poisoning the same year his collected poems were published?
237. In painting, what is the term for the degree of lightness or darkness in a color?
238. Where would you find the Elgin Marbles?
239. Name the world's largest art gallery?
240. In 1854, Which Bronte sister married Reverend A B Nicholls?

Quiz 49

241. From which of Shakespeare's plays is this line: "All the world's a stage____"
242. Which tavern was the favorite haunt of Falstaff in Shakespeare's Henry IV?
243. Who wrote Gone with the Wind?
244. A large painting or decoration done on a wall.
245. Whose life was the subject of James Boswell's biography, published in 1791?

Quiz 50

246. What did Winston encounter in room 101?
247. What American author became a British citizen in 1927?
248. What was the name of Charles Dickens' last novel unfinished at his death?
249. Who painted The Blue Boy?
250. French artist who devised the 'Pointillism' style of painting and whose first major work was Bathers at Asnieres which now hangs in the National Gallery, London.

Quiz 51

251. What did A E Houseman's initials stand for?
252. During which decade did the Impressionists movement first come to prominence?
253. Where is the Louvre?
254. Which US dramatist was once married to Marilyn Monroe and penned the plays Death of a Salesman and The Crucible?
255. Born in Malaga in 1881, this artist famously had a 'Blue Period'.

Quiz 52

256. The fictional Overlook Hotel in The Shining by Stephen King is based on what real-life hotel?
257. Who wrote the Barsetshire Novels?
258. Who wrote The Gulag Archipelago?
259. How many plays is Shakespeare generally credited with today?
260. What was Dante's last name?

Quiz 53

261. Whose smile remained after the rest of it had vanished?
262. Which member of the Monty Python Team wrote children's books about "Erik the Viking?"
263. What is the fourth book in the Harry Potter series?
264. In the book The Secret Diary of Adrian Mole, what was the name of Adrian's girlfriend?
265. Which of her characters did Agatha Christie dislike the most?

266.   Gandalf's Elven name.
267.   A realistic style of painting in which everyday life forms the subject matter, as distinguished from religious or historical painting.
268.   What term, in which the artist seeks to depict not objective reality but rather the subjective emotions and responses that objects and events arouse, refers to early 20th-century northern European art?
269.   Which famous sculptor was refused entry to the French Academy three times?
270.   What nationality was Joseph Conrad?

Quiz 55

271.   Who kills Nancy in Dickens' novel Oliver Twist?
272.   This girl hid from the Nazis in Amsterdam.
273.   What painting movement originated in New York City and emphasized spontaneity and freedom?
274.   What is the nationality of Picasso?
275.   In which book did four ghosts visit Scrooge?

Quiz 56

276.   This early American statesman and inventor wrote the book, Fart Proudly?
277.   What artistic style means wild beast?
278.   Which gallery has exhibitions in London & St Ives, Cornwall?
279.   Who created Lord Peter Wimsey?
280.   What book begins with the famous line: "The mole had been working very hard all the morning, spring-cleaning his little home?"

Art & Literature

TRIVIA

Answers

Answers – Quiz 1

1. HG Wells
2. Stephen Hawking
3. Andy Warhol
4. Romanticism
5. Nabis

Answers – Quiz 2

6. Thomas Harris
7. Jeremy Clarkson
8. Postimpressionism
9. A Christmas Carol
10. T E Lawrence

Answers – Quiz 3

11. Edgar Rice Burroughs
12. Gilbert & Sullivan
13. As You Like It
14. Daniel Defoe
15. Monochrome

Answers – Quiz 4

16. Edgar Degas
17. Dr Samuel Johnson
18. Ernest Hemingway
19. The Hitchhiker's Guide to the Galaxy
20. Frank McCourt

Answers – Quiz 5

21.   Little Men
22.   Ulysses By James Joyce
23.   An Albatross
24.   Surrealism
25.   13 & Three Quarters

Answers – Quiz 6

26.   Dune
27.   Greyfriars
28.   Joan Rowling
29.   Polonius (Hamlet, Act I, Scene III)
30.   Art noveau

Answers – Quiz 7

31.   The Midwitch Cuckoos
32.   Realism
33.   Iliad
34.   William Wordsworth
35.   Edgar Wallace

Answers – Quiz 8

36.   Pilgim's Progress
37.   Romanesque
38.   Ebenezer Scrooge
39.   Shangri-La
40.   Conceptual art

Answers – Quiz 9

41. Carving
42. Fahrenheit 451
43. Corinthian
44. The Eisteddfod
45. Earnshaw

Answers – Quiz 10

46. Orson Scott Card
47. J.D. Salinger
48. The Night Watch
49. Sir Arthur C. Clarke
50. Woodstock

Answers – Quiz 11

51. Robert Bloch
52. Isaak Dinesen
53. A Collage
54. Engraving
55. Monet

Answers – Quiz 12

56. Artie Shaw
57. Uncle Remus
58. Gesso
59. John Le Carre
60. William Heath Robinson and Rube Goldberg

Answers – Quiz 13

61. Joanne Kathleen
62. William Faulkner
63. Palette
64. Impasto
65. Art Deco

Answers – Quiz 14

66. Frederic Bazille
67. Minimalism
68. The Hound of The Baskervilles
69. The use of words which sound like the event they describe, such as a bang
70. The Tempest

Answers – Quiz 15

71. George Stubbs
72. The Picture of Dorian Gray
73. Acrylic
74. Dick Francis
75. The eight

Answers – Quiz 16

76. Edvard Munch
77. Diction
78. Quotations from the Works of Chairman Mao Tse-Tung
79. Twelfth Night
80. A Piroutte

Answers – Quiz 17

81.	Kenneth Grahame
82.	Ash Can School
83.	Caricature
84.	Gollum
85.	Tempera

Answers – Quiz 18

86.	Anne Rice
87.	Ms
88.	Thomas Pynchon
89.	The Hunchback Of Notre Dame
90.	Mount Doom

Answers – Quiz 19

91.	Suprematism
92.	Oliver Twist
93.	Nick Hornby
94.	Cruella De Vil
95.	Naïve art

Answers – Quiz 20

96.	Catherine Cookson
97.	Botticelli
98.	Better Homes and Gardens
99.	Leonardo da Vinci
100.	Architecture

Answers – Quiz 21

101.   Westminster Abbey
102.   Wagner
103.   Polyptych
104.   Modeling
105.   Color field painting

Answers – Quiz 22

106.   David Hockney
107.   Noel Coward
108.   The Railway Children
109.   2001, A Space Odyssey
110.   Inspector Morse

Answers – Quiz 23

111.   Highlight
112.   Pathetic fallacy
113.   The Bolshoi Ballet
114.   Nietzsche
115.   Wheel of Time

Answers – Quiz 24

116.   Op art
117.   Jonathan Swift
118.   Trompe l'oeil
119.   Anne Hathaway
120.   Harry Potter And The Philosophers Stone

Answers – Quiz 25

121.	Arabian Nights
122.	Alex Haley
123.	Mrs Malaprop
124.	In open air
125.	Figure

Answers – Quiz 26

126.	Pride & Prejudice
127.	Aquatint
128.	Kiri Te Kanawa
129.	Ballet
130.	Vincent Van Gogh

Answers – Quiz 27

131.	Kurt Vonnegut
132.	Jurassic Park
133.	Baroque
134.	William
135.	Jane Austen

Answers – Quiz 28

136.	Charlotte, Emily & Anne
137.	Anna Sewell
138.	Surgeon
139.	Antonio
140.	Michelangelo!!

Answers – Quiz 29

141. Mary Ann Cross (Née Evans)
142. Harry Potter & The Deathly Hallows
143. French
144. Sir Thomas More
145. His pink period

Answers – Quiz 30

146. Persuasion
147. Anne McCaffrey
148. Phileas Fogg
149. Sue Towsend
150. Kite

Answers – Quiz 31

151. Surrealism
152. Folk art
153. James Whistler
154. Pablo
155. Beat

Answers – Quiz 32

156. John Constable
157. Toulouse- Lautrec
158. Terry Pratchett
159. Vincent Van Gogh
160. Renaissance

Answers – Quiz 33

161.   David and Leigh Eddings
162.   Stevenson
163.   Banquo's
164.   (Georges Remi) Herge
165.   Thomas Gray

Answers – Quiz 34

166.   Dr. Seuss
167.   Tom Clancy
168.   Moby Dick, the great white whale
169.   The Water Babies
170.   Foreshortening

Answers – Quiz 35

171.   Dr Spock (No Kidding)
172.   Beatrix Potter
173.   James Herriot
174.   Satan
175.   Wash

Answers – Quiz 36

176.   Artful Dodger
177.   Dorothy
178.   The Waltz
179.   Chiaroscuro
180.   Aldous Huxley

Answers – Quiz 37

181. Albert Camus
182. Major
183. La Boheme
184. Muggle
185. A Tale of Two Cities

Answers – Quiz 38

186. T.S. Eliot
187. 101 Dalmations
188. Baroque
189. Sense and Sensibility
190. Art deco

Answers – Quiz 39

191. A certifiable lunatic
192. C.S. Forester
193. Drypoint
194. Stravinsky
195. DH Lawrence

Answers – Quiz 40

196. Dr Zhivago
197. Wormtongue
198. Rococco
199. The Metaphysical Poets
200. A. A. Milne

Answers – Quiz 41

201.   Charcoal
202.   Oscar Wilde
203.   Madame Butterfly
204.   Mannerism
205.   Bertolt Brecht

Answers – Quiz 42

206.   Abel Magwitch
207.   Peter Pan
208.   G.K. Chesterton
209.   Penguin
210.   Ballet Dancing

Answers – Quiz 43

211.   Batman
212.   Alex Ferguson
213.   Enid Blyton
214.   Prokofiev
215.   Edward Lear or Lewis Carroll

Answers – Quiz 44

216.   Aldous Huxley
217.   Saki
218.   Shadowfax
219.   Emile Zola
220.   The Ents

Answers – Quiz 45

221.	Futurism
222.	Howard's End
223.	Constable
224.	Badger
225.	Jo, Meg Beth & Amy

Answers – Quiz 46

226.	The lucky country
227.	Peter Ustinov's
228.	Daphne du Maurier
229.	Henry VI, part 2
230.	Bram Stoker

Answers – Quiz 47

231.	Robotics
232.	Lord Snooty and His Pals
233.	Photorealism
234.	Pastel
235.	Neoclassicism

Answers – Quiz 48

236.	Dylan Thomas
237.	Values
238.	The British Museum
239.	Paris, The Louvre
240.	Charlotte

Answers – Quiz 49

241. As You Like It
242. The Boar's Head
243. Margaret Mitchell
244. Mural
245. Samuel Johnson

Answers – Quiz 50

246. Rats
247. T S Eliot
248. The Mystery Of Edwin Drood
249. Gainsborough
250. Georges Seurat

Answers – Quiz 51

251. Alfred Edward
252. 1870s
253. Paris, France
254. Arthur Miller
255. Pablo Picasso

Answers – Quiz 52

256. The Stanley Hotel in Estes Park, Colorado
257. Anthony Trollope
258. Alexander Solzhenitsyn
259. Thirty seven
260. Alighieri

Answers – Quiz 53

261.   The Cheshire Cat's
262.   Terry Jones
263.   The Goblet of Fire
264.   Pandora
265.   Hercule Poirot

Answers – Quiz 54

266.   Mithrandir
267.   Genre painting
268.   Expressionism
269.   August Rodin
270.   Polish

Answers – Quiz 55

271.   Bill Sykes
272.   Anne Frank
273.   Abstract expressionism
274.   Spanish
275.   A Christmas Carol

Answers – Quiz 56

276.   Benjamin Franklin
277.   Fauvism
278.   The Tate Gallery
279.   Dorothy L Sayers
280.   The Wind In The Willows

Entertainment

TRIVIA

DID YOU KNOW?

It costs less than a dollar to charge your phone all year.

Quiz 1

1. Who wrote the operas The Magic Flute and The Marriage of Figaro?
2. Which famous TV horse was able to talk?
3. In what game are Jiggies, Jinjos, and Feathers collected?
4. Which gypsy swing guitarist almost had their left hand destroyed by fire when they were young?
5. FTP stands for what?

Quiz 2

6. Name the first video art game ever released.
7. What was the hometown of Fred, Wilma, Barney, and Betty?
8. What did ROB (the old NES peripheral) stand for?
9. Josie and the what?
10. Which toy was originally made from an animal's bladder?

Quiz 3

11. Name Mega Man's sister?
12. Which detective duo featured in Mystery at Devil's Paw?
13. Which exercises are supposed to improve oxygen consumption & increase circulation?
14. What was the first console the "Duke Nukem" game was available on?
15. Super Street Fighter II introduced which character?

Quiz 4

16. Name Fred Flintstone's best friend and neighbor?
17. What does the acronym "NES" stand for?
18. Which group had hits with "He's So Fine", "One Fine Day" and "A Love So Fine?"
19. Name the third opponent in Super Smash Bros?
20. Who played Fox Mulder in the X-Files?

Quiz 5

21. Green Lantern's alter ego?
22. What video game begins with Koma Pigs stealing a bracelet?
23. What new female fighter is introduced in Virtua Fighter 4?
24. Which play was written while the playwright lived at 632 St. Peter Street in New Orleans?
25. What was Nintendo's first arcade game?

Quiz 6

26. Where does Gonzo from the Muppet Show come from?
27. Which comedy duo did the famous, "Who's on first?" routine?
28. Group of heroes led by Dick Grayson.
29. Which series from the 2000s featured the characters Sheldon and Leonard?
30. The Minus World of Super Mario Bros. is a never-ending version of what stage?

Quiz 7

31. Where do the Munster's live?
32. The quote "You spoony bard!" is from what game?
33. What was Citizen Kane's dying word?
34. How many dots are on a Twister mat?
35. In which opera does Leporello entertain a vengeful jilted lover?

Quiz 8

36. To which elementary school did TV's Brady Bunch go?
37. What does the statue of Oscar stand on?
38. What is the name of the cloud-riding, glasses-wearing koopa in the Super Mario Bros. series?
39. Which British game is known as checkers in the USA?
40. Name the dog in the Yankee Doodle cartoons.

Quiz 9

41. What is Celine Jules's favorite food?
42. Who created and wrote 'The West Wing'?
43. Personal merry-go-round guaranteed to make you dizzy?
44. Andy Capp's favorite pub is run by whom?
45. Name Mexico's fastest mouse?

Quiz 10

46. The signature move of the Bombs in Final Fantasy is what?
47. What is Nintendo's Mario's last name?
48. Who plays the voices of Dr. Nick and Moe in 'The Simpsons'?
49. Which game occurs on the mythical island of Koholint?
50. Which famous actress was Tommy Lee married to before Pamela Anderson?

Quiz 11

51. Who played 'ouboet' in the first TV series of 'Orkney Snork Nie'?
52. What was Sega's first home console system?
53. In the original Contra, "S" would get you which gun?
54. What were Wilma Flintstone and Betty Rubble's surnames before they were married?
55. In the TV show, "House" who played "Thirteen?"

Quiz 12

56. Sony's video recorder was known as what?
57. What does "poco a poco" mean?
58. Which highly regarded TV drama was based around a dysfunctional family running a funeral parlor?
59. Which board game involves climbing and sliding.
60. Name Sally Brown's sweet baboo?

Quiz 13

61. Which cartoon first featured sound?
62. Which chess term means "in passing?"
63. TV show: "American _____?"
64. The ranking system in Chess is called...?
65. Which famous musical director worked for Square's Final Fantasy series?

Quiz 14

66. Who were Lucy and Ricky's next door neighbors and best friends?
67. Who is the main character from Nintendo's Earthbound?
68. What is Tina Turner's real name?
69. Who did Larry Hagman portray in the TV series Dallas?
70. In the Marvel comics, who was Thanos's sibling?

Quiz 15

71. Name all main characters from each Final Fantasy 2, and 4-10.
72. Who won the 2002 Academy Award for best actress in a leading role, for "Monster's Ball?"
73. The "Shaia" inventors feature in which TPG series
74. What is Kenny G's actual surname?
75. What was the game by Sega Genesis about two aliens looking for their spaceship called?

Quiz 16

76. What was the original name of The Little Rascals?
77. What fictional character is found naked and wrapped in plastic in Twin Peaks?
78. Who is James Bond's often returning nemesis?
79. Who invented the hovercraft?
80. What turn of phrase did Clark Kent's boss often use?

81. What was Charles Schultz originally going to call Peanuts?
82. Who made the first home video game system?
83. In "Breaking Bad" which actor played Walter White?
84. Which manned aircraft first exceeded the speed of sound?
85. Which company first made Donkey Kong?

Quiz 18

86. Which place do Rocky and Bullwinkle go to play football?
87. Name the first game cartridge to include a battery backed save feature?
88. What is a "koopa?"
89. A Gibbons' catalogue was used to buy what?
90. What item's sound effect was removed from Smash Brothers when it was imported to the US

Quiz 19

91. Name Barbie's pink sports car.
92. What was the name of the Jaguar prior to 1945?
93. Jean De Bruhoff created what character?
94. Which cube puzzle was created by a Hungarian mathematician in the 1970s?
95. Name the final bosses from each Final Fantasy games 1-8.

Quiz 20

96. In Bodley Mansion in Castlevania II: Simon's Quest, what body part is discovered?
97. What was Rare's first game?
98. Nolan Bushnell founded the video arcade chain that now goes by which name?
99. The shooter game Salamander is better known in the U.S. by which name?
100. "The Wire" was set in which American city?

Quiz 21

101. "Is it animal, vegetable, or mineral" is the start of which game?
102. What name was given to the genre of rock from the US Pacific Northwest at the start of the 1990s?
103. Which advertising campaign was the line "I can't believe I ate the whole thing" used for?
104. Which game featured plastic animals eating marbles?
105. What was Marilyn Monroe's birth name?

Quiz 22

106. From what did the word FORTRAN originate?
107. How much cash do you begin the game 'Wall Street Kid' with?
108. Which old Chinese game uses 156 small rectangular tiles?
109. In the StarFox team, who betrays the group to join StarWolf?
110. What was Jethro Tull before giving his name to a British rock group?

Quiz 23

111. Who created the The Masked Ball opera?
112. A pair of aces & a pair of eights is also known as what?
113. In 80's television, What did "HHOH" stand for?
114. In which game do you meld groups of three or more cards with the same rank or suit?
115. The Greatest Show On Earth refers to what?

Quiz 24

116. Where did Mighty Mouse's superpowers come from?
117. What were balloons originally made of?
118. In Castlevania 2, what is the most powerful whip in?
119. Where does Link find himself in Majora's Mask?
120. What TV comedy is set at the Sacred Heart teaching hospital?

Quiz 25

121. Atari competitor that featured better graphics?
122. What Nintendo development team is led by Shigeru Miyamoto?
123. Who is Mega Man's creator?
124. What do you call a number between 1 and 18 in Roulette?
125. What was George of the Jungle always running into?

Quiz 26

126. What was Daffy Duck's usual closing line?
127. Who was the ranger who was always chasing Yogi Bear?
128. What was the name of the witch in the TV show Emu's World?
129. This game has 361 intersections?
130. In the original All-C Saga game, Mandy and Matthew are killed by whom?

Quiz 27

131. What is Smokey Stover employed as?
132. The first artificial satellite on earth was what?
133. In TV, what did IMF stand for?
134. Who was George Costanza in "Seinfeld" played by?
135. Who is the wingman in Star Fox Team?

Quiz 28

136. To marry Blondie, what did Dagwood give up?
137. Which track is unlocked in "Excite Bike 64" upon completing the tutorial?
138. In Japan, what are Final Fantasy Legend 1-3 known as?
139. Who are Dennis the Menace's next door neighbors?
140. Which network series was first devoted only to rock music?

Quiz 29

141. In Dead or Alive 2, Hayabusa informs you that "If your soul is imperfect," what?
142. Who invented Tetris?
143. What was the name of Barney and Betty Rubble's son?
144. In the "Extreme Battle" mini-game in Resident Evil 2, what characters are selectable?
145. What is your character's name in the "Legend of Zelda" series?

Quiz 30

146. Who wrote the song, "Pac-Man Fever?"
147. What are names of the two brothers in the Double Dragon games?
148. What was launched on the 4th December 1996?
149. In Chrono Trigger, who is the "Master of War?"
150. What are a chessboard's horizontal rows called?

Quiz 31

151. If you're killing a goomba, what game are you playing?
152. What is the name of the PlayStation controller that uses two analog joysticks?
153. What is the prequel to the movie Psycho?
154. What object did you need to get to the secret room in Atari's Adventure?
155. What TV show follows a family who moves into a haunted house in Los Angeles?

Quiz 32

156. What fuzzy animal does Croc rescue?
157. What TV show made flip up sunglasses popular?
158. Plastic vehicle equipped with spin-out brake.
159. Who played Garth in Wayne's World?
160. Talking toy that helped you do well on spelling tests.

161.	What does CR-ROM stand for?
162.	What actor plays Aragorn in Peter Jackson's version of The Lord of the Rings?
163.	Who is Mega Man's traditional nemesis?
164.	Car racing card game with a French name is called what?
165.	Which castles do you need the bridge to explore completely in the game, Adventure?

Quiz 34

166.	Name the first gym leader you fight in Game Boy's Pokémon?
167.	On aircraft what do the letters VTOL mean?
168.	Where was The King and I set?
169.	In Joust, what animal is your mount?
170.	Who built a supercomputer to work out the digits of Pi?

Quiz 35

171.	Name Warren Beatty's sister?
172.	Don Rickles' nickname was what?
173.	Who was the photographer for the Daily Planet?
174.	What post-apocalyptic TV series has defined the zombie horror genre?
175.	What does ASCII stand for?

Quiz 36

176.	Name the central character in the first Street Fighter?
177.	Who said "All life begins and ends with Nu____at least this is my belief for now____?"
178.	Who is Goemon's sidekick in Mystical Ninja?
179.	Any number between 19 & 36 in roulette
180.	Who Ozzie's energetic sister in the first All-C Saga game?

181.   Baduk is a player on which board?

182.   This comic strip was banned from "Stars and Stripes?"

183.   Name of the Family Circus's dog.

184.   John Wayne's real name is...?

185.   Who plays the eldest sister in TV's Charmed?

Quiz 38

186.   What is Li'l Abner's preferred drink?

187.   Who was Olive Oyl engaged to before Popeye?

188.   Who was Hagar the Horrible's dog?

189.   What happened to the residents when Bowser Koopa took control of the Mushroom Kingdom?

190.   The hybrid pinball/video game in the Pac-Man series was called what?

Quiz 39

191.   Who is the leading manufacturer of toy cars?

192.   Who created the British sci-fi TV series Black Mirror?

193.   Who is the only unmarried female suspect in the game "Clue?"

194.   In the The Brady Bunch, what was Cindy's doll called?

195.   In Sesame Street, which two characters were roommates?

Quiz 40

196.   In M.A.S.H. what is Hawkeye's full name?

197.   What are Tinky Winky, Dipsy LaLa and Po?

198.   Where do the Jetsons live?

199.   Who is Beetle Bailey's sister?

200.   What does HTML stand for?

Quiz 41

201. What supernatural horror TV show follows five siblings in a haunted house?
202. What does LED stand for?
203. Porky Pig had a girlfriend named _____.
204. What do the initials B.B. stand for in B.B. King's name?
205. Who programmed Roller Coaster Tycoon?

Quiz 42

206. What sci-fi horror Netflix series is based in Hawkins, Indiana?
207. Who was Carl in Five Easy Pieces before going to Walton's Mountain?
208. What number is the Pokémon "Scyther" in the Pokémon GameBoy games?
209. Who is the main character in the DeathQuest series?
210. What is the reason behind the layout of the QWERTY keyboard?

Quiz 43

211. What is a Hurdy-Gurdy?
212. What does the 'x' mean when referring to the speed of a CD-rom (e.g. 32x)?
213. Who invented Tetris?
214. What is the drummer's name in The Muppet Show?
215. On what non-Nintendo console can you find Zelda games?

Quiz 44

216. This popular card game's name is Spanish for "one."
217. What's the first video game ever to contain an "Easter Egg?"
218. Mundane toy that involved sticking plastic pieces on scenes.
219. The Nintendo 64 was titled under what name during production?
220. What was the name of the restaurant in the TV series Happy Days?

Entertainment TRIVIA Answers

Answers – Quiz 1

1. Wolfgang Amadeus Mozart
2. Mr. Ed
3. Banjo-Kazooie
4. Django Reinhardt
5. File Transfer Protocol

Answers – Quiz 2

6. Computer Space
7. Bedrock
8. Robotic Operating Buddy
9. Pussycats
10. Balloon

Answers – Quiz 3

11. Roll
12. Hardy, The Hardy Boys
13. Aerobics
14. Duke Nukem 64
15. Cammy

Answers – Quiz 4

16. Barney Rubble
17. Nintendo Entertainment System
18. The Chiffons
19. Fox McCloud
20. David Duchovny

Answers – Quiz 5

21. Hal Jordan
22. Tomba!
23. Vanessa Lewis
24. A Streetcar Named Desire
25. Radarscope

Answers – Quiz 6

26. Outer space
27. Abbott and Costello
28. New Titans
29. The Big Bang Theory
30. 42037

Answers – Quiz 7

31. 1313 Mockingbird Lane
32. Final Fantasy IV
33. Rosebud
34. Thirty
35. Don Giovanni

Answers – Quiz 8

36. Dixie Canyon Elementary
37. A reel of film
38. Lakitu
39. Draughts
40. Chopper

Answers – Quiz 9

41.   Baby rabbit risotto
42.   Aaron Sorkin
43.   Sit n spin
44.   Jack and Jill
45.   Speedy Gonzalez

Answers – Quiz 10

46.   Exploder
47.   Mario
48.   Hank Azaria
49.   Link's Awakening
50.   Heather Locklear

Answers – Quiz 11

51.   Frank Opperman
52.   Sega Master System
53.   Spread Gun
54.   Slaghoople and Mcbricker
55.   Olivia Wilde

Answers – Quiz 12

56.   Betamax
57.   Little by little
58.   Six Feet Under
59.   Chutes(Snakes) and ladders
60.   Linus

Answers – Quiz 13

61.   Steamboat Willie
62.   En passant
63.   Bandstand
64.   Elo
65.   Nobuo Uematsu

Answers – Quiz 14

66.   Fred and Ethel
67.   Ness
68.   Anne Mae Bullock
69.   J.R. Ewing
70.   Ero

Answers – Quiz 15

71.   Frionel, Cecil, Butz, Terra, Cloud, Squall, Zidane, and Tidus
72.   Halle Berry
73.   Lufia
74.   Gorelick
75.   ToeJam and Earl

Answers – Quiz 16

76.   Our Gang
77.   Laura Palmer
78.   Ernst Stavro Blofeld
79.   Sir Christopher Cockerell
80.   Great Caesar's Ghost!

Answers – Quiz 17

81.	Li'l Folks
82.	Magnavox
83.	Bryan Cranston
84.	Bell X-1
85.	Nintendo

Answers – Quiz 18

86.	What'samatta University
87.	The Legend of Zelda
88.	A turtle
89.	Stamps
90.	The Beam Sword

Answers – Quiz 19

91.	Vette
92.	SS
93.	Babar the Elephant
94.	Rubik
95.	Chaos, Emperor from Hell, Dark Cloud, Zeromus, Deathgyunos, Kefka, Sephiroth, and Ultimecia

Answers – Quiz 20

96.	An eye
97.	Slalom
98.	Chuck E. Cheese's
99.	Life Force
100.	Baltimore

Answers – Quiz 21

101.	20 questions
102.	Grunge
103.	Alka Seltzer
104.	Hungry hungry hippos
105.	Norma Jean Mortenson

Answers – Quiz 22

106.	Formula Translation
107.	500000
108.	Mah jongg
109.	Pigma Dengar
110.	Agriculturist

Answers – Quiz 23

111.	Giuseppe Verdi
112.	Dead man's hand
113.	Hammer House Of Horrors
114.	Rummy
115.	Barnum & Bailey Circus

Answers – Quiz 24

116.	Supermarket
117.	Animal bladders
118.	Flame Whip
119.	Termina
120.	Scrubs

Answers – Quiz 25

121. Intellevision
122. EAD
123. Dr. Light
124. Manque
125. A tree

Answers – Quiz 26

126. You're despicable!
127. Rick
128. Grotbags
129. Go
130. Simetra

Answers – Quiz 27

131. Fireman
132. Sputnik 1
133. Impossible Mission Forces
134. Jason Alexander
135. Falco Lombardi

Answers – Quiz 28

136. A family inheritance
137. Classic NES Excite Bike
138. SaGa 1-3
139. Mr and Mrs Wilson
140. American Bandstand

Answers – Quiz 29

141. Living will be difficult
142. Alexi Pazhitnov
143. Bam Bam
144. Claire, Leon, Ada, and Chris
145. Link

Answers – Quiz 30

146. Buckner and Garcia
147. Billy and Jimmy
148. Mars Pathfinder
149. Spekkio
150. Ranks

Answers – Quiz 31

151. Super Mario Bros.
152. Dual Shock
153. Bates Motel
154. The dot
155. American Horror Story

Answers – Quiz 32

156. The Gobbos
157. A Different World
158. Big wheel
159. Dana Carvey
160. Speak n spell

Answers – Quiz 33

161. Compact Disk Read Only Memory
162. Viggo Mortenson
163. Dr. Wily
164. Mille borne
165. Black and white Castles

Answers – Quiz 34

166. Brock
167. Vertical Take off and landing
168. Siam (Thailand)
169. An ostrich
170. Chudnovsky

Answers – Quiz 35

171. Shirley MacLaine
172. Mr. Warmth
173. Jimmy Olsen
174. The Walking Dead
175. American Standard code for Information Interchange

Answers – Quiz 36

176. Ryu
177. Nu
178. Ebisumaru
179. Passe
180. Treli

Answers – Quiz 37

181. Goban
182. Beetle Bailey
183. Barf
184. Marion Morrison
185. Shannon Doherty

Answers – Quiz 38

186. Kickapoo joy juice
187. Bluto
188. Snert
189. They became bricks and powerup blocks
190. Baby Pac-Man

Answers – Quiz 39

191. Hot wheels
192. Charlie Brooker
193. Miss Scarlett
194. Kitty Carrie All
195. Bert and Ernie

Answers – Quiz 40

196. Benjamin Franklin Pierce
197. The Teletubbies
198. The Skypad Apartments
199. Lois (of Hi and Lois)
200. Hyper Text Markup Language

Answers – Quiz 41

201.	The Haunting of Hill House
202.	Light Emitting Diode
203.	Pet
204.	Blues Boy
205.	Chris Sawyer

Answers – Quiz 42

206.	Stranger Things
207.	Waite
208.	123
209.	Lucretzia
210.	To slow down typing rates and prevent jamming

Answers – Quiz 43

211.	A Fiddle
212.	Times (faster than standard speed)
213.	Alexey Pazhitnov
214.	Animal
215.	Philips CD-I

Answers – Quiz 44

216.	Uno
217.	Adventure
218.	Colorforms
219.	Project Reality
220.	Arnolds

Movies

TRIVIA

DID YOU KNOW?

1 OUT OF EVERY 4 AMERICANS HAS APPEARED ON TV IN THEIR LIFETIME.

Quiz 1

1. Whose scary movie character has the real name of Charles Lee Ray
2. What popular Disney film tells the story of an ice queen and her sister?
3. The Single "Up Where We Belong" is taken from which film?
4. In the Harry Potter film franchise, what does the Hogwarts motto "Draco dormiens nunquam titillandus" mean?
5. What is the name of the Volkswagen in the film, The Love Bug?

Quiz 2

6. Name the 1996 sequel to "Terms of Endearment?"
7. "Happy Days" was inspired by the nostalgia created by which 1974 film?
8. In "Forrest Gump" who loved shrimp?
9. John McClane was the hero in which eighties movie?
10. "Hey Stella!" is a line from which 50s movie?

Quiz 3

11. Which plant was Uma Thurman's character in Batman & Robin named for?
12. Later acted by Sarah Michelle Geller on TV, who was played by Kirsty Swanson in a movie?
13. On what did Dorothy's house land in The Wizard Of Oz?
14. A love scene in Honey, I Shrunk The Kids occurs inside what?
15. Which horror movie killer's look is based on the painting "Scream" by Edvard Munch?

Quiz 4

16. "Snakes, I hate snakes" is a line from which film?
17. The theme tune for the movie The Spy Who Loved Me was sung by who?
18. Which film stars Robert Downey Jr. where superheroes team up to fight the villain, Thanos?
19. What 1981 film with an athletic theme won the Oscar for Best Film in 1982?
20. How many storm troopers were there on screen in Star Trek?

Quiz 5

21. In the 80s movie Absolute Beginners, who was acted by David Bowie?
22. Name the 2 main characters in the movie Life?
23. Who directed The first Halloween movie
24. What does Scarlett invest in Gone with the Wind?
25. What movie features the famous line: "You wouldn't be able to do those awful things to me if I weren't still in this chair!"

Quiz 6

26. "Jurassic Park III was directed by who?
27. Who was the actor playing Charlie in the TV version of Charlie's Angels?
28. Which planet does Anakin Skywalker come from?
29. Which actor won an Oscar for her part in Cold Mountain?
30. Who sang "New York New York" in the film of the same name?

Quiz 7

31. What Rizzo's real name in the movie, Grease?
32. Which actor said the line, "Love means never having to say you're sorry?"
33. Which film starred Winona Ryder and Susan Sarandon about the March sisters?
34. 'Mookie' was a character in which film?
35. Who played Kris Kringle in the original 1947 version of Miracle on 34th Street?

Quiz 8

36. Name the film starring Rosie O'Donnell, Rita Wilson and Meg Ryan?
37. What was Han Solo's ship in Star Wars called?
38. Where is Das Boot set?
39. The 1954 film White Christmas was made with what new Paramount format?
40. Which movie with John Candy was about The Jamaican Bobsleigh Team?

Quiz 9

41. Finish this tag line from the trailer for the film Alien. "In space no one can_____."
42. Name John Cazale's last film?
43. Name the film that began the trend of wearing cutoff sweatshirts over the shoulder?
44. Four Weddings and a Funeral later had "an equal, not a sequel." What was it called?
45. Name the actor playing Lois Lane in the 1978 "Superman" movie.

Quiz 10

46. Which kind of creature is Templeton in Charlotte's Web?
47. Starring Goldie Hawn & Meryl Streep, this 1992 film was about 2 women taking extreme measures to preserve their looks.
48. "Either this man is dead or my watch has stopped." is a line by Groucho Marx. In which film did he say it?
49. In which horror movie did Johnny Depp make his film debut?
50. What was Steven Spielberg's 1975 first hit?

Quiz 11

51. Harry Potter keeps which kind of animal?
52. Who did Alec Guinness play in Star Wars?
53. Who did Martin Landau play in Tim Burton's 1994 film about Ed Wood
54. Which 1988 film saw Bruce Willis battling against a group of terrorists that rudely interrupted a Christmas party
55. What movie did Robert Vaughan, Richard Chamberlain and Robert Wagner all die in?

Quiz 12

56. What was Melissa Matheson's contribution to E.T.?
57. In what 1970s movie did Dustin Hoffman play Carl Bernstein?
58. What movie features a villain named Han who only has one hand?
59. Jeremy Irons, Lindsay Lohan and Bette Davis have all played the same type of character. What type of character was it?
60. Which film did James Dean die during the filming of in 1955?

Quiz 13

61. What unique gift did Harry Potter get for Christmas in his first semester at Hogwarts School?
62. Name the first film to get the whole cast Oscar-nominated?
63. Tall Dark And Gruesome is the autobiography of which star?
64. What French town does Robbie die in in Atonement?
65. In the movie Godzilla, what is the Japanese name for Godzilla?

Quiz 14

66. Which James Bond movie takes place over Christmas?
67. What popular Christmas film is known for the line, "Every time a bell rings, an angel gets its wings"?
68. How many films are there in the Jaws series
69. In the 1996 film of Romeo and Juliet, who was Juliet played by?
70. In the movie Casablanca, which actor played the part of Sam, the pianist who was asked to "play it again"?

Quiz 15

71. Which comic strip did Bill The Cat originally feature in?
72. What kind of car did Don Mclean drive in American Pie?
73. The thinnest film is made from which metal?
74. What speed would the bus in Speed blow up at?
75. In a 1974 movie, who was Kissing In The Back Row?

Quiz 16

76. Which Harry Potter actor also starred in Dracula?
77. What film is thought to be the worst film ever made?
78. In It's A Wonderful Life how do you know that an angel has gotten their wings?
79. Which actor played "Robin" to Val Kilmer's "Batman?"
80. Who starred in the movie "The Mask?"

Quiz 17

81. What was both a 1992 horror movie and a 2006 hit by Christina Aguilera?
82. Robert Mitchum acted in the 60's original, and Robert de Niro in the remake in 1991. What was the title of both movies?
83. Where did Alex Leamas come from?
84. In the 1999 version of The Mummy, what is the mummy called?
85. In Herbie Fully Loaded, who plays Maggie Payton's father?

Quiz 18

86. Gimme Shelter notoriously captured which festival?
87. Who won a 1955 Oscar for The King and I?
88. Who stars in The Usual Suspects?
89. Who originally played Obi-Wan Kenobi in Star Wars?
90. Who sang the theme song for From Russia With Love?

Quiz 19

91. Who played the part of the Tokyo underworld boss O-Ren Ishii in Kill Bill I and II?
92. In the Adventures of Robin Hood who is Errol Flynn fighting for?
93. Name the second movie Olivia Newton John and John Travolta starred in together?
94. A succession of 48 baby pigs were used in the title role for the 1995 movie hit _____
95. James Dean starred in three films. What were they?

Quiz 20

96. Who is Owen Wilson's brother?
97. In the comedy movie, The Adventures of Priscilla, Queen of the Desert, what is Priscilla?
98. Which British actor won the Best Actor Oscar in the 80s?
99. Who played the medium Oda Mae Brown in Ghost?
100. How much did John Carpenter's original Halloween movie make? A. 40M, B. 50M or was it C. 60M?

Quiz 21

101. Which comic book hero patrols Gotham City?
102. Which British actor has used a unique voice or accent for every one of their characters?
103. What made the crew sick in Airplane?
104. How many times was Richard Burton nominated for an Oscar?
105. Coolio had a 1995 hit with which song from Dangerous Minds?

Quiz 22

106. In the 1957 film Showboat, who starred as June?
107. Who played Lee Christmas in The Expendables?
108. What kills Alex Guinness in The Ladykillers?
109. The dream sequence in which Hitchcock film was inspired by the works of Salvador Dali?
110. Who played Juno MacGuff in the 2007 film Juno?

Quiz 23

111. Name the second Carry On film?
112. In It's a Wonderful Life, what's the name of George Bailey's angel?
113. Who has played a villain in the films Patriot Games, Goldeneye, National Treasure, and Don't Say A Word?
114. Which actress starred in King Kong in 1933?
115. Hannibal Lecter liked to eat what with liver?

Quiz 24

116. What 1994 movie focuses on Egyptian hieroglyphs and a structure in Giza?
117. Who played Frankenstein's monster in the 1931 film Frankenstein
118. Which cross-eyed lion inspired the Dakari television series?
119. Who played Princess Leia in Star Wars?
120. Jim Carey Played Lloyd Christmas in what movie?

Quiz 25

121. Crouching Tiger, Hidden Dragon takes place during which dynasty?
122. What movie is the flux-capacitor from?
123. Who did Ben Stiller play in Mystery Men?
124. In a famous metal music mockumentry, what was the name of the band who "turned it up to 11?"
125. Who played Che Guevara in the film Evita?

Quiz 26

126. Name Ashley Wilkes' plantation in Gone With the Wind?"
127. Captain Jack Sparrow has a key catch-phrase in the Pirates of the Caribbean films? What is it?
128. What movie was Orson Wells nominated for four Oscars for?
129. Who won an Oscar for her first film role in Mary Poppins?
130. Who played the part of Brad Pitt's police partner in "Seven?"

Quiz 27

131. What is Tom Cruise's real name?
132. 'Which British group recorded the song "You Sexy Thing" for the film, The Full Monty?
133. What movie shows a couple trying to visit each of their divorced parents during Christmas?
134. Which python tries to kill Mowgli in The Jungle Book?
135. Name the first 3-D film.

Quiz 28

136. Who plays Gisele in the Fast and Furious film series?
137. What movie did Barbra Streisand win her second Oscar for?
138. Mr. Bigglesworth was a character in which movie?
139. Elton John appeared as a character called "The Pinball Wizard" in what rock opera?
140. Name the space shuttles in Armageddon?

141.   "It's as big as a house" is a line in which 70s film?
142.   Who played the preacher in the rock film Tommy?
143.   In American Hot Wax, who was Jay Leno's character?
144.   Name Elwood's brother from The Blues Brothers?
145.   Michael Hutchence played a terrible punk singer in which 80s movie?

Quiz 30

146.   Who wrote and directed the 2010 film, The Way?
147.   What color is Spock's blood in Star Trek?
148.   Dr. Egon Spengler is a character in which horror film?

Movies TRIVIA Answers

Answers – Quiz 1

1. Chucky
2. Frozen and Frozen 2
3. An Officer And A Gentleman
4. Never tickle a sleeping dragon
5. Herbie

Answers – Quiz 2

6. Morning Star
7. American Graffiti
8. Bubba
9. Die Hard
10. A Streetcar Named Desire

Answers – Quiz 3

11. Poison Ivy
12. Buffy the Vampire Slayer
13. The Wicked Witch of the East
14. Lego Brick
15. Ghost face from Scream

Answers – Quiz 4

16. Raiders Of The Lost Ark
17. Carly Simon
18. Avengers: Endgame
19. Chariots of Fire.
20. None (It was Star Wars)

Answers – Quiz 5

21. Vendice Partners
22. Eddie Murphy and Martin Lawrence
23. John Carpenter
24. Sawmill
25. What ever happened to Baby Jane?

Answers – Quiz 6

26. Joe Johnston
27. John Forsythe
28. Tatooine
29. Renee Zellweger
30. Liza Minelli

Answers – Quiz 7

31. Betty
32. Ali MacGraw
33. Little Women
34. American Hot Wax
35. Edmund Gwenn

Answers – Quiz 8

36. Sleepless in Seattle
37. Millennium Falcon
38. On a submarine
39. VistaVision
40. Cool Runnings

Answers – Quiz 9

41. Hear you scream
42. The Deer Hunter
43. Flashdance
44. Notting Hill
45. Margot Kidder

Answers – Quiz 10

46. He is a rat
47. Death Becomes Her
48. A Day at the Races
49. A Nightmare on Elm Street
50. Close Encounters

Answers – Quiz 11

51. His snowy owl, Hedwig
52. Obi-Wan Kenobi
53. Bela Lugosi
54. Die Hard
55. The Towering Inferno.

Answers – Quiz 12

56. Scriptwriter.
57. All the Presidents Men
58. Enter the Dragon
59. Twins
60. Giant

Answers - Quiz 13

61. An invisibility cloak
62. Who's Afraid of Virginia Woolf
63. Christopher Lee
64. Dunkirk.
65. Gojira

Answers - Quiz 14

66. On Her Majestys Secret Service
67. It's a Wonderful Life
68. 4 (Jaws 1, 2, 3 & Jaws The Revenge)
69. Claire Danes
70. Dooley Wilson.

Answers - Quiz 15

71. Bloom County
72. Chevy (Chevrolet)
73. Gold
74. 50 miles per hour.
75. The Drifters

Answers - Quiz 16

76. Gary Oldman
77. The list is long but Attack of the Killer Tomatoes is often
     referred to as the worst movie ever.
78. A Bell Rings
79. Christopher O'Donnell
80. Jim Carrey

Answers – Quiz 16

81.   Candyman
82.   Cape Fear
83.   In from the cold. The Spy Who Came In From The Cold.
84.   Imhotep
85.   Michael Keaton

Answers – Quiz 17

86.   Altamont
87.   Yul Brynner
88.   Kevin Spacey
89.   Alec Guiness
90.   Matt Munro

Answers – Quiz 18

91.   Lucy Liu
92.   Richard I.
93.   Two of a Kind
94.   Babe
95.   A Rebel Without a Cause, East of Eden, Giant

Answers – Quiz 19

96.   Luke Wilson.
97.   Bus
98.   Ben Kingsley
99.   Whoopi Goldberg
100.   B (50 Million)

Answers – Quiz 20

101.   Batman and Robin
102.   Gary Oldman
103.   The fish
104.   Seven
105.   Gangsta's Paradise

Answers – Quiz 21

106.   Ava Gardner
107.   Jason Statham
108.   A railway signal
109.   Spellbound
110.   Ellen Page

Answers – Quiz 22

111.   Carry on, Nurse
112.   Clarence (Oddbody)
113.   Sean Bean
114.   Fay Wray
115.   Fava Beans

Answers – Quiz 23

116.   Stargate
117.   Boris Karloff
118.   Clarence
119.   Carrie Fisher
120.   Dumb & Dumber

Answers – Quiz 24

121.	Ching
122.	Back to the Future
123.	Mr. Furious
124.	Spinal Tap
125.	Antonio Banderas

Answers – Quiz 25

126.	Twelve Oaks
127.	Savvy?
128.	Citizen Kane
129.	Julie Andrews.
130.	Morgan Freeman

Answers – Quiz 26

131.	Thoma Cruise Mapother, IV
132.	Hot Chocolate
133.	Four Christmases
134.	Kaa
135.	Bwana Devil

Answers – Quiz 27

136.	Gal Gadot
137.	A Star is Born
138.	Austin Powers
139.	Tommy
140.	Freedom and Independence

Answers – Quiz 28

141.   Close Encounters of the Third Kind
142.   Eric Clapton.
143.   Mookie
144.   Jake
145.   Dogs In Space

Answers – Quiz 29

146.   Emilio Estevez
147.   Green
148.   Ghostbusters

Music

TRIVIA

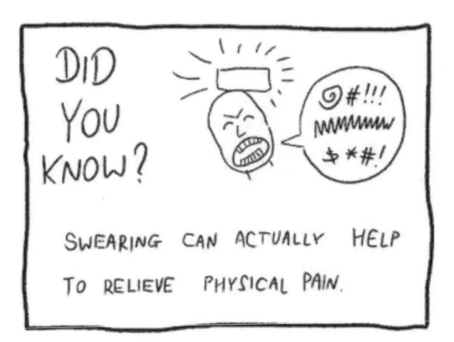

Quiz 1

1. What style of dancing was popularized with rap music?
2. What three words came just before "land that I love" in the 1938 Irving Berlin song?
3. "I am the eggman, they are the Eggmen, I am _____ _____ (2 Words)
4. Aretha Franklin was the first woman inducted into what?
5. Which 1996 single sold a then-record 420,000 copies in its first week of release

Quiz 2

6. How much, to within £5, was a weekend ticket for the Reading 98 concert?
7. Which duo asked "Are You Sure" in 1961?
8. About which jazz player was "Ain't Misbehavin'?"
9. Who were the two members of the pop duo Wham?
10. Whose 1991 autobiography was called And the Beat Goes On?

Quiz 3

11. What was Jamaican singer Barry Biggs' highest song entry to the charts, making No. 3 in 1976?
12. There have only been 2 No.1 singles that have rhymed "Eskimo" with "Arapahoe" name them.
13. The Beatles' "All You Need Is Love" from the 60s began with what?
14. What America song contains the lyric "You take what you want and I"ll take the sunshine?"
15. The movie Back to the Future featured a song entitled "Back in Time" by which band?

Quiz 4

16. What was the title of Ike and Tina Turner's only album?
17. Which singer is known as The Wicked?
18. Which guitarist used a sixpence to play his instrument?
19. What is Johnny Rotten's real name?
20. Which actress was Paul McCartney's girlfriend before Linda Eastman?

Quiz 5

21. What is the title of the 70s England World Cup team's official song?
22. "I'll Be Missing You" featured which Faith?
23. John Parr sang about what "Fire" from the film of the same name
24. In the 60s, who was "Shakin' All Over?"
25. "Also Sprach Zarathustra" was the music for which Stanley Kubrick film?

Quiz 6

26. In the song "You've Lost That Loving Feeling" which two body parts are first mentioned?
27. How much did the Beatles sue Nike for after Nike used the song "Revolution" in one of their commercials?
28. Who took the starring role in Grease in 1997?
29. What inflatable featured in Pink Floyd's 1977 tour?
30. Name the last single released by John Lennon.

Quiz 7

31. Which record label did Simply Red record with in the 90's?
32. Who was John Lennon's father?
33. What was the title of Cyndi Lauper's Re-released 80's classic album?
34. What links David Cassidy, The Monkees, and KISS?
35. The word Xylophone comes from the Greek words for what?

36. Who has used names such as "69 Psyche," "Paperclip People" & "Innerzone Orchestra?"
37. George and Felix Powell wrote which popular WWI song?
38. Which ex-member of the Latin teen group Menudo enjoyed worldwide success in 1999?
39. Who did The Byrds ask to "Play A Song For Me" in 1965?
40. What was a Christmas No 1 in both 1975 and 1991?

Quiz 9

41. What "Snoopy Vs. The Red Baron" follow-up was made by The Royal Guardsmen?
42. What was the first UK number one of Robbie Williams' solo career?
43. Did Mike Oldfield have a "Shadow Of Light" Or A "Moonlight Shadow?"
44. Who won best international female artist at the 2005 Brit awards?
45. Which three groups did Tony Burrows appear on Top Of The Pops with?

Quiz 10

46. The Motels removed The "L" from Lover, making it _____
47. Did Johnny Hates Jazz sing "Shattered Dreams" Or "Dreaming Of You?"
48. The Beatles covered the song "Chains." Who was the original artist?
49. In 1988, someone fell to his death from a window in Amsterdam. Who was it?
50. Which Oxford poetry Professor's lyrics were rejected For Les Miserable?

Quiz 11

51. During their 1964 world tour, who filled in for the Beatles' Ringo Starr?
52. What are The Band Aston, Marvin JB & Oritse also known as?
53. What was the Ringo-designed Discover card's introductory interest rate in 1996?
54. Which rock star once tried to bite the head off a bat during a gig?
55. What does FRAM stand for?

Quiz 12

56. What didn't Voice Of The Beehive want us to do in 1988?
57. What name does Damon Gough perform under?
58. In 1980, who made a special brew?
59. Name the first George Harrison composition recorded by the Beatles?
60. Born Roberta Streeter, this artist wrote their first single about a man's suicide in "Ode To Billy Joe."

Quiz 13

61. A Cellarful Of Noise was whose autobiography?
62. This US singer was married to Debbie Reynolds, Elizabeth Taylor & Connie Stevens.
63. Which instruments are also known as kettledrums?
64. These two spent 12 weeks on the charts with a re-mixed Surfari's track.
65. Which British producer worked on Madonna's Ray Of Light album?

66.   Bach, Handel and Vivaldi are associated which music era?
67.   For what reason did The Jackson 5 change their name to The Jacksons?
68.   Herb Alpert was backed by what band?
69.   What function Franz Schubert perform at Beethoven's funeral?
70.   Which Beach Boy joined the Beatles on their visit to the Maharishi?

Quiz 15

71.   Who sang "When I'm Dead And Gone?"
72.   In the song "Wake Up Little Suzie" What time do they wake up?
73.   What "Rolling Stone" record was voted the best album of 1976?
74.   Whose trumpet did the talking in "This Guys In Love With You?"
75.   What is Paul McCartney's estimated worth?

Quiz 16

76.   "It's late September and I really should be back at school, I know I keep you amused but I feel I'm being used?" was a line by which 70s singer?
77.   Where did the first US live Beatles concert take place?
78.   The album Incense and Peppermints was written by who?
79.   Bjork was originally a member of which band?
80.   What was Stevie Wonder's first album after getting control of his work In 1972?

Quiz 17

81.   Name the lead singer of "Visage."
82.   In music, what did Simon Fuller get the sack from in 1997?
83.   Which Guns N' Roses video did Arnold Schwarzenegger appear in?
84.   Who recorded the album Handsworth Revolution?
85.   Who said "Go West" in 1993?

Quiz 18

86. Name the 60's singer born in Johannesburg, whose birth name is Michael Lubowitz.
87. Who used his wife's car crash compensation money to pursue music full time?
88. "The Boy Looked At Johnny" was written by which two journalists?
89. Who said they were "The Wild One?"
90. Which image is on the front of 10cc's album "The Original Soundtrack?"

Quiz 19

91. Who was the lead singer for Teardrop Explodes?
92. Paul McCartney recorded duets with which two Motown artists?
93. What is the world's best-selling album of all time?
94. Name the Apple label's first single.
95. Name the female trio who released "Wide Open Spaces" in 1998?

Quiz 20

96. In 1974, who did Eric Clapton not shoot?
97. Frank Sinatra had 2 No.1s in the 60's. What were they?
98. What are the 2 figures wearing on the 1978 album cover of Never Say Die by Black Sabbath
99. Finish the name of this Christina Aguilera track "Genie In A ...?"
100. Who was the Bay City Rollers' original bassist?

Quiz 21

101. What was Mike Berry's comeback single that reached No.9 in 1980?
102. In 1972 who sang to "All The Young Dudes?"
103. Who had their debut album with "Piper At The Gates Of Dawn?"
104. Which composer wrote the score for Gentleman Prefer Blondes and Funny Girl?
105. What year was the U2 album "War" released?

Quiz 22

106.   Which instrument did Dave of The Dave Clark Five play?
107.   Which fiddle-playing singer is backed by his band Union Station?
108.   What was the stage name of Kajagoogoo's Chris Hamill?
109.   Where did Horst Jankowski take his piano for a walk in 1965?
110.   According to the lyrics of the B52's song "Love Shack" what was their Chrysler as big as?

Quiz 23

111.   What is the title song From Back To The Future?
112.   Who brought fame to a disco lady in 1976?
113.   Who "Let The Dogs Out?"
114.   Which song and artists sang this line: "only hope can keep me together, love can mend your life, but love can break your heart?"
115.   The presenters of Swap Shop released a single. What did they call their band?

Quiz 24

116.   What song was voted the most annoying song of the 2000s?
117.   Who recorded albums entitled Mystery, The Beat Goes On and Near The Beginning?
118.   Who recorded the 1994 song "If you go"?
119.   Whose 1979 debut album was called Inflammable Material?
120.   Which family heartthrob told us he was the author of The Record in 1975?

121. Who sang the opening song in The Italian Job?
122. This Australian composer's Incomplete 8th Symphony is world famous?
123. Which song features the line "One Dream One Soul, One Prize, One Goal?
124. Which British opera festival was started in 1934?
125. What was the signature tune of The Duke Ellington Band, written by Billy Strayhorn?

Quiz 26

126. Which declaration brought The Beastie Boys onto the charts in 1987?
127. Mary Hopkins won which TV talent show?
128. According to Billboard, which artist was the top-selling album artist in the 1970's?
129. Who Bought XFM In 1998?
130. What were Judas Priest's two no 12 records In 1980?

Quiz 27

131. Which band's abbreviated name was "Carter TUSM?"
132. Name Paul McCartney's first solo No.1 In 1984.
133. Who sang lead vocals for Lynyrd Skynyrd?
134. What is this Hawaiian small 4-string instrument?
135. What sporting star is mentioned in the Simon & Garfunkel song "Mrs. Robinson?"

Quiz 28

136. What was the thirteenth album released by Chicago?
137. Who was the lead singer & producer for Cameo?
138. What was Madonna's first UK number one single?
139. Who are the lead singers of the band "Full Metal Racquets?"
140. Length of shortest Beatles track?

Quiz 29

141. What leisure complex was founded in Nashville by country star Conway Twitty?

142. Which 1970s song does this line come from: "Well I know I've been out of style, for a short while, but I don't care how cold you are?"

143. Finish this James Brown title: "Say It Loud_____"

144. What is the significance of 6 July 1957 to the Beatles?

145. What's the smallest grand piano?

Quiz 30

146. Who sang the song "Danger Zone" from Top Gun?

147. What instrumental piece did Bruce Johnson take us down in 1977?

148. With which group do you associate David Ruffin & Eddie Kendricks?

149. Who organized the legendary 1972 Bickershaw Festival starring The Grateful Dead, Captain Beefheart, & Donovan?

150. From what do the Doobie Bros take their name?

Quiz 31

151. What was the name of ABC's first album?

152. What relation is Eagle Eye Cherry to Neneh Cherry?

153. What did the Beatles' "The Girl That's Driving Me Mad" have?

154. How in the world of music are Julia Volkova & Lena Katina generally known?

155. Who did Eric Clapton fall in love with despite her being married to one of The Beatles?

Quiz 32

156. Name the Christmas number one in 1995.
157. In "Oh What A Beautiful Morning" how high does the corn grow?
158. The B52's were formed in what US city?
159. Alex Turner is the lead singer with which band?
160. Tchaikovsky, Mendelssohn, and Chopin are associated with which music period?

Quiz 33

161. Which Police track got to no.2 on its re-entry in 1979?
162. Which 1960's group sang a song inspired by Alice in Wonderland?
163. Which hot dance classic did The Trammps bring us?
164. In a standard orchestra line-up which musicians sit immediately to the conductor's left?
165. Who is the author of High Fidelity, a tale set in an 80's record store?

Quiz 34

166. The Kane Gang split to become who?
167. What did Cher's baby do in 1966?
168. Who was the lead singer of the Plasmatics?
169. Which trumpeter born in 1961 enjoys equally successful Jazz & Classical Careers?
170. In which country was Olivia Newton John born?

Quiz 35

171. Which theme tune sang by Matt Monro & composed by John Barry, came to us with love?
172. Who was the lead singer with Cockney Rebel?
173. Which 1970 album cover featured a former Beatle and his newborn child?
174. Who did Paul McCartney write the song "Hey Jude" for?
175. Which British dance act was masterminded by Jazzy B & Nellee Hooper?

Quiz 36

176. What Christmas carol was originally banned by the Catholic church for being too sexual?
177. Which future pop star attended the scene of Eddie Cochran's fatal car crash in 1960 in his job as a police officer?
178. Longest chart life of any Beatles single?
179. Janis Joplin died in 1970, how did she die?
180. What did Brenda Lee want to jump over in 1961?

Quiz 37

181. What is the connection between Johnny Logan & Sean Sherrard?
182. John Waite was lead singer for what band?
183. How high was the first ever music chart in 1952, Top 10, Top 12, Top 20, Top 100?
184. Name the song performed both by Julie Covington in 1973 and by Madonna in 1996?
185. Whose 1993 debut single was "Bombtrack?"

Quiz 38

186. Name the bestselling Classical album of all time.
187. What was Nick Cave's band called before it was The Bad Seeds?
188. Who had the final UK number one of 2018 with "Sweet but Psycho?"
189. Name Pink Floyd's "Crazy Diamond?"
190. "Are You Gonna Go My Way" was asked by whom in 1993?

Quiz 39

191. Maracas are what?
192. What was the first No.1 for The Searchers?
193. Which is the most broadcast record ever and has held this record since 1977 and why?
194. How many Beatles biographies are registered at the Library of Congress
195. Which style of Jazz was pioneered by Charlie Parker & Dizzy Gillespie?

Quiz 40

196. Who were Mark Farner, Mel Schacher and Don Brewer?
197. Which of Madonna's albums featured a duet with Prince called "Love Song?"
198. Which 2 Singers married in 1969, divorced in 1975, & recorded one last album together in 1995?
199. What connects Bob Dylan, Absolutely Fabulous, and Julie Driscoll?
200. The label is Bludgen Riffola; name the band.

Quiz 41

201. In "Teenage Depression" who would join Eddie if he quit his town?
202. The musicals Brigadoon and My Fair Lady were penned by which duo?
203. Who were "Big in Japan?"
204. "Wild Thing" was sung by who In 1966?
205. What was the first name of the group Chicago?

206.   Who is the guitarist for the rock group Genesis?

207.   Who first played Evita on stage?

208.   Name the Andrew Lloyd Webber musical set during Belfast's Troubles in the early 1970's?

209.   Whose debut single was a cover of a Smokey Robinson tune and former No.1 for The Temptations?

210.   Who backed Bruce Hornsby?

Quiz 43

211.   Who named Sid Vicious?

212.   Who was Starry Eyed in 1960?

213.   Who currently holds the record of 134 weeks on the charts in one year?

214.   Who took a Eurovision song contest entry to No.2 in 1969 and what was it?

215.   How were Showaddywaddy discovered?

Quiz 44

216.   Who was the singer of "Jet Airliner?"

217.   In the title of a 1973 Gary Glitter single which word appeared three times?

218.   In 2006 who became the first British solo artist for eight years to top the US charts?

219.   According to the song by Katie Melua where are there 4 million bicycles?

220.   In which year did Gerry & The Pacemakers achieve three No.1's?

Quiz 45

221. What is the singer Bjork's nationality?
222. Which lyricist worked with Richard Rogers on such songs as "Blue Moon," "Where Or When," & "My Funny Valentine?"
223. Who became the first UK singer to win Eurovision?
224. Who sang about Rosie, Caroline & Desiree?
225. Name the first female DJ for Radio One.

Quiz 46

226. What was the name of Lobo's Dog after 1971?
227. The original members of Joy Division later formed which group?
228. Who came back to Hello, Dolly! for the 30th Anniversary Revival in 1994?
229. Who was lead vocalist for Dawn?
230. How old was Smokey Robinson when "Got a Job" was released?

Quiz 47

231. Who sang with The Dakotas?
232. What Spice Girl did Missy Elliot sing with on "I Want You Back?"
233. Who married Jamie Redknap In 1998?
234. Who gave us the story of the blues?
235. Who keeps a ten bob note up his nose?

Quiz 48

236. What links Ron Pigpen McKernan, Keith Godcheaux & Brent Myland?
237. What song has the line "I've been going out with a girl, her name is Julie?"
238. Who had a monkey gone to heaven in 1989?
239. Who had a No.1 hit in 1967 with "Let The Heartaches Begin?"
240. Whose 1996 debut album was entitled First Band On The Moon?

241. On Celine Dion's Let's Talk About Love album, name the only song that has a foreign title?
242. In "Is This The Way To Amarillo" who are the first 2 people to join Peter Kay on his journey?
243. What band used "The Firebird" by Stravinsky at the start of their concerts?
244. The first version of "Je T'aime"___. By Moi Non Plus was recorded as a duet between Serge Gainsbourg and who?
245. Name the Queen album featuring a silver cover with a picture of the band wearing leather jackets.

Quiz 50

246. What part of New York City was immortalized in Bob & Earl's dance song?
247. The duo Erasure consisted of Vince Clark and which other singer?
248. Which Irish Band is led by Dolores O'Riordan?
249. The Spice Girls Had 3 UK No.1's in 1996, 1997, 1998 with which songs?
250. "Fire" By The Prodigy was released by which record label?

Quiz 51

251. According to Frank Loesser in 1966, what was a secretary not?
252. Who sang "Puff The Magic Dragon?"
253. "Push Pineapple, Shake The Tree" is a line from which song?
254. Which pair had a leaky bucket in 1961?
255. To where did Steely Dan bid "Toodle-oo?"

256.   Who does Davey Jones claim to love in the 60s Monkees song "Here comes Tomorrow?"

257.   The rise of Cuban music in the late 90's was represented by which album?

258.   Which instrument did James Last start out with?

259.   Who was the lead Singer of "Destiny's Child?"

260.   In 1980, what did Air Supply run out of?

Quiz 53

261.   Which single hit No.2 on the UK charts in 1967 and ended a run of eleven consecutive number ones?

262.   Who Sang "I Wanna Sex You Up?"

263.   How many artists have covered "Yesterday?"

264.   What name was on the front of the first Motown office in Detroit?

265.   Which guitarist joined RCA in 1947 where he helped further the careers of Don Gibson and Elvis Presley?

Quiz 54

266.   In 1970, what type of band was Freda Payne linked with?

267.   Shorty Long had a brief solo career with a Tamia Motown Classic. Which one?

268.   "Peter George St John De Baptiste De La Salle" are middle names belonging to who?

269.   What sort of shack did the B52's like to stay at?

270.   Who recorded the original version of "Tainted Love?"

Quiz 55

271.   Name the gangs in West Side Story.

272.   When playing the bagpipes, what name is given to the "melody" pipe?

273.   By what name are Rod Stewart, Ron Wood, Ian McLagan, Ronnie Lane & Kenny Jones usually known?

274.   Who was the Osmonds's drummer?

275.   Who fronted Bronski Beat And The Communards?

Quiz 56

276.   To where was Tony Christie asking directions in 1971?

277.   Who had chart success With "Walking Back To Happiness" in 1961?

278.   By what name are "Hodges & Peacock" more commonly known?

279.   Name the songwriters who formed Philadelphia International Records.

280.   What beautiful capital by the sea is wonderful?

Quiz 57

281.   Who performed on both the original and the 20 year remake of Band Aid's "Do They Know It's Christmas?"

282.   Which 3 bands has Johnny Marr been associated with?

283.   What kind of girl took Jamiriquai to No.6 in 1996?

284.   What was the first single to be No 1 for 14 weeks?

285.   Which term defines unaccompanied singing?

Quiz 58

286.   "I Was Working As A Waitress In A Cocktail Bar" is a line from which famous song?

287.   Mick Jagger featured as a Ringmaster on which show?

288.   Who was calling Gloria in 1982?

289.   Which song starts with, "Heaven. I'm in Heaven?"

290.   Which of Beethoven's symphonies was the legendary "Incomplete?"

Quiz 59

291. Tannhauser & Tristan Und Isolde were written by whom?
292. Who wrote Bird On A Wire?
293. Which pop band "Beat The Clock" to number 10 in 1979?
294. Where did Murray Head spend a night?
295. In 2004 Johnny Cash's family tried to stop a song of his from being used in an advert for hemorrhoid cream. What was the song?

Quiz 60

296. Bananarama had what sort of summer in the 1980's?
297. Name Janet Jackson's older sister.
298. Name the club at Richmond's Station Hotel where the Rolling Stones came to the fore.
299. "I've got love in my tummy" follows which line?
300. "Kung Fu Fighting" made which band famous?

Quiz 61

301. Where was the birthplace of Benjamin Britten?
302. What links Chrissie Hynde, & Robert Palmer?
303. "Back In The Saddle Again" was whose theme song?
304. The albums "Kind Of Blue, In A Silent Way, and Bitches Bru & Tutu" were written by whom?
305. Name The Eagles' first No 1 single?

Quiz 62

306. Which children's author appears on the Beatles album Sgt. Pepper's Lonely Hearts Club Band's cover?
307. What is Bo Diddley's also called?
308. Who sang the theme song for "License To Kill?"
309. America's MTV used which song to launch their channel?
310. How long was Iain Macmillan given to shoot the cover of Abbey Road?

311.   Who made up The Million Dollar Quartet?

312.   In "The Ballad of John and Yoko", who helped John and Yoko marry?

313.   How much did ABC reportedly pay for the Beatles Anthology documentary?

314.   How many children did the Beatles collectively have?

315.   Who has "hair of floating sky?"

Quiz 64

316.   Name the ex-member of The Police who made a solo album called XYZ

317.   Name the beach far away in time.

318.   Mark McLoughlin changed his name to what?

319.   What is an English horn more properly called?

320.   Name the artist who picked up an academy Award for Best Film Song in 1971.

Quiz 65

321.   Sheet Music is an album by which artist?

322.   What links Mozart, Beethoven and Schubert with the city of Vienna?

323.   Who wrote Oh Lonesome Me, Sweet Dreams, & I Can't Stop Loving You?

324.   Name the instrument that produced the weird noises on The Beach Boys' "Good Vibrations?"

325.   Which trio won 5 Grammy Awards in 2007?

326. What was odd about the US Top 100 charts in June 1983?
327. Which record label released the first Beatles LP in the US?
328. "Stars in your eyes little one, where do you go to dream" is a line from which song?
329. Which 80s US metal band was fronted by the singer Sebastian Bach?
330. What is the theme song in Midnight Cowboy?

Quiz 67

331. Name the first Black Country singer successful in Nashville?
332. Name the title of Des O Connor's Only No.1 single.
333. An eight-foot bronze statue in Texas memorializes which rock singer?
334. The Stratocaster was made by which guitar manufacturer?
335. Name the Woodpeckers only album?

Quiz 68

336. What links "Windmills Of Your Mind," "Evergreen," and "Take My Breath Away."
337. What run did "Penny Lane" break for The Beatles & why?
338. Who were Bobby Hatfield & Bill Medley?
339. What do the initials of the TV channel TMF actually stand for?
340. Who is generally thought to have produced "Rocket 88" in 1950?

341.   Which opera overture is used as a background to post-Grand Prix champagne celebrations?

342.   What nationality was the singer Roy Orbison?

343.   What single gave The Human League a transatlantic number one?

344.   Which German composer's best known work is the opera Hansel and Gretel?

345.   What was the name of Elvis Presley's manager?

Quiz 70

346.   Which singer did The Family Stone back?

347.   Who did Spice Girl Mel B marry in 1998

Music TRIVIA Answers

Answers – Quiz 1

1. Break Dancing
2. God Bless America
3. The Walrus
4. The Rock & Roll Hall Of Fame
5. Babylon Zoo / Spaceman

Answers – Quiz 2

6. £75
7. The Allisons
8. Fats Waller
9. George Michael & Andrew Ridgely
10. Sonny Bono

Answers – Quiz 3

11. Sideshow
12. Hit Me With Your Rhythm Stick & Chicken Song
13. The French National Anthem/"La Marseillaise".
14. Riverside
15. Big Audio dynamite

Answers – Quiz 4

16. River Deep,Mountain High
17. Wilson Picket
18. Brian May
19. John Lydon
20. Jane Asher

Answers – Quiz 5

21.	Back Home
22.	Evans
23.	St Elmo's Fire
24.	Johnny Kidd And The Pirates
25.	2001 : A Space Odyessy

Answers – Quiz 6

26.	Eyes & Lips
27.	$15 million (terms of the settlement are confidential)
28.	Ian Kelsey
29.	A Pig
30.	I Don't Want to Face It

Answers – Quiz 7

31.	East West
32.	Alfred "Freddie" Lennon
33.	Hey Now (Girls Just Want To Have Fun)
34.	Own TV Program
35.	Wood & Sound

Answers – Quiz 8

36.	Carl Craig
37.	Pack up your Troubles in your Old Kit Bag
38.	Rick Martin
39.	Mr Tambourine Man
40.	Queen's Bohemian Rhapsody

Answers – Quiz 9

41. Return Of The Red Baron
42. Millenium
43. Moonlight Shadow
44. Gwen Stefani
45. Brotherhood Of Man, Edison Lighthouse, White Plains

Answers – Quiz 10

46. Over
47. Shattered Dreams
48. The Cookies
49. Chet Baker
50. James Fenton

Answers – Quiz 11

51. Jimmy Nicol
52. JLS
53. 5.9 percent
54. Ozzy Osbourne
55. Fellow Of The Royal Academy Of Music

Answers – Quiz 12

56. Don't Call Me Baby
57. Badly Drawn Boy
58. Bad Manners
59. Don't Bother Me
60. Robbie Gentry

Answers – Quiz 13

61. Brian Epstein
62. Eddie Fisher
63. Tympani
64. Beach Boys & Fat Boys (Wipeout)
65. William Orbit

Answers – Quiz 14

66. Baroque Period
67. Motown owned the name The Jackson 5, and they were moving to Epic Records.
68. Tijuana Brass
69. He was a pallbearer
70. Mike Love

Answers – Quiz 15

71. McGuiness Flint
72. 4 O'Clock
73. Frampton Comes Alive / Peter Frampton
74. Herb Albert
75. $600 million

Answers – Quiz 16

76. Rod Stewart / Maggie May
77. Washington D.C.
78. Strawberry Alarm Clock
79. The Sugacubes
80. Music On My Mind

Answers – Quiz 17

81. Steve Strange
82. Manager of the Spice Girls
83. You could be Mine
84. Steel Pulse
85. The Pet Shop Boys

Answers – Quiz 18

86. Manfred Mann
87. Howard Jones
88. Tony Parsons & Julie Burchill
89. Bobby Rydell
90. A Cowboy

Answers – Quiz 19

91. Julian Cope
92. Stevie Wonder & Michael Jackson
93. Michael Jackson's Thriller
94. Hey Jude/Revolution
95. Dixie Chicks

Answers – Quiz 20

96. The Deputy
97. Strangers In The Knight / Something Stupid
98. Some Type Of Flight Suits
99. Bottle
100. Alan Longmuir

Answers – Quiz 21

101.	The Sunshine Of Your Smile
102.	Mott The Hoople
103.	Pink Floyd
104.	Jule Styne, last of the Broadway Giants
105.	1983

Answers – Quiz 22

106.	The Drums
107.	Alison Krauss
108.	Limahl
109.	For A Walk In the Black Forest
110.	A Whale

Answers – Quiz 23

111.	The Power Of Love
112.	Johnnie Taylor
113.	The Baha Men
114.	Police / Message In A Bottle
115.	Brown Sauce

Answers – Quiz 24

116.	James Blunt / You're Beautiful
117.	Vanilla Fudge
118.	John Secada
119.	Stiff Little Fingers
120.	David Cassidy / I Write The Songs

Answers – Quiz 25

121.   Matt Monroe
122.   Franz Schubert's
123.   A Kind Of Magic (Queen)
124.   Glyndebourne
125.   Take The "A" Train

Answers – Quiz 26

126.   You Gotta Fight For Your Right To Party
127.   Opportunity Knocks
128.   Elton John.
129.   Capital Radio
130.   Living After Midnight / Breakin' The Law

Answers – Quiz 27

131.   Carter The Unstoppable Sex Machine
132.   Pipes Of Peace
133.   Ronnie Van Zandt
134.   The Ukulele
135.   Joe Dimaggio

Answers – Quiz 28

136.   Chicago XIII
137.   Larry Blackmon
138.   Get Into The Groove
139.   John Mcenroe and Pat Cash
140.   23 Secs / Her Majesty / from Abbey Road

Answers – Quiz 29

141.	Twitty City
142.	David Essex / Gonna Make You A Star
143.	I'm Black & I'm Proud
144.	The day John Lennon met Paul McCartney
145.	A Baby Grand

Answers – Quiz 30

146.	Kenny Loggins
147.	Pipeline
148.	The Temptations
149.	Jeremy Beadle
150.	A marijuana joint, also known as a Doobie

Answers – Quiz 31

151.	The Lexicon Of Love
152.	Half brother
153.	A Ticket To Ride
154.	Tatu
155.	Patti Boyd Harrison

Answers – Quiz 32

156.	Michael Jackson / Earth Song
157.	As high as an elephant's eye
158.	Athens, Ga
159.	Arctic Monkeys
160.	Romantic period

Answers – Quiz 33

161. Can't Stand Losing You
162. Jefferson Airplane
163. Disco Inferno
164. First Violin
165. Nick Hornby

Answers – Quiz 34

166. Hue & Cry
167. He Shot Her Down
168. Wendy O Williams
169. Wynton Marsalis
170. Cambridge, England (Went to Oz when she was 5)

Answers – Quiz 35

171. From Russia With Love
172. Steve Harley
173. McCartney / By Paul McCartney
174. Julian Lennon
175. Soul II Soul

Answers – Quiz 36

176. I saw Mommy kissing Santa Claus
177. Dave Dee
178. 19 Weeks / Hey Jude
179. From a heroin overdose
180. The Broomstick

181.   They are the same person
182.   Bad English
183.   Top 12
184.   Don't Cry For Me, Argentina
185.   Rage Against The Machine

Answers – Quiz 38

186.   Currently that's the first Three Tenors album
187.   The Birthday Party
188.   Ava Max
189.   Syd Barrett
190.   Lenny Kravitz

Answers – Quiz 39

191.   Shaken Latin percussion instruments made from gourds with dried beans or peas inside
192.   Sweets For My Sweet
193.   The Carpenters / Calling Occupants, because it's broadcast by N.A.S.A every 3 minutes
194.   177= Beatles, John=69, Paul=23, George=6, Ringo=2
195.   Bebop

Answers – Quiz 40

196.   Grand Funk Railroad
197.   Like A Prayer
198.   George Jones & Tammy Wynette
199.   This Wheel's On Fire
200.   Def Leppard

Answers – Quiz 41

201.   The Hotrods
202.   Alan Lerner and Fredric Loewe
203.   Alphaville
204.   The Troggs
205.   Chicago Transit Authority

Answers – Quiz 42

206.   Mike Rutherford
207.   Elaine Paige
208.   The Beautiful Game
209.   Otis Redding / My Girl
210.   The Range.

Answers – Quiz 43

211.   Johnny Rotten
212.   Michael Holiday
213.   Oasis / 1996
214.   Lulu / Boom Bang A Bang
215.   On the TV show New Faces

Answers – Quiz 44

216.   Steve Miller Band
217.   Love (I Love, You Love, Me Love)
218.   James Blunt
219.   Bejing
220.   1963

Answers – Quiz 45

221. Icelandic
222. Lorenz Hart
223. Sandie Shaw
224. Neil Diamond (Cracklin' Rosie, Sweet Caroline, Desiree)
225. Anne Nightingale

Answers – Quiz 46

226. Boo (Me & you and a dog named Boo)
227. Joy Division
228. Carol Channing
229. Tony Orlando
230. It was released on his 18th birthday

Answers – Quiz 47

231. Billy J. Kramer
232. Mel B / Scary Spice
233. Louise Nerding
234. The Mighty Wah
235. Mean Mr. Mustard

Answers – Quiz 48

236. All keyboardists who died while with The Grateful Dead
237. Jilted John
238. Pixies
239. Long John Baldry
240. The Cardigans

241.   Amar Haciendo El Amor.
242.   Ken & Deirdre (Barlow)
243.   Yes
244.   Brigette Bardot
245.   The Game

Answers – Quiz 50

246.   Harlem (Harlem Shuffle)
247.   Andy Bell
248.   The Cranberries
249.   2 Become 1, Too Much, Goodbye
250.   XL Recordings

Answers – Quiz 51

251.   "A Toy" How To Succeed In Business
252.   Peter, Paul and Mary
253.   Agadoo
254.   Harry Belafonte & Odetta
255.   East St Louis

Answers – Quiz 52

256.   Sandra and Mary
257.   Buena Vista Social Club
258.   Double Bass
259.   Beyonce Knowles
260.   Love (All Out Of Love)

Answers – Quiz 53

261. Penny Lane/Strawberry Fields Forever
262. Color Me Bad
263. 2961
264. Hitsville USA
265. Chet Atkins

Answers – Quiz 54

266. A Band Of Gold
267. Here Comes The Judge
268. Brian Eno
269. A Love Shack
270. Gloria Jones

Answers – Quiz 55

271. Jets & Sharks
272. The CHANTER
273. The Faces
274. Jay Osmond
275. Jimmy Sommerville

Answers – Quiz 56

276. Amarillo (Is this the way to Amarillo?)
277. Helen Shapiro
278. Chas And Dave
279. Gamble & Huff
280. Wonderful Wonderful Copenhagen

Answers – Quiz 57

281.   Bono / U2
282.   The Smiths, The The, Electronic
283.   Cosmic Girl
284.   I Will Always Love you.
285.   A Cappella

Answers – Quiz 58

286.   Don't You Want Me Baby
287.   Rock N Roll Circus
288.   Laura Branigan
289.   Cheek To Cheek
290.   The 10th Symphony

Answers – Quiz 59

291.   Wagner
292.   Leonard Cohen.
293.   Sparks
294.   In Bangkok
295.   The Ring Of Fire

Answers – Quiz 60

296.   Cruel
297.   LaToya
298.   The Crawdaddy
299.   Yummy yummy yummy.
300.   Carl Douglas

Answers – Quiz 61

301.   Lowestoft
302.   UB 40
303.   Gene Autry's
304.   Miles Davis
305.   Best Of My Love.

Answers – Quiz 62

306.   Lewis Carol
307.   Elias Bates (Elias McDaniel)
308.   Gladys Knight
309.   Video Killed The Radio Star
310.   10 Mins

Answers – Quiz 63

311.   Elvis Presley, Jerry Lee Lewis, Carl Perkins & Johnny Cash
312.   Peter Brown
313. $20 million
314.   16
315.   Julia

Answers – Quiz 64

316.   Andy Summers
317.   Echo Beach
318.   Marti Pellow
319.   Cor Anglais
320.   Isaac Hayes (Shaft Theme)

Answers – Quiz 65

321. 10cc
322. They all died there
323. Don Gibson
324. Theremin
325. The Dixie Chicks

Answers – Quiz 66

326. It contained more records by foreigners than Americans for the first time
327. VeeJay Records
328. Land Of Make Believe
329. Skid Row
330. Everybody's Talking

Answers – Quiz 67

331. Charley Pride
332. I Pretend
333. Buddy Holly
334. Fender
335. Emmerdance

Answers – Quiz 68

336. Oscar winning songs
337. A string of 7 No.1's preceded it - (2)
338. The Righteous Brothers
339. The Music Factory
340. The Kings Of Rhythm

Answers – Quiz 69

341.	Bizet's Carmen
342.	USA / Texas
343.	Don't You Want Me Baby?
344.	Engelbert Humperdinck's
345.	Colonel Tom Parker

Answers – Quiz 70

346.	Sly
347.	Jimmy Gulzar

Sports & Leisure TRIVIA

DID YOU KNOW?

TOP EXPORT FROM THE USA IS CARS.
TOP IMPORT TO THE USA IS ALSO CARS.

Quiz 1

1. An archery target has which five colors?
2. Name the first bowler to take more than 300 wickets in test cricket?
3. In 1992, who did David Gower succeed as England's most prolific run scorer?
4. In boxing, who was 'The Clones Cyclone"?
5. The Solheim Cup is the equivalent to which famous sporting cup?

Quiz 2

6. Which Everton fan won the world title in 1991?
7. How many players does a volleyball team have?
8. What is an oxer?
9. Ian Rush said "If I don't drink my milk, I'll only be good enough to play for which football team?"
10. Who did Sue Barker succeed as host of A Question Of Sport?

Quiz 3

11. Who were the two host countries of Euro 2008?
12. How many cards should you be dealt in Gin Rummy?
13. Bjorn Borg won how many consecutive Wimbledon titles?
14. In a game of polo, what is the period of play called?
15. What Chicago Bears running back was known as "The Galloping Ghost?"

Quiz 4

16. Where does The Irish Grand National take place?
17. Who beat Mike Tyson in 1990 to become the World Heavy Weight Boxing Champion?
18. Name the Austrian who won four World Downhill Championships in the 70's?
19. You could Peg Out in which game?
20. In which game might you get a cannon?

Quiz 5

21. Which country held the 1992 Olympics?
22. Who first won the US Masters five times?
23. Whose record did Brian Lara beat when he scored 400 not out in April 2004?
24. Name the Surrey town home to The British National Shooting Centre.
25. Which 2004 darts champion is known as "The Viking" because of his appearance?

Quiz 6

26. Which football club did Paul Gascoigne turn out for?
27. Name the scorer of England's final winning goal against Belgium in the 1990 Football World Cup?
28. Who won the BBC's 1984 Sports Personality of the Year?
29. What is the "perfect score" in a game of Ten Pin Bowling?
30. Which football manager was reprimanded in 2006 after criticizing female officials?

Quiz 7

31. Name three tennis players born in Germany between 1950 And 2000 that won the Wimbledon Men's Singles title?
32. Where do competitors travel down The Brabham Strait?
33. Where did the game of Polo originate?
34. Is an ice hockey puck or a baseball heavier?
35. Who preceded Tiger Woods as the number one ranked golfer in 1998?

Quiz 8

36. "Behind & Banana Kick?" are terms in which sport?
37. What major sporting milestone took place on 6th May 1954?
38. In the schoolboys card game what cancels out a Black Jack?
39. Lepidoptery is better known as what?
40. Name the first black footballer to captain England?

Quiz 9

41. Jaques Villeneuve succeeded who as a driver for Williams?
42. What object is 11-12" long and must weigh at least 50 grams?
43. What links Ray Reardon, Geoff Capes and Christopher Dean?
44. In 1985, Kevin Moran became the first player to do what in an FA Cup final?
45. What is (K) worth in Scrabble

Quiz 10

46. Name the squash shot where the ball hits the side of the wall first
47. You would "Catch a Crab" in which sport?
48. What's the main feature of a speedway motorbike?
49. Which winter sport was introduced as an official event at the 1998 games?
50. Which 2 football players scored For England in the 1986 World Cup Finals? (PFE)

Quiz 11

51. Which American football team won the 2006 Super Bowl?
52. What annual race happens between Putney and Mortlake?
53. The winner of a Formula One Grand Prix is awarded how many points?
54. What is the name for the white outfits used in Karate and Judo?
55. In which sport is Valentino Rossi a leading competitor?

Quiz 12

56. Which swimming stroke is not started by a dive?
57. Betting a Lady Godiva means your stake will be what?
58. "Clickety Click" refers to which number in Bingo
59. "Outcrop," "Big Wall" and "Crag" are all types of what?
60. Which footballer scored six of England's seven goals at the 1986 World Cup Finals?

Quiz 13

61. What was Commonwealth Gold Medalist Judy Simpson's Gladiator name?
62. Which Scottish athlete won Gold for the 100m in the 1980 Moscow Olympics?
63. Which football club's badge is a golden lion on a claret and blue background?
64. What in sport is 7 feet 9 quarter inches (2.375 meters) in length?
65. In ice hockey, how many players in a team?

Quiz 14

66. Who first defeated Frank Bruno in a professional fight?
67. Name the first NHL player to score 50 goals in one season?
68. Who did Stephen Hendry succeed as World No1 in the 1989-90 Snooker season?
69. In backgammon, how many pieces per player are there?
70. British Sport that uses a leather ball hit by a gloved hand?

Quiz 15

71. What testing was first carried out at the1968 Olympics?
72. In what sport do you find a piece of wooden apparatus exactly 17ft long?
73. Who would use a penholder grip?
74. Name football's international governing board.
75. Which tennis player cried on The Duchess of Kent's shoulder during Wimbledon when she lost the final to Steffi Graf?

Quiz 16

76. Name the West Indian Fast Bowler who died in 1999 at the age of 41.
77. Where is the Derby run each year?
78. Who was the first non-British manager to win the English FA Cup?
79. Ibrox Stadium is home ground to which football team?
80. What is 62 feet and 10 inches long and 42 inches wide?

Quiz 17

81. What football player rushed for 2,003 yards in 1973?
82. What martial art debuted at the 2000 Olympic Games?
83. Which course is The Scottish Grand National Run on?
84. How many people are on a Tug-of-War team?
85. 3 balls used in a game of Billiards?

Quiz 18

86. Which class is the lowest weight in professional boxing?
87. Name the England Rugby Union international fined 15,000 pounds for dragging the game into disrepute?
88. What does the ringing of a bell mean in athletic track races?
89. Which sportswear company uses three stripes to signify their brand?
90. According to a 2000 survey, who were the greatest male & female tennis players of all time?

Quiz 19

91. A Rugby League team has how many players?
92. Which Steeplechase did party politics win in 1992?
93. What is the Scottish Football Club named after an Irish Monk called?
94. What is referred to by a "Mashie?"
95. Who won the 2007 title for Men's & Woman's Wimbledon Singles?

Quiz 20

96. How many people are in each crew for The Oxford & Cambridge Boat Race?
97. Name the Yorkshire football team who plays home at Oakwell?
98. Name the Grand Prix Racing Team based in Woking, Surrey.
99. A "biased" is what piece of sporting equipment?
100. What name is given to an American football field?

Quiz 21

101.   Where were the 1964 Summer Olympics held?

102.   What is the official circumference of an Australian football?

103.   Name the cricketer who scored a record 11,174 test runs for Australia.

104.   What is a "Ringer" in horse racing?

105.   This swimmer won 7 gold Medals at the 1972 Olympics.

Quiz 22

106.   Polo consists of 8 periods. What are these periods called?

107.   To what sport do the following terms belong to - "Tight End & Wide Receiver?"

108.   Where were the 1912 Summer Olympics held?

109.   A Steeple Chase Run is run over what distance?

110.   Who beat Arsenal in 2012 to become the UEFA Champions League Winner?

Quiz 23

111.   Where were the 1968 Summer Olympics held?

112.   Where might you find a Chicane?

113.   Who beat Muhammad Ali in 1978 and took his World Heavyweight Title?

114.   How many clubs are allowed in a golf bag?

115.   In darts, from which number under 100, is it impossible to finish with 2 darts?

Quiz 24

116.   Torvill & Dean are famous for which sport?

117.   At which sporting venue would you find Melling Road?

118.   What football team has their home games at Stamford Bridge?

119.   What does the Cricket Umpire signal when they raise both arms aloft?

120.   A game of Field Hockey lasts how long?

Quiz 25

121. Which Jumping event did Carl Lewis often compete in as well as the Sprint?
122. What is the diameter of the circle from which you throw a discus?
123. Who scored the 10,000th goal in the 2001 English Premier league for Tottenham against Fulham?
124. What is completion of a circuit of bases on one hit called in Baseball?
125. In what sport is the Heisman trophy awarded?

Quiz 26

126. How many meters long is an Olympic-sized swimming pool?
127. What is thrown the shortest distance in field athletics?
128. What is Q worth in Scrabble?
129. What is the first event in a decathlon?
130. Who hosted the 2004 Summer Olympic Games?

Quiz 27

131. In boxing what is an illegal punch to the back of the head known as?
132. Pablo Montoya drives for which formula one team?
133. Where is Gabriela Sabatini from?
134. In which sport might you see a double axel?
135. What is Linford Christie's best time for the 100 meters?

Quiz 28

136. For what reason Did Henry Viii Ban the game of Bowls?
137. In 1968 who Made '"The Jump Into The 21st Century?"
138. The motto "Superbia In Proelio" is used by which football club?
139. Which country hosted the 1952 Summer Olympics?
140. What is the controlling body in Flat Racing?

141. Name the first woman to compete in the World Snooker Champion?
142. In boxing, who beat Ken Norton after Muhammad Ali retired in 1979?
143. Name the 3 Athletics events women do not participate in?
144. What was the name of the former sports person who became MP for Falmouth & Cambourne in 1992?
145. A golf ball has how many dimples?

Quiz 30

146. What is the bull's eye worth in outdoor archery?
147. What fruit is depicted on top of the Wimbledon Men's Singles Trophy?
148. In what year did London host the Olympic Games?
149. What goes to the F.A. cup final every year but never has and never will be used?
150. Who won three ladies singles titles at Wimbledon in the 1950's?

Quiz 31

151. Which football team has the shortest name in the English League?
152. Who was Alex Ferguson's team before he became manager of Manchester United?
153. This shooting season starts on "The Glorious Twelfth."
154. What's the highest possible score in darts
155. Rifle shooting & Cross Country Skiing are combined in which sport?

Quiz 32

156. The white marks intersecting each five yard line in American football are called _____.
157. Who was football manager at Southampton, the Rangers and Liverpool in the 1980's & 1990's?
158. What was Australian John Landy the second person to achieve?
159. Which brothers represented England in the 1995 Rugby Union World Cup?
160. Which country does Chelsea Striker Didier Drogba represent at the international level?

Quiz 33

161. This Chess piece always stays on the same color square?
162. Name Martina Navratilova's regular ladies doubles partner in the 1980's?
163. Why some English Football Clubs have triangular corner flags rather than square?
164. Name the Golf stroke 2 under par for the hole.
165. Which 3 teams were knocked out on penalties in the 1998 World Cup final?

Quiz 34

166. What country first won The World Cup & who was the first to host it?
167. Linford Christie was disqualified from the 1996 Atlanta Olympics for what reason?
168. How many players on a baseball team?
169. What do the letters G.A. stand for on netball bibs?
170. Name the Boston-based National Hockey League team in the US?

Quiz 35

171.   What age are the horses in the Epsom Derby?
172.   Who is presently (2020) the President of the Football
        Association?
173.   Which US horse race is run at Churchill Downs?
174.   What would you see someone perform a "Cocked Hat
        Double" in?
175.   How many times did Nick Faldo win The Masters Golf
        Tournament?

Quiz 36

176.   Which club did Jose Mourinho leave in order to become
        manager of Chelsea in 2004?
177.   Hockey team: The Chicago _____.
178.   Who was the first black captain of Great Britain's men's team?
179.   What was Evonne Goolagong's name after marriage?
180.   Which British football club was Christian Gross the manager
        for?

Quiz 37

181.   What did the Inter Cities Fairs Cup change its name to?
182.   What does the term "Kung Fu" mean?
183.   Which football team has played at Wembley more times than
        anyone else?
184.   What was the biggest margin of victory ever in a Triple Crown
        Race?
185.   What is the downwind sail on a yacht called?

186. Which famous athletics world record stood between 1968 & 1991?
187. Which English football team is nicknamed the Tractor Boys?
188. In tennis what have you achieved when you score a point directly from a serve?
189. What is the weight of a cricket ball in ounces?
190. Michael "Eddie the Eagle" Edwards had to have two inches taken off his what when he represented England at the 1988 Winter Olympics?

Quiz 39

191. Kevin Keagan left Liverpool to move to which club?
192. Who is the new team captain on the TV show A Question of Sport?
193. Which British man ran the fastest mile in the 80's?
194. Who did Lennox Lewis beat to win his first world heavyweight title?

Quiz 40

195. Which two London clubs did Bobby Moore play for?
196. How many minutes is each period of hockey?
197. What number is by the side of the number 16 on a dart board (either side)?
198. Who was the Dutchman who became Embassy World Darts Champion In 1998?
199. What country won the first World Cup?
200. Name the hockey trophy awarded to the player demonstrating the best sportsmanship.

Quiz 41

201. First Asian Snooker player to be ranked in The World's Top 10?
202. Mike Tyson was fined $3 million by the boxing association in 1997 for what reason?
203. Which woman swimmer won an individual silver medal for Great Britain in the 1980 Moscow Olympics?
204. What are the only two fences not jumped twice in the Aintree Grand National?
205. What vehicles are involved in the "Tour de France?"

Quiz 42

206. Name 2 British golfers who won the US Masters in the 1990's?
207. In cricket, if an umpire raises their arms above their head how many runs are being signaled?
208. What is Chicago's American Football Team called?
209. How many balls are there in the beginning of a game of Snooker?
210. What award is given to a British Boxing Champion?

Quiz 43

211. Who won the US Super Bowl in 2007?
212. In football, which team is nicknamed the Swans?
213. Who holds the record for the most Grand Prix Wins?
214. Who was the first person to defeat Amir Khan's in 2008?
215. What was Pluto Platter the original name for?

Quiz 44

216. In sport, what has the max dimensions of 60 by 30 meters?
217. Which two sports comprise a Biathlon?
218. In fencing, besides an Epee & Foil what other weapon is used?
219. Who was disqualified for failing a drug test at the 1988 Olympic Games?
220. Who was the heaviest player in England's 2002 World Cup Squad?

221. This 3-letter word refers to a replayed point in tennis?
222. Which sport includes the Halfpipe, the Slopestyle and the Bordercross?
223. Barry McGuigan became a World Champion in which weight category?
224. The 1896 Olympics were held were?
225. This racer was the first American to win the Formula 1 championship.

Quiz 46

226. Where were the 1980 Summer Olympics held?
227. Bridgestone and _____ are the manufacturers for the F1.
228. Name the player Boris Becker beat for his first Wimbledon title.
229. What yachting race was called the Hundred-Guinea Cup until 1851?
230. Ali McCoist first played for which league club?

Quiz 47

231. Who was the second person to score 200 Premiership goals?
232. What is Italy's Formula 1 race course called?
233. Lincoln, East End, Manchester & London are all types of what?
234. In Baseball, where are the Braves from
235. Which annual sporting event occurs between Putney and Mortlake?

Quiz 48

236. Which NHL player was the first to score 50 goals in one season?
237. What sport might you need to perform an Eskimo Roll for?
238. In Three-Day Eventing, what is the first event?
239. Football: The Chicago _____?
240. How many miles are there in a marathon?

241. Name 2 non-American cities that have hosted the modern Summer Olympics.
242. Other than green, what are the colors for the All England Lawn Tennis Club?
243. In what decade was Cricket's first World Cup Final played?
244. In baseball, what is the score of a forfeited game?
245. What team is the most frequent winner of The County Cricket Championships?

Quiz 50

246. Who won the 2008 Lakeside World Darts Championships?
247. In Darts how much would you have scored if you got a "Tic Tac Toe?"
248. Where were the 1928 Olympics held?
249. In Wimbledon, who lost the singles finals to Boris Becker and Pat Cash?
250. Why was The Cheltenham Festival cancelled in 2001?

Quiz 51

251. Why was Number Six Valverde famous in 2006?
252. Which player missed the penalty shot that put England out of the European Championships in 1996?
253. What did Jockey Lester Piggot serve 3 years in prison for?
254. What piece of clothing was banned from Ascot in 1971?
255. What is Sonic in the video game?

256.   Who's the current female world darts champion?
257.   Which 200+ Laps race begins with the words, "Ladies And Gentlemen, Start Your Engines?"
258.   England played football at the weekend but only managed a 0-0, draw against which team?
259.   Which cricketer made the most test match appearances for England?
260.   Name a country in which Badminton is the national sport?

Quiz 53

261.   In Women's Gymnastics, how wide is the beam?
262.   In Rugby, what animal is on the top of the Calcutta Cup?
263.   Where produces the most successful Rally drivers?
264.   In 1994 which West Indian Batsman scored 501 not out in one inning?
265.   Who has won the most gold's in any one Olympics?

Quiz 54

266.   What sport did Conrad Bartelski compete in for Britain?
267.   "Toucher & Dead Length" are terms in which sport?
268.   During strenuous exercise which acid is produced in the muscles?
269.   In Rugby, which league club has won The Challenge Cup the most times?
270.   Which popular sport team started in 1926 as The Savoy Big Five?

271.   In a Hockey Bully Off how many times do sticks need to touch?
272.   Name the players who beat Steve Davis in the 1983 &
        1989 world championship?
273.   What are sheets in regards to a yacht?
274.   In a 1990 test match against India how many runs did Graham
        Gooch score in a treble Nelson?
275.   England and Scotland compete for which Rugby Union Trophy?

Quiz 56

276.   Which Dart's commentator is known for his hyperbole?
277.   Which Football Team is the most frequent winner of The
        European Cup?
278.   Runners pass this famous ship after completing 10km of The
        London Marathon?
279.   Where were the 1964 Summer Olympics held?
280.   Where were the 1972 Summer Olympics held?

Quiz 57

281.   Which team knocked out Liverpool in the 1955-56 FA Cup.
282.   What score follows "Deuce" in tennis?
283.   How many years did it take to build the new Wembley
        Stadium?
284.   Who became the first black manager of a premiership club
        when he took over in 1996?
285.   What 6 weapons are used in a game of Clue?

Quiz 58

286.   Which boxer was the first to be knighted?
287.   The only position in soccer allowed to handle the ball?
288.   Who did Alex Ferguson succeed as manager of Manchester
        United
289.   Which sport has the highest amount of umpires per player?
290.   By what name is the boxer Packy East better known?

291. Who came after Roger Maris for the homerun record in 1961?
292. How many dots are on a standard set of dominoes?
293. Steve Davis reached every final of the Snooker World Championship between 1983 and 1989, but who were the two players who beat him?
294. In 2003, who was declared the BBC's Golden Sports Personality for the last 50 Years?
295. What is the name of Manchester City football club's old home ground?

Quiz 60

296. Name the 4 cities beginning with the letter A that have hosted the Summer Olympics?
297. Who won the 2007 Masters Snooker Final?
298. In hurling, how many points does a player win for a goal?
299. Dick Beardsley won which famous sporting event
300. How many minutes does a Professional World Cup Rugby game last?

Quiz 61

301. Who joined Steve Redgrave in the last three of his Olympic Gold Medals, and later won a fourth Gold himself in 2004?
302. What nationality is the former Snooker World Champion Cliff Thorburn?
303. Name the 2 Major League Baseball Teams in New York.
304. Which player was stabbed on court at Wimbledon by a fan of her chief rival?
305. Which race gained its name from a short dash between 2 churches?

306. In 1988, who came last in the Olympic Ski Jump Finals?
307. Who was Andre Agassi married to from 1997 to 1999?
308. Who was the Premierships highest goal scorer at the start of The 2002/03 season?
309. Who played Muhammad Ali in "The Greatest?"
310. Name the 2 England Football Team players who missed penalties against Portugal in Euro 2004?

Quiz 63

311. Name the highest possible Out Shot in Darts.
312. Where might you score a hit?
313. The Waterloo Cup occurs in which sport?
314. What sport was invented by a group of drinkers at a pub in West Sussex in 1973?
315. Where will you find the terms "Bump, Set, Spike & Pancake?"

Quiz 64

316. The sign language used by bookies is known as what?
317. How many suits are in Mah Jongg?
318. Baseball team: The Houston _____?
319. What is Snooker player Peter Ebdon's strong physical disadvantage?
320. Who hosted The 2004 Summer Olympics?

Quiz 65

321. Which horse won The Grand National in 1992?
322. In which century was The Oxford and Cambridge Boat Race first contested?
323. Name the only 3 countries to have taken part in all of the Summer & Winter Olympic Games.
324. Name The War Dance the All Blacks perform prior to A Match.
325. What is a Japanese sumo wrestling tournament called?

Quiz 66

326. Trundle Hill overlooks which English Race Course?
327. A Pommel Horse is a term in which sport?
328. Who was winner of the F.A. Cup the most times during the 70's?
329. Who won his only Snooker World Championship in 1979?
330. Name the object ball in bowls.

Quiz 67

331. Dart players must stand behind what mark?
332. What is a GS in netball
333. What is played over 4 sets of 15 minutes where only two of seven players can score?
334. Where might you use A Fosbury Flop?
335. This Moroccan Athlete was the first man to run 5000 m in under 13 minutes.

Quiz 68

336. In the 70s and 80s, name 2 Steve's who were record breaking middle distance runners.
337. What animal is on a Ferrari Badge?
338. In which card game might you be dealt a "Yardborough?"
339. What famous race began in 1903?
340. What is the final event in a decathlon?

Quiz 69

341. What is the fastest swimming stroke?
342. Which Premiership Club plays their home games at the JJB Stadium?
343. Which sport takes place in a circle 4.55m in diameter?
344. In 1980 an official was knocked unconscious whilst measuring in the WHHC. What does the acronym WHHC stand for?
345. Who rode Shergar to victory in The Epsom Derby?

Quiz 70

346.   Who was the first football player to score a Hat-Trick in the World Cup finals?

347.   Which Middleweight Boxer is the subject of the film Raging Bull?

348.   In 2005 who was named BBC Sport Personality of the year?

349.   What distance is covered in one circuit of a modern outdoor running track? (In meters)

350.   In 2002, what female host won BBCs Sport Personality of the Year?

Quiz 71

351.   Shirley Crabtree was better known as which larger-than-life character?

352.   Who did Gazza flick the ball over for the Euro 96 goal against Scotland?

353.   Which team defeated the World Champions Argentina in the opening game of 1990 Football World Cup?

354.   Which player won her last tennis Grand Slam Tournament in Paris in 1999?

355.   What was unusual about Ted Schraeder's appearance at Wimbledon in the 1949 tournament?

Quiz 72

356.   What is the technique called by which you right a capsized canoe?

357.   Until 2001, Southampton played at The Dell but have now moved to where?

358.   In Olympic Weight Lifting what are the two methods of lifting?

359.   What do runners pass to each other in a relay race?

360.   Is The Oaks Race a race for colts or fillies?

Quiz 73

361. Canadian football's most coveted trophy.
362. Surname shared by Three Formula One Champions?
363. Which bridge is past first in The University Boat Race?
364. How many stitches does a regulation baseball have?
365. This football team was known as the "Orange Crush."

Quiz 74

366. Hockey team: The Boston _____.
367. Place where Ice Hockey players are sent for breaking rules.
368. Bisley in Surrey is home to which sport?
369. This Scottish Golfer was Captain for Europe's 2002 Ryder Cup Team.
370. Who was the second club to win the English Premier League?

Quiz 75

371. How high is an Olympic Diving Board?
372. What are the sticks in golf called?
373. Who were the first two team Captains for A Question of Sport?
374. This sport has 4 letters and begins with A "T?"
375. Where were the 1936 Summer Olympics held?

Quiz 76

376. This sport event combines Riding, Shooting, Fencing, and Swimming & Running?
377. Name the Blackpool Football Club's home ground?
378. How many clubs were there in the 1997-8 Premier League?
379. The 3 female characters in the game Clue were called what?
380. Alex "Hurricane" Higgins & Jimmy "The Whirlwind" White but what's Ronnie O' Sullivan's nickname?

381.   Monza & Silverstone are venues for which sport?
382.   Until 2008 there were 6 Players to achieve A 147 Break at the Crucible; Ronnie O Sullivan & Ali Carter Both did it. Can you name the other four (PFE)?
383.   Who was the first darts player to receive an MBE in 1989?
384.   Which Billionaire owns Formula One
385.   Which English Football team has the longest one word name?

Quiz 78

386.   What type of bowler might use a Chinaman?
387.   Catherine McTavish made Wimbledon history in 1979. How?
388.   Who won Wimbledon twice with an 8-year gap in between?
389.   The Eskimo Roll can be used in which sport??
390.   When was Shergar kidnapped?

Quiz 79

391.   Ascot was built in which year?
392.   Who was thrown out of 1995 Wimbledon games after he hit a Ball Girl with a ball?
393.   What is the score of a forfeited softball game?
394.   How many points would be scored by "Potting The Black" in a Perfect 147 Snooker Break?
395.   James Naismith is best known for what?

Quiz 80

396.   In what sport does the ball have a diameter of at least 42.67 millimeters and weigh no less than 45.93 grams?
397.   You would tug on your ear during which game?
398.   Who did Mike Tyson beat for his first Heavy Weight Title?
399.   At which sport might you see a crucifix?
400.   Name one of the three years in which The Olympics were cancelled?

Quiz 81

401. Location of the 1988 Olympics?
402. Over which distance did Steve Ovett win Olympic Gold?
403. This baseball team won 37 World Series in the 20th Century?
404. How much did Newcastle pay to get Alan Shearer?
405. Number of dominoes in a full set?

Quiz 82

406. Which sporting event of 1985 attracted 18.6 million early morning viewers?
407. Who won a boxing gold medal in the super heavyweight division at Sydney in 2000?
408. Name the first woman to run a mile in less than 5 minutes?
409. Which title has been won by the rider who wears the polka dot jersey in the Tour De France?
410. What was Matthew Simmons in the news for in 1995?

Quiz 83

411. This former World Boxing Champion was jailed in May 2006 for dangerous driving.
412. Who was Formula One's World Champion in 1996?
413. September 28th 1996 is a famous date in horse racing? Why?
414. Which Ex-Eastenders actor was the Ghostwriter of David Beckham's Autobiography?
415. Hockey team: The St. Louis _____.

416.   Name the start and finish points for The University Boat Race?
417.   Liverpool won the Champion's League, who scored the first three Liverpool goals?
418.   What sport was officially banned in Scotland three times between 1457 and 1502?
419.   Which sporting milestone occurred at Iffley Road, Oxford in May 1954?
420.   In 1926, what did Gertrude Ederle become the first woman to do?

Quiz 85

421.   What is the last event in a decathlon?
422.   What is a boxer who leads with his right side?
423.   Ian Botham's middle name is what?
424.   Who did Boris Becker beat in The Wimbledon Final?
425.   What sport uses a broom?

Quiz 86

426.   Which country won the most Gold Medals in the 2008 Olympics (Bonus Pt. For How many)
427.   Who won the 1974 WBC Light Heavyweight Title?
428.   Both Arsenal & Chelsea had something in 1928 that no other team had. What was it?
429.   In professional football, the crossbar of a goal is how high?
430.   What is a Petanque more commonly known as what?

Quiz 87

431.   Stirling Moss won the World Championship how many times?
432.   In Australian Football how many members of one team can be on the field at once
433.   How many disciplines are in Men's Gymnastics?
434.   Who was the first head coach of the Dallas Cowboys?
435.   How many meters does a competitor have to run in a decathlon?

436. Who lost the World Snooker Finals from 1990 to 1994?
437. Banderillas are used in which blood sport?
438. Who threw their Olympic Gold Medal into a river in Kentucky after he was refused a meal because of his skin color?
439. Who was the "Sultan of Swat?"
440. Which American Football team is known as The Chargers?

Quiz 89

441. Where were the 2008 Summer Olympics held?
442. Which country won the Woman's World Cup Final in 2007?
443. What is Eric Bristow's nickname?
444. Name the motorcyclist also known as (Foggy)?
445. Colin Jackson played in which athletic event?

Quiz 90

446. Hockey team: The Montreal _____.
447. What is Toxophily?
448. What was Mathew Simmons in the news for in 1995?
449. Who was the winner of the 2006 Young Persons BBC Sports Personality of the Year Award?
450. How many jumps are in The Grand National?

Quiz 91

451. Maximum score possible in Ten Pin Bowling?
452. A Biathlon contains which events?
453. What is the average viewing figure for A Question Of Sport?
454. Which woman won their last Wimbledon Singles Title in 1975?
455. How did Baron Pierre De Coubertin's contribute to sport?

456. Which three race courses make up the five English horse racing (Classics)?
457. Who did John McEnroe beat 6-2, 6-2, 6-2 in 1983?
458. In which game might you find A Dummy?
459. This county cricket team plays home games at Grace Road.
460. She was the only woman to win an athletics gold medal for Britain in the Barcelona Olympics in 1992.

Quiz 93

461. The 800 meters at the 1980 Moscow Olympics was won by which athlete?
462. In Baseball who is behind Home Plate?
463. Which horrific sporting event happened on Saturday the 28th of June 1997?
464. In Netball, what does the C stand for?
465. Harvey Smith, Nick Skelton and Rob Hoekstra are known for which sport?

Quiz 94

466. Which is the most valuable property you can land on in Monopoly?
467. Which boxing division is between flyweight and featherweight?
468. Which brothers played for England in the 1995 Rugby Union World Cup and appeared with their Mother in a Pizza Hut advert?
469. Facing The Music is the autobiography of which sporting couple?
470. Who was England's captain when they won the World Cup in 1966?

471.   Who hosted the 1920 Olympics?
472.   In Tennis what did Gunther Parche become notorious for in 1993?
473.   Which game uses hoops?
474.   When and where did Canadian Ben Johnson Famously lose his Olympic Title, World Record & Gold Medal by failing a drug test at The Summer Olympics?
475.   Name the only Australian to win The Wimbledon Men's Singles in the 1980's?

Quiz 96

476.   Competitive Swimming includes Butterfly, Breast Stroke, Back Stroke, and one other event. What is it?
477.   At The Snooker World Championships who made the first 147 break?
478.   Who lit the Olympic Torch for the 2000 Sydney Olympics
479.   How many numbers does a roulette wheel have?
480.   Who suffered boxing defeats to Tim Witherspoon, Mike Tyson & Lennox Lewis?

Quiz 97

481.   Who was third to score 100 goals in the English Premiership after Dwight York & Jimmy Floyd Hasselbaink?
482.   What UK leisure activity is the most fatal?
483.   Who sank in the 1978 boat race?
484.   Which club won the most European cups in the 90s?
485.   How many feet high is a badminton net?

486.   Name the NFL team whose defensive unit held the nickname "The Purple People Eaters."

487.   Which golfer is El Ninio?

488.   In boxing what is a TKO?

489.   What type of wood are Cricket Stumps generally made from?

490.   Curling Stones are generally made from which type of rock?

Quiz 99

491.   Who has played first team football for Liverpool 658 times and Wales 67 times?

492.   Which Premiership footballer's real name is Sulzeer?

493.   Harry Redknapp managed which club before West Ham?

494.   Which UK Football Team are nicknamed The Owls?

495.   Finish the sequence: (Red, Blue, White, Black, and Orange).

Quiz 100

496.   What do the letters PB next to an athlete's name mean?

497.   Which sports ball is the heaviest?

498.   Who was the youngest baseball player to throw a no-hitter?

499.   The name of what model Ferrari means "Redhead?"

Sports & Leisure

TRIVIA

Answers

Answers – Quiz 1

1. Gold, Red, Blue, Black, White
2. Fred Truman
3. Geoffrey Boycott
4. Barry McGuigan
5. The Ryder Cup

Answers – Quiz 2

6. John Parrott
7. 6 Players
8. A type of jump in show jumping
9. Accrington Stanley
10. David Coleman

Answers – Quiz 3

11. Austria & Switzerland
12. 10 Cards
13. 5
14. A Chukka
15. Harold Grange

Answers – Quiz 4

16. Fairyhouse
17. James Buster Douglas
18. Franz Klammer
19. Cribbage
20. Billiards, pool or snooker

Answers – Quiz 5

21.	Barcelona, Spain
22.	Jack Nicklaus
23.	Matthew Hayden's
24.	Bisley
25.	Andy Fordham

Answers – Quiz 6

26.	Lazio
27.	David Platt
28.	Torvill & Dean
29.	300
30.	Mike Newell

Answers – Quiz 7

31.	Boris Becker , John McEnroe & Michael Stich
32.	Brands Hatch
33.	Persia (Iran)
34.	An Ice Hockey puck
35.	Greg Norman

Answers – Quiz 8

36.	Australian Football League
37.	First Sub 4 Minute Mile
38.	A Red Jack
39.	Butterfly Collecting
40.	Paul Ince

Answers – Quiz 9

41.   David Coultarde
42.   A relay baton
43.   Were all policemen
44.   Get sent off
45.   5 Points

Answers – Quiz 10

46.   A Boast
47.   Rowing
48.   No brakes
49.   Snow Boarding
50.   Gary Lineker & Peter Beardsley

Answers – Quiz 11

51.   New England Patriots
52.   Oxford & Cambridge Boat Race
53.   Ten Points
54.   GI (Geeeeee)
55.   Motorcycling

Answers – Quiz 12

56.   BackStroke
57.   5 Pound
58.   66
59.   Rock Climbing
60.   Gary Lineker

Answers – Quiz 13

61.   Night Shade
62.   Alan Wells
63.   Aston Villa
64.   The Oche in darts
65.   20 (18 players and two officials on the bench)

Answers – Quiz 14

66.   James Bonecrusher Smith
67.   Maurice Richard <-- pronounced "Reeee-shard"
68.   Steve Davis
69.   15 Pieces
70.   Fives

Answers – Quiz 15

71.   Sex Testing
72.   (Caber Toss)
73.   A Table Tennis Player
74.   FIFA
75.   Jana Novotna

Answers – Quiz 16

76.   Malcolm Marshall
77.   Epsom
78.   Ruud Gullit
79.   Rangers Football Club
80.   Ten Pin Bowling Alley

Answers – Quiz 17

81. OJ Simpson
82. Tae Kwon Do
83. Ayr
84. 8 People
85. White,Spot,Red

Answers – Quiz 18

86. Straw Weight
87. Lawrence Dallaglio
88. The Last Lap
89. Adidas
90. Bjorn Borg. Martina Navratlilova

Answers – Quiz 19

91. 13 Players
92. Grand National
93. St. Mirren
94. A type of golf club
95. Roger Federer & Venus Williams

Answers – Quiz 20

96. 9 = 8 Rowers & 1 Cox
97. Barnsley
98. McClaren
99. A Crown Green Bowl
100. The Gridiron

Answers - Quiz 21

101.	Tokyo, Japan
102.	27-28 Inches
103.	Alan Border
104.	Illegally replacing a horse
105.	Mark Spitz

Answers - Quiz 22

106.	Chukkers
107.	American Football (Gridiron)
108.	Stockholm, Sweden
109.	3,000 meters
110.	FC Barcelona

Answers - Quiz 23

111.	Mexico City, Mexico
112.	On a motor race track
113.	Leon Spinks
114.	14
115.	99

Answers - Quiz 24

116.	Ice Skating / Ice Dance
117.	Aintree Race Course
118.	Chelsea
119.	A Six
120.	70 Minutes

Answers – Quiz 25

121.	Long Jump
122.	2.5m
123.	Les Ferdinand
124.	A Home Run
125.	American football

Answers – Quiz 26

126.	50 meters
127.	Shot
128.	10 points
129.	100 meters
130.	Greece (Athens)

Answers – Quiz 27

131.	A Rabbit Punch
132.	Mclaren
133.	Argentinian
134.	Ice Skating
135.	9.87

Answers – Quiz 28

136.	To force people to take up archery
137.	Bob Beamon
138.	Manchester City
139.	Helsinki, Finland
140.	The Jockey Club

Answers – Quiz 29

141.	Alison Fisher
142.	Larry Holmes
143.	Hammer, Pole Vault, Triple Jump
144.	Sebastian Coe
145.	336

Answers – Quiz 30

146.	25
147.	A Pineapple
148.	2012
149.	The Losers Ribbons
150.	Maureen Connolly

Answers – Quiz 31

151.	Bury
152.	Aberdeen
153.	Grouse Shooting
154.	167
155.	The Biathlon

Answers – Quiz 32

156.	Hash marks
157.	Graeme Souness
158.	A sub four-minute mile
159.	Rory and Tony Underwood
160.	Ivory Coast

Answers – Quiz 33

161.   The Bishop
162.   Pam Shriver
163.   Because they've won the F.A Cup
164.   An Eagle
165.   England , Italy , Holland

Answers – Quiz 34

166.   Uruguay & Uruguay
167.   2 false starts
168.   9 players
169.   Goal attack
170.   The Boston Bruins

Answers – Quiz 35

171.   Three years old
172.   Prince William
173.   The Kentucky Derby
174.   Snooker Table
175.   3 (1989, 90 , 96)

Answers – Quiz 36

176.   Porto
177.   Blackhawks
178.   Kris Akabusi
179.   Cawley
180.   Spurs

Answers – Quiz 37

181.   UEFA Cup
182.   Leisure Time
183.   Leyton Orient
184.   31 lengths by Secretariat
185.   The Spinnaker

Answers – Quiz 38

186.   Bob Beamans Long Jump
187.   Ipswich
188.   An ace
189.   5.5 - 5.75 ounces
190.   His chin

Answers – Quiz 39

191.   Hamburg
192.   Frankie Dettorie
193.   Steve Cram
194.   Nobody, Riddick Bowe relinquished his title
195.   West Ham & Fulham

Answers – Quiz 40

196.   Twenty
197.   8 or 7
198.   Raymond Barneveld
199.   Uruguay, July 3o, 1930
200.   The lady byng trophy

Answers – Quiz 41

201.	James Wattana
202.	He bit off Evander Holyfield's ear
203.	Sharron Davies
204.	The Water Jump & The Chair
205.	Bicycles

Answers – Quiz 42

206.	Nick Faldo & Ian Woosnam
207.	6 Runs
208.	Bears
209.	22 including the cue ball
210.	A Lonsdale Belt

Answers – Quiz 43

211.	Indianapolis Colts
212.	Swansea
213.	Alain Prost
214.	Breidis Prescott
215.	The Frisbee

Answers – Quiz 44

216.	An Ice Skating Rink
217.	Cross Country Skiing & Rifle Shooting
218.	The Sabre
219.	Ben Johnson
220.	David Seaman

Answers – Quiz 45

221.	Let
222.	Snowboarding
223.	Featherweight
224.	Athens, Greece
225.	Phil Hill

Answers – Quiz 46

226.	Moscow, U.S.S.R.
227.	Michelin
228.	Kevin Curren
229.	The America's Cup
230.	St Johnstone

Answers – Quiz 47

231.	Andy Cole
232.	Monza
233.	Dartboards
234.	Atalanta
235.	The University Boat Race

Answers – Quiz 48

236.	Maurice Richard
237.	Canoeing & Kayaking
238.	Dressage
239.	Bears
240.	26 miles, 385 yards

Answers – Quiz 49

241.   London , Paris or Athens
242.   Purple
243.   1970's
244.   36770
245.   Yorkshire

Answers – Quiz 50

246.   Mark Webster
247.   Darts (180)
248.   Amsterdam, The Netherlands
249.   Ivan Lendl
250.   Foot & Mouth Disease

Answers – Quiz 51

251.   Won The Grand National
252.   Gareth Southgate
253.   Tax evasion
254.   Hot Pants
255.   A Hedgehog

Answers – Quiz 52

256.   Trina Gulliver
257.   The Indianapolis 500
258.   Macedonia
259.   Graham Gooch
260.   Malaysia & Indonesia

Answers – Quiz 53

261. 4 Inches
262. Elephant
263. Finland
264. Brian Lara
265. Mark Spitz (Swimming)

Answers – Quiz 54

266. Downhill Skiing
267. Lawn or Indoor Bowls
268. Lactic
269. Wigan (15)
270. The Harlem Globetrotters

Answers – Quiz 55

271. 3 Times
272. Dennis Taylor, 1985 Joe Johnson, 1986
273. Ropes
274. 333
275. Calcutta Cup

Answers – Quiz 56

276. Sid Waddell
277. Real Madrid (6 Times)
278. Cutty Sark
279. Tokyo
280. Munich, West Germany

Answers – Quiz 57

281.   Burnley
282.   Advantage
283.   7 Years
284.   Ruud Gullit
285.   Candlestick, Lead Pipe, Dagger, Spanner, Rope, Revolver

Answers – Quiz 58

286.   Sir Henry Cooper
287.   Goalkeeper
288.   Ron Atkinson (Red Ron)
289.   Tennis (15-1)
290.   Bob Hope

Answers – Quiz 59

291.   Mickey Mantle
292.   168 Pips
293.   Dennis Taylor & Joe Johnson
294.   Steve Redgrave
295.   Maine Road

Answers – Quiz 60

296.   Athens , Amsterdam , Antwerp & Atlanta
297.   Ronnie O'Sullivan
298.   3 Points
299.   London Marathon
300.   80 Mins

Answers – Quiz 61

301.   Matthew Pinsent
302.   Canadian
303.   Yankees & The Mets
304.   Monica Seles
305.   Steeple Chase

Answers – Quiz 62

306.   Eddie (The Eagle) Edwards
307.   Brooke Shields
308.   Alan Shearer
309.   Muhammad Ali
310.   David Beckham & Darius Vassell

Answers – Quiz 63

311.   170 (t20 t20 Bull)
312.   Battleships
313.   Crown Green Bowls
314.   Lawnmower Racing
315.   Volleyball

Answers – Quiz 64

316.   Tic Tac
317.   3 Suits
318.   Astros
319.   He is color blind
320.   Greece / Athens

Answers – Quiz 65

321. Party Politics
322. 19th
323. Great Britain , France and Switzerland
324. The Haka
325. A Basho

Answers – Quiz 66

326. Good Wood
327. Gymnastics
328. Arsenal
329. Terry Griffiths
330. Jack

Answers – Quiz 67

331. The Oche
332. Goal Shooter
333. Net Ball
334. High Jump
335. Said Aouita

Answers – Quiz 68

336. Steve Cram & Steve Ovett
337. Horse/Stallion
338. Bridge (No Card Over 9)
339. The Tour de France
340. The 1500 meters

Answers – Quiz 69

341.   The Crawl
342.   Wigan Athletic
343.   Sumo Wrestling
344.   World Haggis Hurling Championships
345.   Walter Swinburn

Answers – Quiz 70

346.   Geoff Hurst
347.   Jake Le Motta
348.   Andrew Murray
349.   400 Metres
350.   Paula Radcliffe

Answers – Quiz 71

351.   Big Daddy
352.   Colin Hendry
353.   Cameroon
354.   Steffi Graff
355.   He played whilst smoking a pipe

Answers – Quiz 72

356.   Eskimo Roll
357.   St Mary's
358.   Clean & Jerk, The Snatch
359.   Baton
360.   Fillies

Answers – Quiz 73

361. Grey Cup
362. Hill (Damon, Graham & Phil)
363. Hammersmith
364. 108
365. The Denver Broncos

Answers – Quiz 74

366. Bruins
367. The Sin Bin
368. Rifle Shooting
369. Sam Torrance
370. Blackburn Rovers

Answers – Quiz 75

371. 10m
372. The Flag
373. Henry Cooper, Cliff Morgan
374. Golf!!!!
375. Berlin, Germany

Answers – Quiz 76

376. The Pentathlon
377. Bloomfield Road
378. 20
379. Mrs. White, Miss Scarlet, Mrs. Peacock
380. Ronnie "The Rocket" O Sullivan

Answers – Quiz 77

381.	Formula One Racing
382.	Cliff Thorburn, Jimmy White, Mark Williams, Steven Hendry
383.	Eric Bristow
384.	Bernie Ecclestone
385.	Middlesbrough

Answers – Quiz 78

386.	A Legspin Bowler
387.	First Female Empire
388.	Jimmy Connors
389.	Canoeing
390.	1983

Answers – Quiz 79

391.	1711
392.	Tim Henman
393.	36708
394.	112
395.	Inventing Basketball

Answers – Quiz 80

396.	Golf Ball
397.	Charades
398.	Trevor BerBick
399.	Gynmastics (The Rings)
400.	1916, 1940, 1944

Answers – Quiz 81

401.   Seoul, South Korea
402.   800 Meters
403.   New York Yankees
404.   15 Million
405.   28

Answers – Quiz 82

406.   Embassy World Snooker (Taylor & Davis)
407.   Audley Harrison
408.   Diane Leather
409.   King Of The Mountains
410.   He was kung Fu kicked by Eric Cantona

Answers – Quiz 83

411.   Naseem Hamed
412.   Damon Hill
413.   Frankie Dettori won 7 races in one day at Ascot
414.   Tom Watt (Lofty)
415.   Blues

Answers – Quiz 84

416.   Putney & Mortlake
417.   Stephen Gerrard, Vladimir Smicer & Xabi Alonsco
418.   Golf
419.   Roger Bannister ran the first 4-minute mile
420.   Swim across The English Channel

Answers – Quiz 85

421.	1500 meters
422.	A South Paw
423.	Terrence
424.	Kevin Curran
425.	Curling

Answers – Quiz 86

426.	China (51)
427.	John Conteh
428.	Numbered Shirts
429.	8 Feet
430.	Boules

Answers – Quiz 87

431.	Never
432.	18
433.	6 (Vault, Rings, Floor, High Bar, Para Bars, Horse)
434.	Tom Landry
435.	2110 (100,110,400,1500)

Answers – Quiz 88

436.	Jimmy White
437.	Bull Fighting
438.	Casius Clay / Muhammed Ali
439.	Babe Ruth
440.	San Diego Chargers

Answers – Quiz 89

441.   Beijing / China
442.   Germany (Beat Brazil 2.0)
443.   The Crafty Cockney
444.   Carl Foggarty
445.   110m Hurdles

Answers – Quiz 90

446.   Canadians
447.   Archery
448.   Eric Cantona Kung Fu Kick
449.   Theo Walcott
450.   30 Jumps

Answers – Quiz 91

451.   300 Points
452.   Cross Country Skiing & Shooting
453.   8 Million
454.   Billy Jean King
455.   He founded the Olympic movement in 1892

Answers – Quiz 92

456.   Doncaster , Epsom & Newmarket
457.   Chris Lewis
458.   Bridge
459.   Leicestershire
460.   Sally Gunnell

Answers – Quiz 93

461.   Steve Ovett
462.   The Catcher
463.   Evander Holyfield's Ear was bitten off by Mike Tyson
464.   Center
465.   Show Jumping

Answers – Quiz 94

466.   Mayfair
467.   Batamweight
468.   Rory & Tony Underwood
469.   Jane Torvill & Christopher Dean
470.   Bobby Moore

Answers – Quiz 95

471.   Antwerp, Belgium
472.   Stabbed Monica Seles
473.   Croquet
474.   1988, Seoul / Korea
475.   Pat Cash

Answers – Quiz 96

476.   Freestyle
477.   Cliff Thorburn
478.   Cathy Freeman
479.   37 - (0-36)
480.   Frank Bruno

Answers – Quiz 97

481.   Thierry Henry
482.   Fishing
483.   Cambridge
484.   AC Milan
485.   5ft

Answers – Quiz 98

486.   The Minnesota Vikings
487.   Sergio Garcia
488.   Technical Knock Out
489.   Ash
490.   Granite

Answers – Quiz 99

491.   Ian Rush
492.   Sol Campbell
493.   Bournemouth
494.   Sheffield Wednesday
495.   Black and White (Grey Hounds)

Answers – Quiz 100

496.   Personal Best
497.   (Ten Pin Bowling)
498.   Amos Rusie, he was 20 years and 2 months old.
499.   Tetarossa

Made in the USA
Middletown, DE
25 August 2020